The Origins of the Foundation Stories Genre in the Hebrew Bible and Ancient Eastern Mediterranean

GUY DARSHAN
guy.darshan@mail.huji.ac.il
Hebrew University of Jerusalem, Jerusalem 91905, Israel

This article examines two types of foundation narrative prevalent in the biblical literature in light of as-yet-undiscussed parallels from ancient Greek and Mediterranean texts. The first type, embodied in the Genesis narratives and Greek genealogical traditions, portrays the founders as leaving a distant land to settle peacefully in a new land. The second is exemplified by the central hexateuchal theme of the Israelites' migration to Canaan by dispossessing the native population as well as the Dorian migration traditions. Several factors indicate that the foundation story genre also became central and foundational in other small kingdoms around the Mediterranean—as indicated, for example, by the Phoenician-Luwian inscriptions referring to *bt Mpš/Mopsus* and related classical sources. The popularity of the genre in the ancient Mediterranean is striking in light of the fact that, while experiencing tribal migrations and wanderings, the great Mesopotamian and Egyptian kingdoms never represented themselves as "immigrants." It is suggested that this genre may have emerged with the rise of the new, small-scale kingdoms in the Mediterranean basin toward the end of the second millennium B.C.E. The Phoenician and Greek colonization enterprises of the first third of the first millennium B.C.E. in particular increased awareness of the newly emerging states and focused attention on ethnic identity.

The biblical narratives of the patriarchal wanderings and settlement in Canaan recorded in the Pentateuch and the book of Joshua exhibit close parallels in genre and form to the Greek foundation (κτίσις) stories. Moshe Weinfeld has drawn attention to the fact that, while ancient Near Eastern literature contains no examples of this genre, accounts focusing on the migration of the founding father/group

---

I am grateful to Prof. Alexander Rofé, Prof. Deborah Levine Gera (both of The Hebrew University of Jerusalem), and Prof. Carolina López-Ruiz (The Ohio State University), who commented on earlier versions of this paper.

to a new land and the beginning of a new nation are prevalent in the ancient Greek literary world:[1]

> As is well known, most of the genres of biblical literature have their counterparts in the ancient Near East. Creation stories, genealogies, legal codes, cultic instructions, temple-building accounts, royal annals, prophecies, psalms, wisdom literature of various kinds—all are widely attested in the cognate literatures from Mesopotamia, the Hittites, and the Egyptians. The only genre lacking such counterparts is that of stories about the beginning of the nation and its settlement, which are so boldly represented in the Patriarchal narratives and the accounts of the Exodus and the conquest of the Land.... On the other hand, this genre would be expected in the Greek sphere, which like Israel was based on colonization and founding of new sites.[2]

Rather than recounting the adventures of a mighty hero, these foundation stories address the origin and identity of an ethnic community and are based on traditions held by people who perceived themselves to be the offspring of the founding fathers. These stories are designed to explain where they came from and how their city was established, or their tribal provenance.

The most widespread form of these Greek stories relates to the foundation of colonies abroad. Devoting most of his attention to this form, Weinfeld argues that the similarity these stories exhibit to the pentateuchal traditions reflects the reality common to the settlement of new cities in Canaan and the Greek colonies and "regulations for settlement in a new place that were generally accepted throughout the Mediterranean area."[3] Quite clearly, however, not all the details given in these stories necessarily derive from contemporary historical circumstances or conventions controlling settlement and city building. As in every literary artifact,

---

[1] Weinfeld, *The Promise of the Land: The Inheritance of the Land of Canaan by the Israelites* (Taubman Lectures in Jewish Studies; Berkeley: University of California Press, 1993), 1–51. See also idem, "The Promise to the Patriarchs and Its Realization: An Analysis of Foundation Stories," in *Society and Economy in the Eastern Mediterranean (c. 1500–100 B.C.): Proceedings of the International Symposium Held at the University of Haifa from the 28th of April to the 2nd of May 1985* (ed. M. Heltzer and E. Lipiński; OLA 23; Leuven: Peeters, 1988), 353–69; idem, "The Pattern of the Israelite Settlement in Canaan," in *Congress Volume: Jerusalem 1986* (ed. J. A. Emerton; VTSup 40; Leiden: Brill, 1988), 270–83; idem, "Historical Facts behind the Israelite Settlement Pattern," *VT* 38 (1988): 324–32. See also Peter Machinist, "Outsiders or Insiders: The Biblical View of Emergent Israel and Its Contexts," in *The Other in Jewish Thought and History: Constructions of Jewish Culture and Identity* (ed. Laurence J. Silberstein and Robert L. Cohn; New Perspectives on Jewish Studies; New York: New York University Press, 1994), 35–60, esp. 48–54; John Pairman Brown, *Israel and Hellas* (3 vols.; BZAW 231, 276, 299; Berlin: de Gruyter, 2000), 2:214–24; Nili Wazana, "Natives or Immigrants: The Perception of the Origins of Israel and Other Peoples in the Bible" (in Hebrew), in *Shai le-Sara Japhet: Studies in the Bible, Its Exegesis and Its Language* (ed. Mosheh Bar-Asher et al.; Jerusalem: Bialik Institute, 2007), 37–59.

[2] Weinfeld, *Promise of the Land*, 1–2.

[3] Ibid., 40–41.

their authors were at liberty to select information from their sources when fashioning their own works. The recurrent motifs, themes, and patterns we find are thus more likely to reflect at times literary considerations and ideological beliefs rather than historical realities. More significantly, the stories of the Greek colonies are not strictly analogous to the central pentateuchal migration traditions—none of which depicts sending a delegation from the homeland to found a new settlement.

Neither Weinfeld nor subsequent biblical scholars appear to have paid any attention to other Greek traditions that recount the establishment of cities and the formation of ethnic groups within the homeland itself. Like the biblical traditions, these Greek sources relate to a primordial "mythic" era and describe the foundation process in terms of migration rather than colonization. I wish to examine here the affinities between these texts and the biblical accounts in order to reveal the distinctive literary parallelism between them and the historical background underlying the formation of this genre within these two ancient Mediterranean cultures. This issue is of particular interest in light of the fact that, while the great ancient Near Eastern kingdoms of the third and second millennia B.C.E. (in Mesopotamia, Egypt, and Anatolia) were familiar with tribal and clan wanderings and migrations—some of the nomadic groups on occasion even ruled these ancient kingdoms—they did not produce any examples of this literary genre. The questions I thus seek to address here are the following: How did this genre arise and why did it occupy a central place in Greek and Israelite culture?

I. Two Types of Foundation Narrative in the Hebrew Bible and Their Greek Parallels

The biblical texts contain two principal forms of the foundation narrative. The first is reflected in the patriarchal narratives in Genesis, which portray an early ancestor leaving a faraway land to settle in a new land. Although he is a foreigner in his new place of residence, this forefather acquires a foothold in the country, gaining the respect of the local inhabitants. Over the course of generations, his descendants populate the land and become its local inhabitants. This model corresponds most closely to the Greek genealogical traditions of the eponymous progenitors of the Greek tribes.

The second type is exemplified by the central hexateuchal narrative—namely, the exodus from Egypt and the conquest of Canaan. According to this model, a large group of settlers migrates to a new country, and their settlement is achieved via warfare and dispossession of the native population. The closest Greek analogy to this type is found in the traditions regarding the migration of the Dorians and the return of the Heraclids to the southern Peloponnese.

A. Founding-Father Settlement Type

The first model consists of four principal elements: (1) The founding father leaves an early cradle of civilization. (2) He arrives at a new location where he lives as a foreigner among the local populace. (3) During his wanderings or in his new place of residence he acquires legal status by erecting an altar or buying land or a burial plot (either with money or in exchange for military assistance, etc.). (4) He eventually becomes the progenitor of a nation or a local ruler, and the group to whom the narrator belongs regards him as their original ancestor and is frequently called after his name.

The first biblical example of this literary type is the Abraham cycle.[4] (1) Abraham arrives in Canaan from a distant cultural center, from Ur of the Chaldeans (Gen 11:28, 31 [P]) in southern Mesopotamia—or from Haran in northern Mesopotamia (Gen 24:4, 7, 10; cf. 12:1; 27:43; 28:10; 29:4)—and settles in the land.[5] (2) At this point in time, Canaan is inhabited by a local population, among whom Abraham dwells as a foreigner (Gen 13:7; cf. 12:6 [J]; 23:1–20 [P]). (3) During his sojourn in Canaan, he acquires a foothold in the land—by purchasing the Cave of Machpelah in Hebron (Genesis 23) according to P or by wandering in places that de facto constitute the boundaries of the Israelite culture—Shechem, Bethel, and Ai in the Ephraimite allotment and the Negeb and Beersheba in the Judahite inheritance according to the Yahwistic thread. In some of these locations he erects an altar (Gen 12:7–8) or plants a tree (Gen 21:33). (4) The account concludes with his assimilation and implies, via a divine promise, that he will become the ancestor of the group residing in the land in the author's own day.

Greek stories similarly speak of a wandering forefather who, at an early point in time, arrives from a distant place and settles in a location whose inhabitants will later bear his name. The account of Xuthus—son of Hellen, brother of Dorus and Aeolus, and grandson of Deucalion, the hero of the Greek flood myth—exhibits precisely this pattern (Hesiod F 9 M-W; Hellanicus *FGH* 4 F 125; Apollodorus 1.7.3). According to the *Catalogue of Women* and other Greek genealogical traditions, Xuthus was the father of the Ionians and Achaeans, having begotten Ion and

---

[4] For the Abraham cycle, see, e.g., Jean-Louis Ska, "Essai sur la nature at la signification du cycle d'Abraham (Gn 11,27–25,11)," in *Studies in the Book of Genesis: Literature, Redaction and History* (ed. A. Wénin; BETL 155; Leuven: Peeters, 2001), 153–77; Ronald S. Hendel, *Remembering Abraham: Culture, Memory, and History in the Hebrew Bible* (Oxford: Oxford University Press, 2005), 31–43.

[5] P in fact combines the two traditions regarding Abraham's origin, the family dwelling in Haran after leaving Ur of the Chaldeans, whence Abraham leaves for Canaan following his father's death (Gen 11:31–32; 12:4b–5). See John Skinner, *A Critical and Exegetical Commentary on Genesis* (2nd ed.; ICC; Edinburgh: T&T Clark, 1930), 239. For Gen 15:7 as a post-P text, see, e.g., Ludwig Schmidt, "Genesis xv," *VT* 56 (2006): 251–67; Jean-Louis Ska, "Some Groundwork on Genesis 15," in idem, *The Exegesis of the Pentateuch: Exegetical Studies and Basic Questions* (FAT 66: Tübingen: Mohr Siebeck, 2009), 67–81.

Achaeus through Creusa, daughter of the Athenian king (cf. Hesiod F 10a. 20–24 M-W).[6] Euripides preserves details of Xuthus's story in his tragedy devoted to Ion, Xuthus's son: (1) Xuthus migrated from northern Greece to Athens, where he married the daughter of the king, Erechtheus (Euripides, *Ion* 57–64, 289–98; Conon *FGH* 26 F 1; Strabo 8.7.1; Pausanias 7.1.2).[7] (2) There he lives as a foreigner, "No citizen, but a stranger from foreign land [οὐκ ἀστὸς ἀλλ' ἐπακτὸς ἐξ ἄλλης χθονός]" (Euripides, *Ion* 290; cf. 63–64). (3) He gives military assistance to the Athenians, thereby gaining the king's daughter in marriage and status in the land (*Ion* 58–64, 294–98). (4) In due course, he becomes king and is regarded as one of the fathers of the Ionians who dwelt in Athens and the Greek cities, while his son Ion is "founder of the land of Asia [κτίστορ' Ἀσιάδος χθονός]" (*Ion* 74).[8]

As Herodotus (7.94) notes, this account is paralleled in the legend of Danaus's settlement in Argos. According to the core of this narrative, the paths of Belus's two sons, Danaus and Aegyptus, diverge: (1) In the wake of their split, Danaus and his daughters leave a cradle of civilization, sailing from the shores of Egypt to Argos.[9] (2) Danaus reaches Argos when a local king known either as Galenor or Pelasgus (representing the local pre-Hellenic population) is on the throne and wins the support of the local populace. In his new location, the forefather is a foreigner and alien, lacking any ability to fight the native residents and drive them from their land—his only desire is to receive hospitality.[10] (3) Danaus is also said to have established cultic places, erecting an image of Athena of Lindos at Rhodes on his

---

[6] See also Herodotus 5.66; 7.94; 8.44; Apollodorus 1.7.3; Strabo 8.7.1; Pausanias 1.31.3; 2.14.2; 7.1.2. Cf. Euripides, *Melanippe Wise* F 665a–c.9–11(Mette); and see Euripides, *Fragments: Aegeus-Meleager* (ed. and trans. C. Collard and M. Cropp; LCL; Cambridge, MA: Harvard University Press, 2008), 578–79. For the story of Ion's birth, see, e.g., Nicole Loraux, "Kreousa the Autochthon: A Study of Euripides *Ion*," in *Nothing to Do with Dionysos? Athenian Drama in Its Social Context* (ed. John J. Winkler and Froma I. Zeitlin; Princeton: Princeton University Press, 1990), 168–206; Katerina Zacharia, *Converging Truths: Euripides' Ion and the Athenian Quest for Self-Definition* (Mnemosyne Supplement 242; Leiden: Brill, 2003), 66–76 and below.

[7] See also Jan N. Bremmer, "Myth as Propaganda: Athens and Sparta," *ZPE* 117 (1997): 9–17, esp. 10–11; cf. Robert Parker, "Myths of Early Athens," in *Interpretations of Greek Mythology* (ed. Jan N. Bremmer; London: Routledge, 1987), 187–214, esp. 206–7.

[8] For Ion's lineage in Euripides, see n. 52 below.

[9] In a later period, Hellenistic authors—such as Hecataeus of Abdera—recognizing the similarity between Danaus and Moses, conflated them; see, e.g., Doron Mendels, "Hecataeus of Abdera and a Jewish 'Patrios Politeia' of the Persian Period (Diodorus Siculus XL,3)," *ZAW* 95 (1983): 96–110.

[10] Aeschylus, for example, portrays Danaus's daughters as ξέναι (*Suppl.* 277); see Edith Hall, *Inventing the Barbarian: Greek Self-Definition through Tragedy* (Oxford Classical Monographs; Oxford: Oxford University Press, 1989), 136–40. The appearance of the Danaids as foreigners is reflected also in fifth-century B.C.E. art; see Margaret C. Miller, "Barbarian Lineage in Classical Greek Mythology and Art: Pelops, Danaos and Kadmos," in *Cultural Borrowings and Ethnic Appropriations in Antiquity* (ed. Erich S. Gruen; Oriens et Occidens 8; Stuttgart: Steiner, 2005), 68–89, esp. 75–79.

way to his permanent abode and building a temple and image at Argos.¹¹ (4) In time, he becomes king of the city, creating a new dynasty in Argos, and the subsequent generations of the local inhabitants come to be known by his name (Apollodorus 2.1.4; Pausanias 2.16.1; 2.19.3).

Recognition of the topos of the founding father who settles in a place and establishes a bloodline for himself there allows us to classify the pentateuchal traditions concerning Jacob under this category as well. Although Jacob returns to his homeland after having been forced to flee, rather than setting out from one place for a new land, the well-known passage recited at the offering of the first fruit—"My father was a fugitive Aramean. He went down to Egypt with meager numbers and sojourned there; but there he became a great and very populous nation" (Deut 26:5)—indicates that, during the biblical period, Jacob was regarded as having been a "Syro-Canaanite refugee" seeking a place in which to settle.¹²

Independent traditions that apparently were originally linked to either Abraham or Isaac were subsequently integrated into a complex genealogical lineage that included additional founding fathers. Thus, over the course of time it was recounted that Jacob, who was born to Isaac in Canaan, departed for Aram and thence returned to Canaan. Reading between the lines, we can distinguish traces of the legend that depicted him as a founding father and settler according to the model of Abraham: (1) Jacob reaches Canaan from a distant land—either Haran or, according to P, Padan-aram. (2) Like Abraham, he lives there as a foreigner. He purchases the land on which his tent lies from Hamor, the father of Shechem, one of the local inhabitants (Gen 33:19), who, according to one tradition (Genesis 34), asks for his daughter Dina in marriage, suggesting that the two families intermarry (Gen 34:9–10).¹³ (3) Jacob erects pillars in various cities in Canaan, which, as in the Yahwist account of Abraham, symbolize the Israelite centers of settlement.¹⁴ His name is associated in particular with Bethel—the central sanctuary of the kingdom of Israel—where, according to P, God reveals himself to Jacob and changes his

---

¹¹ For Lindos, see Herodotus 2.182; Marmor Parium *FGH* 239 A 9; Diodorus Siculus 5.58.1; Strabo 14.2.11; Eusebius, *Praep. ev.* 3.8. For Argos, see Pausanias 2.19.3

¹² For the meaning of the phrase ארמי אבד in the light of the Akkadian equivalent *Arame ... munnabtu* and the historical background of the eighth and seventh centuries B.C.E., see Jeffrey H. Tigay, *Deuteronomy* דברים: *The Traditional Hebrew Text with the New JPS Translation* (JPS Torah Commentary; Philadelphia: Jewish Publication Society, 1996), 240; Richard C. Steiner, "The 'Aramean' of Deuteronomy 26:5: *Peshat* and *Derash*," in *Tehillah le-Moshe: Biblical and Judaic Studies in Honor of Moshe Greenberg* (ed. Mordechai Cogan et al.; Winona Lake, IN: Eisenbrauns, 1997), 127–38.

¹³ Weinfeld, *Promise of the Land*, 112. In its extant form, however, Genesis 34 appears to be a late composition; see, e.g., Alexander Rofé, "Defilement of Virgins in Biblical Law and the Case of Dinah (Genesis 34)," *Bib* 86 (2005): 369–75.

¹⁴ Rather than the erection of altars attributed to Abraham in J, these traditions speak of pillars (Gen 31:45; 35:14, 20; cf. Gen 33:20). See Skinner, *Genesis*, 416.

name to Israel (Gen 35:9–13, 15). (4) Eventually, Jacob/Israel becomes the progenitor of the nation in the land that will be named after him, in which he both lived and was buried. Significantly, while in our extant text Jacob does not remain in Canaan but goes down to Egypt, we find numerous hints of other traditions according to which he and his descendants settled in Canaan along the lines of the founding-father settlement pattern—thus, for example, the well-known story of the sons of Ephraim in Chronicles, which describes a continuous settlement in the land (1 Chr 7:20–29).[15] According to these traditions, Ephraim was born not in Egypt (Gen 48:5–8) but in Canaan, where he begat sons who were killed by the men of Gath (1 Chr 7:21) and a daughter, Sheerah, who built several cities in Canaan (1 Chr 7:24).[16]

The close correspondence between the Greek and biblical stories of a founding father and his settlement in a new location are particularly striking in light of the fact that this genre is not found in the literature of the great ancient Near Eastern cultures—Mesopotamia, Egypt, and Hatti. Despite being familiar with actual and reported wanderings and migrations, these kingdoms never represented themselves as "immigrant" cultures or possessed foundation stories regarding their ancestors.[17] The ancient Near Eastern literary accounts of wanderers—on occasion even those who lived in Canaan as nomads—always conclude with the hero's return to his place of origin, the focus lying firmly on his peregrinations rather than his establishment of a new tribe or race. These literary accounts thus lack the final and most central element of the foundation pattern, namely, acquisition of rights to the new land and the creation of a new ethnic group that regards the hero as its progenitor and is known by his name.

Thus, for example, the Egyptian *Story of Sinuhe* recounts how its protagonist, a top-ranking Egyptian official, flees to Canaan, where, after wandering for some time, he eventually settles in the north of the country.[18] He receives the daughter of the local tribal head in marriage and eventually becomes ruler, living there for

---

[15] See Sara Japhet, "Conquest and Settlement in Chronicles," *JBL* 98 (1979): 205–18; Alexander Rofé, "The Family-Saga as a Source for the History of the Settlement" (in Hebrew), *ErIsr* 24 (1993): 187–91, and below.

[16] Esau, Jacob's brother, is also described as a founding father in a tradition preserved by P. While Deut 2:9–11 portrays the Edomites as a large group who arrived from elsewhere and drove out the ancient inhabitants (2:12), the Priestly tradition depicts Esau as a nomadic ancestor who settled quietly among the ancient inhabitants of Seir (Genesis 36), marrying local women (36:12, 14, 20, 22). After time had passed, the local population came to be called by his name (36:14).

[17] See the bibliography cited in Claus Westermann, *Genesis 12–36: A Commentary* (trans. John J. Scullion; Minneapolis: Fortress, 1985), 94–95.

[18] For the *Story of Sinuhe*, see, e.g., Günter Burkard and Heinz J. Thissen, *Einführung in die altägyptische Literaturgeschichte* (3 vols.; Einführungen und Quellentexte zur Ägyptologie 1, 3, 6; Münster: Lit, 2007), 1:114–23; *COS* 1.38. For the motif of Canaan as a land of refuge, see John Baines, "Interpreting Sinuhe," *JEA* 68 (1982): 31–44; Raymond Westbrook, "Personal Exile in the Ancient Near East," *JAOS* 128 (2008): 317–23.

many years and bequeathing his status to his sons. At the end of his life, however, his wish is to be buried in his homeland, and the Egyptian pharaoh welcomes him back with great honor. This story clearly focuses on the hero rather than on the local inhabitants.[19]

Canaan is also referred to as a temporary land of refuge by Idrimi, king of Alalakh, who declares in a royal inscription that he fled his father's house in Aleppo and went to live among the Apiru in Canaan, until he managed to return and rule in Syria.[20] Idrimi returns thus to his homeland rather than remaining to rule in Canaan. Like the *Story of Sinuhe*, this inscription does not reflect the viewpoint of one who puts down roots in Canaan. These texts thus clearly diverge from both the Greek and the biblical accounts, which represent the wanderer as a national ancestor and which conclude with his establishment of a permanent residence and the foundation of a new nation or city.

B. Migration of an Ethnic Group and Land-Conquest Type

The second biblical foundation-narrative type deals with the migration of a large group of people. Here the story is not one of an individual founding father who establishes a new bloodline but concerns a collective, such as a tribe or people, that leaves one place to settle in a new land under the guidance of a founding leader. In contrast to the previous type, which usually concludes with the gradual and peaceful assimilation of the immigrant, this form of migration frequently ends in warfare against the local populace, who are driven out by the newcomers.

The central hexateuchal story that details the exodus from Egypt and the entry into Canaan falls into this category.[21] While the extant text of Exodus contains at least two sequential narratival strands and numerous traditions, we can delineate the basic lines as they appear to have been known in ancient Israel. The account begins with the enslavement of the Israelites in Egypt (Exodus 1–2), in the wake of which God reveals himself to Moses (Exod 3:1–4:17; 6:1–7:5), promising to rescue the people from their bondage, bring them into Canaan (Exod 3:8 [J]), and give them the land (Exod 6:8 [P]). During their wanderings in the wilderness, they encounter various delays, as well as several failed attempts to gain the possession

---

[19] The Egyptian *Tale of Two Brothers* similarly relates how the younger, Bata, flees from his older sibling, Anubis, to the "Valley of the Cedar," apparently in Lebanon; see Susan Tower Hollis, *The Ancient Egyptian 'Tale of Two Brothers': A Mythological, Religious, Literary, and Historico-Political Study* (2nd ed.; Oakville, CT: Bannerstone, 2008). For the location of the Valley of Cedar, see Alan H. Gardiner, "Tanis and Pi-Ra'messe: A Retraction," *JEA* 19 (1933): 122–28.

[20] See esp. Edward L. Greenstein, "Interpreting the Bible by Way of Its Ancient Cultural Milieu" (in Hebrew), in *Understanding the Bible in Our Times: Implications for Education* (ed. M. L. Frankel and H. Deitcher; Studies in Jewish Education 9; Jerusalem: Magnes, 2003), *61–*73. See also the bibliography in *COS* 1.148.

[21] For various examples, such as the tribal foundation stories of Manasseh and Dan, see Rofé, "Family-Saga," 187–91.

pledged to them (Num 14:40–45). Ultimately, however—as portrayed in Joshua in particular—they drive out the local inhabitants and settle in the land.

Greek literature contains numerous examples of this story type. While it is represented in all the foundation stories of the Greek colonies in the Mediterranean, relating how these colonies were established by groups of settlers led by a founder, as noted above the closest parallel to the biblical example is found in the account of the foundation of settlements in the Greek homeland. The most prominent instance is the story of the return of Heracles' sons (the Heraclids) and the migration of the Dorians to Sparta.

The legends about Sparta's early era refer to it as the city of Menelaus, the brother of Agamemnon and husband of Helen of Troy, on whose account the Trojan War broke out. However, during the period in which Sparta was a Greek city-state, the majority of the city's inhabitants regarded themselves not as descending from Menelaus's bloodline but as the descendants of Heracles and the Dorians from northern Greece. The poet Tyrtaeus, a Spartan who lived during the second half of the seventh century B.C.E., preserves a tradition according to which Zeus himself gave (δέδωκε) the city to the Dorians and Heraclids (F 2.12–15 West = P.Oxy. 2824 = Strabo 8.4.10):

> For the son of Cronus, spouse of Hera of the beautiful crown,
> Zeus himself, has given this city to the Heracleids,
> in company with whom we left windy Erineus,
> and came to the broad island of Pelops.[22]

As is well known, similar language of the giving of the land to the people occurs on numerous occasions in God's revelation to Abraham and the other patriarchs in Canaan (Gen 13:15–17; 15:18; 17:18) and in Egypt (Exod 6:8).

According to the Greek traditions, Sparta was given to Heracles' sons in the wake of their father's assistance to Tyndareus, the Spartan king of the Menelaus dynasty, in regaining the throne following his banishment from the city. At this juncture, Heracles was promised that one day he and his offspring would return to Sparta to rule (Diodorus Siculus 4.33.51; Pausanias 2.18.7). After Heracles' death, his descendants wandered the earth for a period of three generations, seeking refuge, in various places, from Heracles' adversaries. Although several explanations of this circumstance exist, all the traditions concur that the Heraclids were predestined to be exiled from the homeland promised to them for a period of three generations (e.g., Herodotus 9.26; Apollodorus 2.8.2). In the continuation of the Dorian story, the fourth generation of Heracles' descendants allied themselves with the sons of Aegimius, the son of Dorus, the early king of the Dorians, when the

---

[22] αὐτὸς γὰρ Κρονίων καλλιστεφάνου πόσις Ἥρης / Ζεὺς Ἡρακλείδαις ἄστυ δέδωκε τόδε, / οἷσιν ἅμα προλιπόντες Ἐρινεὸν ἠνεμόεντα / εὐρεῖαν Πέλοπος νῆσον ἀφικόμεθα. See also Irad Malkin, *Myth and Territory in the Spartan Mediterranean* (Cambridge: Cambridge University Press, 1994), 33–36.

Dorians were still living in northern Greece (Thucydides 1.12.3; Diodorus Siculus 4.37.3–4; Apollodorus 2.8.3). With the Dorians' assistance, the Heraclids succeeded in killing Tisamenus, Orestes' son, driving the legendary royal house out of Sparta. They took control of the Peloponnese and established a series of city-states, including Sparta, Argos, and Messene.

The motif of return in the fourth generation occurs also in the story of Danaus and the Argivian genealogy discussed above. According to this tradition Io was taken to Egypt by Zeus, and, after three generations had passed, her fourth-generation descendant, Danaus, finally made his way back to Argos and became king. In this story, Danaus is therefore not a migrant but a returnee to his "homeland" in the fourth generation.

The motif of the restoration of the people in the fourth generation occurs also in biblical texts—reflected, for example, in the priestly genealogy in the Pentateuch. Jacob's sons went down to Egypt, and one of his great-grandsons, Moses (son of Amram, son of Kohath, son of Levi) led his descendants back to Canaan (Exod 6:14–27). Another well-known example is found in the Covenant of the Pieces (Genesis 15), when God reveals himself to Abraham and tells him: "Know well that your offspring shall be strangers in a land not theirs, and they shall be enslaved and oppressed … and they shall return here in the fourth generation, for the iniquity of the Amorites is not yet complete" (Gen 15:13, 16).[23] According to this verse, the Israelites are required to wait three generations until God can remove the local populace from the land.

Both the Israelites and the Dorians, therefore, possess a tradition according to which their settlement commences after three generations of waiting in an area far removed from the land given to them by their god. Both traditions also conclude with a military attack against the local populace. The analogy between the Dorian and Israelite accounts is particularly striking in light of the fact that archaeological and historical evidence attests that the settlement of both in their own land was not accomplished through a massive military campaign against the local populace but via a gradual spreading and the occupation of deserted and long-abandoned sites. This suggests that the parallelism is a function not of similar historical circumstances but of literary and conceptual patterns.[24] I will return to this point below.

---

[23] Since the number "four hundred years" (Gen 15:13) is inconsistent with the period of three or four generations (15:16), it appears to represent an attempt to adjust the period of three generations to the Priestly tradition, according to which "the time that the children of Israel dwelt in Egypt was four hundred and thirty years" (Exod 12:40). Alternatively, it may reflect a divergent perception of the length of a generation, that is, one hundred years, as has been suggested in the past on the basis of uncertain classical parallels (Varro, *Ling. lat.* 6.11; cf. Ovid, *Metam.* 12.188). See the survey by Skinner, *Genesis*, 282.

[24] For the Israelite settlement processes, see, e.g., Nadav Na'aman, "The 'Conquest of Canaan' in the Book of Joshua and in History," in *From Nomadism to Monarchy: Archaeological and Historical Aspects of Early Israel* (ed. Israel Finkelstein and Nadav Na'aman; Jerusalem: Yad Izhak

II. The Origins of the Mediterranean Foundation Stories

The number of literary parallels between the Greek and Israelite foundation stories and the absence of this genre from the literature of the great ancient Near Eastern empires make it difficult to assume that the affinities between them are coincidental or merely reflect similar patterns of thought. At the same time, the similarities cannot be the consequence of direct literary influence—in either direction. A broader examination of the features of the genre as it occurs across the Mediterranean may therefore help us to understand the analogies between different instances of the genre, the development of the pattern, and the process whereby the foundation story became a central literary type in the region.

A. Other Mediterranean Migration and Settlement Stories

While the genre is not known in the literature of the great empires of the period and area, additional examples of foundation narratives appear to have circulated throughout the Mediterranean—beyond the Greek and Israelite worlds—during the first third of the first millennium B.C.E. Although few such texts have been preserved from the neighboring cultures and kingdoms during this period, some of the traditions embedded in the Greek and biblical writings suggest that other nations also regarded themselves as "immigrants" and newcomers to their current place of residence.

The book of Amos contains hints of a tradition concerning a Philistine migration from Caphtor and an Aramean migration from Kir (Amos 9:7). Deuteronomy also appears to preserve similar foundation traditions concerning the Moabites (2:9–11), Edomites (2:12, 22), Ammonites (2:20–21), and Philistines (2:23). All these brief notations exhibit the same pattern: the land was originally inhabited by an ancient local populace that was driven out by "newcomers" arriving from a different place.[25] The Moabites displaced the Emim, the Ammonites the

---

Ben-Zvi, 1994), 218–81; William G. Dever, *What Did the Biblical Writers Know and When Did They Know It? What Archaeology Can Tell Us about Ancient Israel* (Grand Rapids: Eerdmans, 2001). For the Dorian immigration, see esp. Jonathan M. Hall, *Ethnic Identity in Greek Antiquity* (Cambridge: Cambridge University Press, 1997), 111–42.

[25] The same pattern of a "young" nation meeting an ancient population described as giants occurs also in the story of the spies (Num 13:22, 28, 32–33; cf. Josh 11:21–22; 14:12–15; 15:12–14). The notion that the ancient inhabitants of the land were giants appears in a slightly different form in Greek texts: cf. Herodotus 1.69; Pausanias 1.35.5–6; 8.29.3; 8.32.5. For giants in the ancient Near East and the Hebrew Bible, see now Brian R. Doak, *The Last of the Rephaim: Conquest and Cataclysm in the Heroic Ages of Ancient Israel* (Boston: Ilex Foundation, 2012).

Zamzummim (Rephaim/Anakites[26]), the Edomites the Horites,[27] and the Philistines (Caphtorim) the Avvim.[28] While all these traditions have been preserved in the biblical texts, the possibility cannot be dismissed that at least some of them reflect ideas held by the other nations themselves.[29] Similar accounts of other Mediterranean peoples have also been preserved in classical literature, such as the legends of the establishment of Carthage by Phoenician settlers and Rome by Aeneas after he left Troy in Asia Minor.[30] Alongside these we find a lengthy list of foundation narratives that recount the formation of Greek colonies across the Mediterranean from the first third of the first millennium B.C.E. onwards.[31]

In recent decades, new epigraphic findings appear to hint at the existence of additional foundation stories of this type from the kingdom of Que. All these findings are associated with one of the prominent protagonists from the territory in which the kingdom of Que was located. This hero, known as *Mpš* in Phoenician or Mopsus in the classical sources, was a well-known figure in the region of southwestern Asia Minor.[32] The majority of the stories relating to Mopsus recount his

---

[26] The tradition regarding the presence of the Rephaim in the eastern Transjordan is apparently alluded to also in the Ugaritic *Incantation to Rapiu an Eternal King* (*rpu mlk 'lm*) (*KTU* 1:108); see N. Wyatt, *Religious Texts from Ugarit: The Words of Ilimilku and His Colleagues* (2nd ed.; Biblical Seminar 53; Sheffield: Sheffield Academic Press, 2000), 395–98, and the bibliography cited there.

[27] See Gen 36:20–30 and n. 16 above.

[28] See also Gen 10:14, which appears to be based on Amos 9.

[29] Wazana notes that the inscription of Mesha the Moabite king, which describes the men of Gad as dwellers in the country of Ataroth "from ancient times [מעלם]" (*KAI* 181.10), indicates that he regarded himself and the Moabites as newcomers—in contrast to the indigenous Gadites ("Natives," 49–50).

[30] For the traditions regarding the foundation of Carthage, see Werner Huss, *Geschichte der Karthager* (Handbuch der Altertumswissenschaft 3.8; Munich: Beck, 1985); Deborah Gera, *Warrior Women: The Anonymous Tractatus de Mulieribus* (Mnemosyne Supplement 162; Leiden: Brill, 1997), 126–40; María E. Aubet, *The Phoenicians and the West: Politics, Colonies, and Trade* (trans. Mary Turton; 2nd ed.; Cambridge: Cambridge University Press, 2001), 214–18. For the traditions concerning Aeneas, see, e.g., G. Karl Galinsky, *Aeneas, Sicily, and Rome* (Princeton Monographs in Art and Archaeology 40; Princeton: Princeton University Press, 1969); Sergio Casali, "The Development of the Aeneas Legend," in *A Companion to Vergil's Aeneid and Its Tradition* (ed. Joseph Farrell and Michael C. J. Putnam; Malden, MA: Wiley-Blackwell, 2010), 37–51.

[31] A rich literature exists on the Greek colonization phenomenon; see, e.g., Gocha R. Tsetskhladze, ed., *Greek Colonisation: An Account of Greek Colonies and Other Settlements Overseas* (2 vols.; Mnemosyne 193; Leiden: Brill, 2006–8).

[32] For a survey of the classical sources regarding Mopsus, see Ilya S. Yakubovich, *Sociolinguistics of the Luwian Language* (BSIEL 2; Leiden: Brill, 2009), 154–56; Jacques Vanschoonwinkel, "Mopsos: Légendes et réalité," *Hethitica* 10 (1990): 185–211; Carolina López-Ruiz, "Mopsos and Cultural Exchange between Greeks and Locals in Cilicia," in *Antike Mythen, Medien, Transformationen und Konstruktionen* (Fritz Graf Festschrift; ed. Ueli Dill and Christine

wandering with his men in western Asia Minor eastward along the southern Cilician coast and the border region of northern Syria (see Herodotus 7.91; Strabo 14.4.3; Pausanias 7.3.7). Xanthus of Lydia, who collected traditions regarding Mopsus that circulated in Lydia, tells us that Mopsus (Μόξος in the Lydian dialect) even reached the southern shores of the Levant (*FGH* 765 F 17 = Athen. 346e).[33] Several cities in southwestern Asia Minor, such as Mopsuestia and Mopsucrene, were named after him.[34]

Two bilingual (Phoenician-Luwian) inscriptions and a newly discovered trilingual (Phoenician-Akkadian-Luwian) inscription from the same region to which Mopsus is said to belong in the Greek literary traditions have now revealed that this figure, who appears to have been a mythic Greek hero, was in fact the founder of a historical royal dynasty. The first bilingual inscription—the Azatiwada inscription (*KAI* 26), dated to the end of the eighth century B.C.E.—describes how the king of the Danunians brought Azatiwada to power.[35] Its details correspond to those given in Tiglath-pileser III's inscription, which refers to Urikku, king of Que, as well as to those in Sargon II's 718 B.C.E. inscription, which speaks of the appointment of the prince of Adana by the king of Que.[36] The land inhabited by the Danunians was therefore Que, and Azatiwada the prince or top-ranking official appointed.

While the Phoenician text refers to the "house of *Mpš*" (I, 16; II, 15; III, 11), the parallel Luwian text speaks of "the house of Mukasa [*mu-ka-sá-sá-na* DOMUS-*nì-i*]" (XXI, 108–13, LVIII, 324–30).[37] Although the term *bt mpš* was unclear when the Phoenician text was originally deciphered, the Luwian version makes it clear

---

Walde; Berlin: de Gruyter, 2009), 382–96. For the traditions of Mopsus as a prophet or seer, see [Hesiod], *Melampodia* F 278 M-W (= Strabo 14.1.27); cf. Apollodorus, *Epitome* 6.2. See Jan N. Bremmer, "Balaam, Mopsus and Melampous: Tales of Travelling Seers," in *The Prestige of the Pagan Prophet Balaam in Judaism, Early Christianity and Islam* (ed. George H. van Kooten and Jacques van Ruiten; TBN 11; Leiden: Brill, 2008), 49–67.

[33] The form Μόξος appears also in Nicolaus of Damascus (*FGH* 90 F 16).

[34] *Scholia* to Dionysius Periegetes 1.850; Eusebius *Chronicon* p. 60b (*Eusebius Werke*, vol. 7, *Die Chronik des Hieronymus* [ed. Rudolf Helm; Berlin: Akademie, 1956]). See also Philo H. J. Houwink Ten Cate, *The Luwian Population Groups of Lycia and Cilicia Aspera during the Hellenistic Period* (DMOA 10; Leiden: Brill, 1961), 46–47.

[35] For the Azatiwada inscription, see, e.g., K. Lawson Younger Jr., "The Phoenician Inscription of Azatiwada: An Integrated Reading," *JSS* 43 (1998): 11–47; John D. Hawkins, *Corpus of Hieroglyphic Luwian Inscriptions* (Studies in Indo-European Language and Culture n.s. 8; Berlin: de Gruyter, 2000), 1:45–68, and the bibliography mentioned in *COS* 2.31.

[36] See Hayim Tadmor, *The Inscriptions of Tiglath-Pileser III, King of Assyria: Critical Edition, with Introduction, Translations and Commentary* (Publications of the Israel Academy of Sciences and Humanities, Section of Humanities; Jerusalem: Israel Academy of Sciences and Humanities, 1994), 54–55 n. 8; Edward Lipiński, *Itineraria Phoenicia* (OLA 127; Leuven: Peeters, 2004), 116–30; Anna M. Jasink and Mauro Marino, "The West-Anatolian Origins of the Que Kingdom Dynasty," *SMEA* 49 (2007): 407–26.

[37] Hawkins, *Corpus*, 51, 56.

that it alludes to the Asia Minor hero Mopsus/Moxus mentioned in the Greek sources.[38] The phrase "house of *Mpš* (Mopsus)" refers to the founder of the dynasty, Mopsus—along the same lines as the biblical terms "house of Jacob/Israel" or "house of David."

The expression has subsequently also been found on two additional inscriptions in southern Turkey, published very recently. One of these is a trilingual (Phoenician-Luwian-Akkadian) inscription from İncirli, the second a bilingual inscription from Çineköy. Although discovered in 1993, the former has still not been published in full in an official text—the only available version is Stephen A. Kaufman's preliminary publication in 2007.[39] Here, too, the ruler of Que is identified as the "king of the Danunians" (front 2; left 17, 25; back 17), who is related to the "house of *Mpš*" (front 8, 10). The kingdom of Que—known up until this point from Akkadian and Aramaic inscriptions and the biblical text (1 Kgs 10:28; 1 Chr 1:16)—appears here for the first time in Phoenician as *mlk Qw* (front 9; back 10; right 1).[40]

The bilingual inscription from Çineköy was discovered close to the Turkish city of Adana in 2000.[41] The most important detail in this inscription for our purposes lies in the parallelism between the Phoenician "Danunians" in line 9 and the Luwian "Hiyawa [*hi-ia-wa/i-sa-ha-wa/i* (URBS)]" in line 7 (cf. lines 1–3). While the Phoenician text employs the old term "Danunians" in reference to the people of this country, the Luwian parallel speaks of this kingdom as "Hiyawa."[42] This undoubtedly reveals the etymology of the name of "Que," which up until this discovery had remained obscure.[43] This inscription thus attests that the name Que represents the eastern pronunciation of the Luwian Hiyawa.

The name Hiyawa is most probably linked to the "Ahhiyawa" referred to in second-millennium B.C.E. Hittite inscriptions as an important national group in

---

[38] See, for example, one of the first attempts to translate the term as "house of refreshment": J. Leveen and C. J. Moss in R. D. Barnett, J. Leveen, and C. J. Moss, "A Phoenician Inscription from Eastern Cilicia," *Iraq* 10 (1948): 64.

[39] Kaufman, "The Phoenician Inscription of the Incirli Trilingual: A Tentative Reconstruction and Translation," *Maarav* 14 (2007): 7–26.

[40] None of these occurrences is certain, however; see Kaufman, "Phoenician Inscription," 22.

[41] Recai Tekoğlu and André Lemaire, with I. Ipek and A. Kazim Tosun, "La bilingue royale Louvito-Phénicienne de Çineköy," *Académie des inscriptions & belles-lettres* 3 (2000): 961–1000. See also Lipiński, *Itineraria Phoenicia*, 127–28; Gary M. Beckman, Trevor R. Bryce, and Eric H. Cline, *The Ahhiyawa Texts* (SBLWAW 28; Atlanta: Society of Biblical Literature, 2011), 263–66.

[42] The name "Danunians" is also known from an earlier period, occurring in the El-Amarna letters from the second half of the fourteenth century B.C.E. (EA 151), as well as in the Hittite correspondence between Ḫattušili III and Rameses II (KBo XXVIII 25)—apparently being one of the early names of this land and its inhabitants. See also below.

[43] Prior to the discovery of this inscription, other etymological proposals for the name "Que" had been proposed; see Hawkins, *Corpus*, 40.

the Aegean that threatened the Hittite hegemony in western Asia Minor.[44] Although scholars dispute the precise identity of the Ahhiyawan kingdom, it is commonly accepted today that the name lies behind the term "Achaean," one of the generic names in the Homeric texts for the Greek heroes. The location of the Ahhiyawan center also remains disputed. While the natural candidate is Mycenae in the interior of the Aegean territory, the Ahhiyawans also appear to have had some control over the southwestern Anatolian coast.

The Çineköy inscription reveals that the people who established their kingdom in Cilicia and referred to the "house of *Mpš*" (Mopsus) identified themselves as the descendants of the second-millennium Ahhiyawans. This claim is corroborated by Herodotus's statement that "these Cilicians were formerly called Hypachaei [οὗτοι τὸ παλαιὸν Ὑπαχαιοὶ ἐκαλέοντο]" (7.91)—that is, they formed a sort of "Lower Achaea." It is also substantiated by traditions preserved in the Greek sources regarding Mopsus that attest to his wanderings in southeastern Asia Minor eastward toward Cilicia. This cumulative evidence suggests that certain groups in southeastern Asia Minor, who regarded themselves as the offspring of *Mpš*/Mopsus, possessed a tradition that they had arrived from the Ahhiyawan world in west Asia Minor or the Aegean and settled in the region of Cilicia at the end of the second millennium B.C.E., calling the kingdom they established Que (= Hiyawa).[45] The story of migration thus held a central place in their account of the kingdom's history.

B. *The Origins and Diffusion of the Genre*

The majority of the foundation narratives I have presented thus far—relating to the Israelites, Dorians, Aramites, Philistines, Edomites, Moabites, Ammonites, and the kingdom of Que—belong to societies that became states at the end of the second millennium and the beginning of the first millennium B.C.E. with the collapse of the great kingdoms in the region (Egypt, Hatti, and Mycenae). It would thus appear that these cultural and political changes gave rise at some point in their development to a series of foundation stories designed to explain how the new kingdoms emerged in this geographical space.[46]

Yet the fact that these traditions became central and foundational in Israel and the Greek world, as well as in other kingdoms around the Mediterranean, raises

---

[44] For the current state of research into the Ahhiyawa "problem," see Robert Fischer, *Die Ahhijawa-Frage: Mit einer kommentierten Bibliographie* (DBH 26; Wiesbaden: Harrassowitz, 2010); Beckman et al., *Ahhiyawa Texts*, 1–6.

[45] See Margalit Finkelberg, "Mopsos and the Philistines: Mycenaean Migrants in the Eastern Mediterranean," in *Greeks between East and West: Essays in Greek Literature and History in Memory of David Asheri* (ed. Gabriel Herman and Israel Shatzman; Jerusalem: Israel Academy of Sciences and Humanities, 2007), 34–35.

[46] See also Machinist, "Outsiders," 48–54; Wazana, "Natives," 51; cf. Weinfeld, *Promise of the Land*, 18.

questions, since, as noted above, the regions of Mesopotamia, Egypt, and Anatolia also experienced tribal migrations and wanderings during the third and second millennia B.C.E. While several of the nomadic groups even took over the reins of power in these kingdoms of the ancient Near East, these kingdoms never sought to present themselves as "immigrants." On the contrary, they rapidly—and at times even more vehemently than the native populace—assumed a local identity, regarding themselves as the successors and followers of the ancient indigenous culture.[47] We should not be surprised that such migratory populations desired to adopt autochthonous traditions, in view of the fact that migration naturally becomes apologetic when faced with claims to land rights and membership of the local royalty. An ethnic group that states that it has come from elsewhere is liable to encounter opposition from the local populace. Both the Greeks and the Israelites appear to have constantly felt compelled to justify their stories of immigration in some way—by asserting, for example, that they were not foreigners but "returnees" or that the land had been given to them by divine decree.

An additional difficulty arises in light of modern scholarly research. Using archaeological and epigraphic evidence and sociological theories, scholars have convincingly demonstrated that the new, small-scale kingdoms that arose toward the end of the second millennium B.C.E. consisted largely, if not entirely, of native population groups. While migration played some part in their emergence, the stories disseminated by the populaces of the new small states in the Mediterranean regarding massive waves of immigration that led to the physical removal of the ancient inhabitants must, however, be regarded as exaggerated myths rather than historical realities.[48]

We should thus not be surprised that, alongside the literary traditions that depict massive migration, accounts of autochthonous groups who regarded themselves as time-honored residents also circulated among the new small states. While traces of these views have been preserved, in the majority of cases such narratives did not become the central traditions. Thus, for example, the book of Chronicles asserts a continuous Ephraimite settlement in the land (1 Chr 7:20–29), in contrast to the account of Ephraim's birth in Egypt and the arrival of his descendants in

---

[47] Cf. Machinist, "Outsiders," 50–51. For a survey of migration in the ancient Near East, see the studies in Karel Van Lerberghe and Antoon Schoors, eds., *Immigration and Emigration within the Ancient Near East: Festschrift E. Lipiński* (OLA 65; Leuven: Peeters, 1995).

[48] For the Israelites and Dorians, see n. 24 above. For the people of Transjordan, see, e.g., *Studies in the History and Archaeology of Jordan I* (ed. Adnan Hadidi; Amman: Department of Antiquities, Hashemite Kingdom of Jordan, 1982); Randall W. Younker, "Ammonites," in *Peoples of the Old Testament World* (ed. Alfred J. Hoerth et al.; Grand Rapids: Baker, 1994), 300–304. For the Arameans, see Glenn M. Schwartz, "The Origins of the Arameans in Syria and Northern Mesopotamia: Research Problems and Potential Strategies," in *To the Euphrates and Beyond: Archaeological Studies in Honour of Maurits N. van Loon* (ed. O. M. C. Haex et al.; Rotterdam: Balkema, 1989), 275–91; Guy Bunnens, "Syria in the Iron Age: Problems of Definition," in *Essays on Syria in the Iron Age* (ed. Guy Bunnens; ANESSup 7; Louvain: Peeters, 2000), 3–19.

Canaan (Gen 48:5-8).⁴⁹ Other groups of Israelites also appear to have possessed traditions concerning their original presence in Canaan rather than their having come up from Egypt. Thus, for example, while the Kenizzites and Calebites are described on numerous occasions as prominent Judahite clans whose ancestors were among the leaders of the people who left Egypt (see Num 32:12; Josh 14:6, 14; 15:17; Judg 1:13; 3:7-11), other texts imply that they formed part of the local populace that inhabited Canaan before the Israelites' arrival (Gen 15:19-21; 1 Sam 25:2-3; 30:14). These traditions suggest that they were local tribes living in the area of Hebron, Debir, and southern Judah who assimilated into the kingdom of Judah at some point. When their traditions were incorporated into the pan-Israelite tradition over time, they, too, were represented as having come up from Egypt. A similar process is evident among the Kenites, who, at the same time as being listed among the local populace—alongside the Canaanites and Amorites in Gen 15:19-20 and the Amalekites in Num 24:20-21, and linked to Moses and his father-in-law (Judg 4:11; cf. 1 Sam 15:6)—are also described as settling the land together with the Judahites (Judg 1:16).

As with the Israelites, not all the Greeks regarded themselves as immigrants, and some of them also possessed autochthonous traditions alongside migration ones. The Athenians, for example, endeavored to present themselves as the indigenous inhabitants of the territory to which the city belonged. This idea appears to have become firmly fixed in the fifth century B.C.E., when Athens sought to strengthen its position as leader of the alliance against the Persians and was part of the effort to represent the city as the earliest and most preeminent of the Greek cities.⁵⁰ Herodotus even appears to have concluded from these claims that the Athenians were not Hellenes in origin at all but "Pelasgic"—that is, the early inhabitants of the land (1.57-58). At the same time, Athenians were also regarded as Ionians who claimed that their original place of habitation was Achaea in the northern Peloponnese. After they were driven out of that territory by the Achaeans, the Ionians migrated to their well-known historical place of residence.⁵¹ As noted above, Xuthus, who begat Ion, the father of the Ionians, is similarly said to be a wanderer who reached Athens in his travels. According to Euripides, however, who prefers the autochthonous tradition, Xuthus was only Ion's adoptive parent, and Ion was regarded as the son of Creusa on his mother's side and the descendant of the kings of Athens who came out of the ground (*Ion* 266-68), while Ion's real father was Apollo.⁵²

---

⁴⁹ For the tribal foundation traditions of the Manassites (Num 32:39, 41-42), see Rofé, "Family-Saga," 187-91; cf. Weinfeld, *Promise of the Land*, 60, 71-72.

⁵⁰ Vincent J. Rosivach, "Autochthony and the Athenians," *CQ* 37 (1987): 294-306; J. M. Hall, *Ethnic Identity*, 51-56; Sara L. Forsdyke, "'Born from the Earth': The Political Uses of an Athenian Myth," *JANER* 12 (2012): 119-41.

⁵¹ Herodotus 1.145; 7.94; Pausanias 7.1.24; cf. Strabo 8.1.2; 8.7.1-4.

⁵² Parker, "Myths," 207, 213-14 n. 80; Loraux, "Kreousa," 168-206; Zacharia, *Converging Truths*, 55-56 and passim; Kevin H. Lee, *Euripides Ion* (Warminster: Aris & Phillips, 1997), 35-36.

Likewise, while the inhabitants of Sparta claimed to be the offspring of the Dorians and Heraclids who conquered the Peloponnese by force and drove out the early dynasty of the Atreidae, they also sought to create a link with the glorious mythic past—as indicated by the cultic sites and dedicatory inscriptions from the end of the eighth century B.C.E. dedicated to Menelaus and Helen that have been discovered in the city. In similar fashion, when the Spartans imposed their leadership on the remainder of the Greek cities during the Persian war, they appealed to their status as Agamemnon's heirs (Herodotus 7.159), even though, according to other traditions, they had been responsible for removing his dynasty from the Peloponnese.[53]

As we saw above, the people of the "house of *Mpš*," who refer to their kingdom as Hiyawa (Que), preserved a migration tradition according to which they were the descendants of the inhabitants who had in the past dwelled in western Asia Minor or the Aegean. The name "Danunians," however, already appears in sources from the region from the second half of the second millennium B.C.E., suggesting that they were the earliest inhabitants of this region of Cilicia, in the period prior to the changes that occurred at the end of the Bronze Age.[54] Since the name "Danunians" is used interchangeably in the royal inscriptions for "Que" and the "house of *Mpš*," it is reasonable to assume—as archaeological findings corroborate—that Que was also populated by peoples who maintained their long-established presence.[55]

It thus cannot be taken for granted that a people who arrived in a new place continued to recount their migratory traditions. We might have expected that the new nations that emerged in the Mediterranean at the beginning of the first millennium B.C.E. would replace their migratory traditions with claims of indigeneity similar to those made by the "autochthonous" groups of the society—as has happened since time immemorial among the ancient kingdoms in the region (who themselves experienced population movement and migration). How, then, is the fact that these societies transformed their migration accounts into the central stories of the kingdoms of the region to be explained? What caused these kingdoms to adopt such "settler" traditions as their formative narratives?

Two proposals can be raised in this regard. First, the migration myths appear to have been rooted in the new kingdoms and city-states, becoming formative narratives as part of their national and social attempt to dissociate themselves from the political and organizational structures that existed in the space prior to their emergence during the second millennium B.C.E. Despite the migration of peoples and the changes of power in Mesopotamia or Egypt, no such phenomenon of discontinuity occurred in either of these realms, and the political and national structure remained unaltered down to the Persian period. Although these traditions do not

---

[53] Malkin, *Myth and Territory*, 46–66.
[54] See n. 42 above.
[55] Assaf Yasur-Landau, *The Philistines and Aegean Migration at the End of the Late Bronze Age* (Cambridge: Cambridge University Press, 2010), 163; cf. Beckman et al., *Ahhiyawa*, 266.

accord well with claims to land rights, when a society seeks to separate itself from the old order, the immigration traditions tend to reinforce a sense of uniqueness and superiority over those who perceive themselves as belonging to the old order and ancient administration.[56]

Second, in the first third of the first millennium B.C.E.—in particular from the ninth and eighth centuries onward—the Phoenician and Greek worlds began to experience a trend toward large-scale colonization throughout the Mediterranean. At the same time, new foundation and migration myths appear to have developed within these newly formed states in the wake of the new settlements.[57] While the new small-states that arose toward the end of the second millennium B.C.E. consisted largely of native population groups, the new colonies established in the Mediterranean were completely virgin, constituted wholly by migratory ethnic groups planted, by their very nature, in foreign soil. The foundation of these colonies and their establishment undoubtedly created interest in the subject of the formation of cities and kingdoms in the mother country, encouraging the preservation of ancient traditions and their transformation into foundational traditions. This may be the reason why some of the Greek foundation narratives in the mother country are shaped along the lines of the colonies' foundation stories—and so, for example, Pindar calls Sparta a "Dorian colony [Δωρίδ' ἀποικίαν]" (Isthm. 7.12).[58]

The influence of the colony foundation stories on the sense of identity of the cities in the mother country may also serve to explain why migration and foundation narratives flourished among the peoples of the Mediterranean even in places that did not experience the shock waves that shook the region at the end of the second millennium B.C.E., such as among the Phoenicians. The archaeological and literary evidence attests that the Phoenician cities did not suffer significantly from the invasions by the sea people that so devastated the rest of the cities of the Levant.[59] Traces of a foundation and migration story nevertheless still existed among the

---

[56] For other explanations, see Machinist, "Outsiders," 50–51; Wazana, "Natives," 56–58. The suggestion that the foundation stories constitute a mirror image of the "young" nations according to the perception of the oldest kingdoms of the Near East—in particular the Mesopotamian kingdoms—fails to explain why the Israelites, or other groups in the Mediterranean basin, felt a need to differentiate themselves from the old kingdoms in the region in this specific case alone, while in other cases in which biblical and Mesopotamian literature exhibits significant similarities it is customarily attributed to imitation and acceptance of the dominant culture.

[57] For Phoenician colonization, see most recently María Eugenia Aubet, *Commerce and Colonization in the Ancient Near East* (trans. Mary Turton; Cambridge: Cambridge University Press, 2013). For the parallel Greek phenomenon, see n. 31 above.

[58] See Irad Malkin, *Religion and Colonization in Ancient Greece* (Studies in Greek and Roman Religion 3; Leiden: Brill, 1987), 4; Jonathan M. Hall, "Foundation Stories," in Tsetskhladze, *Greek Colonisation*, 2:383–84 and n. 3. For the legend of Cadmus, see Daniel Berman, "The Double Foundation of Boiotian Thebes," *TAPA* 134 (2004): 1–22.

[59] See, e.g., Aubet, *Phoenicians*, 24–25, 29; Glenn Markoe, *Phoenicians* (Peoples of the Past; Berkeley: University of California Press, 2000), 24 and n. 14.

Phoenicians, and Herodotus opens his *History* with this tradition. According to his account, the Phoenicians came to their country from the Red Sea (Ἐρυθρὰ θάλαττα) (1.1; cf. 7.89.2).[60] While this term customarily designates either side of the Indian Ocean in Greek literature, Herodotus generally uses to it refer to the Persian Gulf.[61] He thus asserts that the Phoenicians arrived from the region of southern Mesopotamia, close to the Persian Gulf. Although it is possible to surmise that this narrative is a Greek invention that developed from a popular etymology of the name Phoenicia—"red" in Greek—Herodotus stresses that the tradition is a Phoenician one (ὡς αὐτοὶ λέγουσι). Here, the Phoenicians are described as one of the peoples of the relatively new states in the Mediterranean.

It would thus appear that, among the other causes lying behind the transformation of a migration tradition into a central narrative in many cultures of the eastern Mediterranean was the popularity these accounts possessed among the new colonies and countries established in the region. While the eastern Mediterranean and Levant knew numerous migration and wandering narratives from a relatively early period—such as those in the Idrimi inscription or the Egyptian *Story of Sinuhe*—their primary focus appears to have shifted in the first millennium B.C.E. toward the ethnic identity of the tribe or people. Numerous groups adopted the migration narratives that were circulating among the nomadic societies in the eastern Mediterranean, forging them into a foundation tradition—even when they were not applicable to all members of society—because they corresponded to the ideals embraced by the new states in the region during this period.

While stories of this kind initially flourished independently in each society, these new states were also exposed to conceptual and literary ideas via the cultural exchanges that took place in the early eastern Mediterranean. The origin of the resemblances that we have adduced here may thus lie in the common cultural environment of the Mediterranean. The links between the diverse nations in the area—between neighboring kingdoms, Phoenician and Greek settlers, or settlers and their motherland—must have created the basis for a cultural exchange of foundation stories that contained similar literary types, as well as motifs and ideas from the field of national and ethnic identity.[62]

---

[60] Androsthenes of Thasos, who participated in Alexander the Great's expedition, states that two cities in the area of the Persian Gulf possessed the same name as two Phoenician cities, suggesting that the inhabitants of the latter originated in the Mesopotamia area (*FGH* 711 F 2 = Strabo 16.3.2, cf. Justinus 18.3.1–5).

[61] See David Asheri, Alan B. Lloyd and Aldo Corcella, *A Commentary on Herodotus I–IV* (ed. Oswyn Murray and Alfonso Moreno; Oxford: Oxford University Press, 2007), 74–75.

[62] Irad Malkin has demonstrated the cultural interchange between Phoenician and Greek settlers with respect to the foundation traditions of Melqart and Herakles ("Herakles and Melqart: Greeks and Phoenicians in the Middle Ground," in Gruen, *Cultural Borrowings*, 238–57). See also idem, *A Small Greek World: Networks in the Ancient Mediterranean* (Greeks Overseas; Oxford: Oxford University Press, 2011), 119–42.

III. Conclusion

In this article, I have presented two of the principal models of foundation narratives prevalent in the biblical texts: a founding father who settles in a new place and starts a new bloodline and the migration of a ethnic group that ends in conquest of the new land. Although neither type occurs in the literature of the cultures of the ancient Near East, both were popular in the ancient Greek writings. I have adduced a series of examples from the Greek world that exhibit a significant correspondence with the biblical accounts and to date have not been examined in comparative research. Several factors indicate that these traditions depicting a nation's history in terms of migration and settlement were not the possession of the Greeks and Israelites alone in the Mediterranean but were characteristic of many of the small kingdoms in the region at the beginning of the first millennium B.C.E. The genre appears to have been encouraged by the desire of the new states to separate themselves from the old regimes in the region, and the stories perhaps also owed something to the creation of new colonies in the Mediterranean in the first third of the first millennium B.C.E. onward, a phenomenon that increased awareness of the emergence of new societies and states.

This circumstance in the Mediterranean suggests that the absence of this genre from the literature of the great kingdoms of the ancient Near East is not coincidental. Since the great kingdoms apparently regarded themselves as "veteran," they perceived no need to attribute their identity to an "immigrant" founder. Consequently, this genre did not take written form until the beginning of the first millennium B.C.E. At the same time, in the first third of the first millennium B.C.E. a series of national narratives arose and developed within the new states and the Greek and Phoenician colonies founded during this period. The abundance of traditions promoted the reinforcement and preservation of wandering and migration traditions already prevalent among the seminomadic societies in the region and led to their establishment as foundational narratives. The contact between neighboring states familiarized the peoples of the region with various foundation and settlement stories and led to a cultural exchange.

THE ANCHOR YALE BIBLE

A tradition of excellence in biblical scholarship and a commitment to advancing biblical understanding in the 21st century

The Anchor Yale Bible Commentary Series, a book-by-book translation and exegesis of the Hebrew Bible, the New Testament, and the Apocrypha

The Anchor Yale Bible Dictionary, with more than 6,000 entries from 800 international scholars

The Anchor Yale Bible Reference Library, currently consisting of 34 volumes by foremost scholars from a variety of religious backgrounds who focus on broad biblical themes.

Widely recognized as the flagship of American biblical scholarship, the **Anchor Yale Bible Series** is comprised of:

- Contributions from distinguished authors around the world, representing Protestant, Catholic, Jewish, and Muslim traditions;
- New translations, reflecting the latest knowledge of ancient languages;
- Extensive annotations, including alternative translations;
- Objective treatment of competing theories;
- Commentary to explain texts and clarify difficult passages;
- Historical background as well as up-to-date research;
- Helpful organizing tools including detailed introductions, overviews, and outlines;
- Relevant visual features such as maps, photographs, diagrams, and more.

For more information please visit YaleBooks.com/AnchorYaleBible

Yale UNIVERSITY PRESS

No Future without Moses: The Disastrous End of 2 Kings 22–25 and the Chance of the Moab Covenant (Deuteronomy 29–30)

DOMINIK MARKL
markl@biblico.it
Pontifical Biblical Institute, 00187 Rome, Italy

This article explores the question of why the history of Israel and Judah, according to the books of Kings, ends in disaster (2 Kings 25). Although this question has been intensely discussed, especially since Martin Noth's *Überlieferungsgeschichtliche Studien* (1943), no entirely convincing solution has been offered. The argument suggests a new explanation of the ending of Kings from the perspective of its textual pragmatics. The narrative of the finding of the "book of the torah" during Josiah's reign (2 Kings 22–23) is seen to refer readers emphatically to Deuteronomy. The laconically disastrous end of 2 Kings 24–25 proves the accuracy of Moses' predictions of exile. Readers who wish to know about the possibilities for Israel's future are bound to reread Deuteronomy 29–30, the only text in which Moses refers to the return to the promised land (Deut 30:1–10). They are thereby taken into the dynamics of the Moab covenant (Deuteronomy 29–30). Kings does not console its readers with a happy ending but forces them to turn to Moses' rhetoric of blessing and curse and to make their decision between life and death (Deut 30:15–20).

One of the puzzles of the Hebrew Bible has been the question of why the history of Israel and Judah, according to the books of Kings, ends in disaster (2 Kings 25). Most scholars would probably agree that this ending can be reasonably

This is a revised version of a paper presented at the ProPent meeting in Bass Lake (South Africa) on September 2, 2012. I wish to express my gratitude to Eckart Otto, Thomas Römer, and Ulrich Berges for their inspiring comments. Moreover, I thank Norbert Lohfink, Robert Alter, Garrett Galvin, and Peter Dubovsky for their careful reading of the article and their helpful observations. I am also grateful to Matthew Charlesworth (Nairobi) and David Gill (Berkeley, CA), for proofreading this paper at different stages. Since 2012, I have been a Research Associate at the Department of Old Testament Studies, University of Pretoria, South Africa.

understood as a product of exilic times.¹ The final chapters provide an etiology of exile, while the very last verses, which mention the release and noble treatment of Jehoiachin (25:27–30), may encourage readers to see exile as a state of unexpected opportunities.² Yet many scholars assume that the text of Kings was still open to redaction during Persian times.³ It would have been a simple literary procedure to add a few verses to the end of ch. 25, comparable to the solution that the end of Chronicles provides (2 Chr 36:22–23), to give the entire history of Israel a much more positive interpretation. Such a conclusion might have opened up for readers the hope of a better future.

Yet, at the end of the story, we find ourselves stuck in disaster. Jerusalem and the temple are destroyed and plundered (2 Kgs 25:9–10, 13–17); the upper class of Judah is deported to Babylon (25:11); and the rest of the people have fled to Egypt (25:26). It would not entirely console any contemporary reader that finally the Judean king was released and received an allotment of food "for each day—all the days of his life," as the story is concluded (25:30). Readers are left alone with the burning question as to what the future of God's people could be. Why was there no *Fortschreibung* added to the ending of Kings to indicate clearly the restoration of the people?

I will suggest an explanation of the intriguing ending of Kings from the perspective of its textual pragmatics, which direct readers toward the book of Deuteronomy. The article will unfold in five steps. After a look at previous interpretations

---

¹ Most recently, David Janzen argues for a dating in exilic times, after 562 B.C.E. (*The Violent Gift: Trauma's Subversion of the Deuteronomistic History's Narrative* [LHBOTS 561; London: T&T Clark, 2012], esp. 24–25). See also idem, "The Sins of Josiah and Hezekiah: A Synchronic Reading of the Final Chapters of Kings," *JSOT* 37 (2013): 349–70. In the latter work, Janzen sees in the final chapters a message directed to King Jehoiachin in exile. Many others see in 2 Kings 24–25 an exilic redactor at work, e.g., Hermann-Josef Stipp, "Remembering Josiah's Reform in Kings," in *Remembering and Forgetting in Early Second Temple Judah* (ed. Ehud Ben Zvi and Christoph Levin; FAT 85; Tübingen: Mohr Siebeck, 2012), 225–38, esp. 233; Marvin A. Sweeney, *King Josiah of Judah: The Lost Messiah of Israel* (Oxford: Oxford University Press, 2001), esp. 33–39; Erik Eynikel, *The Reform of King Josiah and the Composition of the Deuteronomistic History* (OtSt 33; Leiden: Brill, 1996), esp. 364.

² See Thomas Römer, "Transformations in Deuteronomistic and Biblical Historiography: On 'Book Finding' and Other Literary Strategies," *ZAW* 109 (1997): 11, where Römer points out parallels with Genesis 37–50, Daniel 2–6, and Esther. See also idem, "Die Anfänge judäischer Geschichtsschreibung im sogenannten Deuteronomistischen Geschichtswerk," in *Die Apostelgeschichte im Kontext antiker und frühchristlicher Historiographie* (ed. Jörg Frey et al.; BZNW 162; Berlin: de Gruyter, 2009), 51–76, esp. 75. David Janzen attributes the "maddening" vagueness at the end of the book to "a time frame when it was impossible to tell what the fate of the Davidide would be." Therefore, the end should be written "in the exile—or possibly in the early post-exilic period" ("An Ambiguous Ending: Dynastic Punishment in Kings and the Fate of the Davidides in 2 Kings 25.27–30," *JSOT* 33 [2008]: 57, 58).

³ Compare Thomas Römer, *The So-Called Deuteronomistic History: A Sociological, Historical and Literary Introduction* (2nd ed.; London: T&T Clark, 2007), 165–83.

of the ending of Kings, I will analyze intertextual connections between the final chapters of Kings and Deuteronomy. I will then discuss Moses' outlook on Israel's future according to Deuteronomy. Against this backdrop, I will be able to suggest a pragmatic understanding of 2 Kings 22–25 and add some hermeneutical perspectives.

I. PREVIOUS INTERPRETATIONS OF THE ENDING OF KINGS

Martin Noth's theory of the Deuteronomistic History (DtrH) prominently emphasized the intricate literary and theological connection between Deuteronomy and the historiography in Kings in his *Überlieferungsgeschichtliche Studien* (1943).[4] Noth interpreted the intention of DtrH with strong emphasis on its ending. According to him, the primary intention of DtrH was to explain the end of history as divine judgment. DtrH, he says, does not envision any hope for the future but presents a definite end. Noth's decisive passage reads:

> Finally we must raise the question of what historical developments Dtr. anticipated for the future. Admittedly his theme is the past history of his people, as written down and, as far as he was concerned, at an end. However, the pre-exilic prophets saw the catastrophe which they predicted not as a final end but as the beginning of a new era. Similarly, Dtr. could have seen the end of the period of history which he depicts as the end of a self-contained historical process, without thinking that his people could go no further; and he could have used the interpretative summaries, which he adds, to answer the question that readily suggests itself: would not the history which he wrote attain its full meaning in the future, in conditions which had yet to develop out of the ruins of the old order, the more so because in Dtr.'s time people were intensely hopeful that a new order of things would emerge from all these catastrophes? It is very telling that Dtr. does not take up this question and does not use the opportunity to discuss the future goal of history. Clearly he saw the divine judgement which was acted out in his account of the external collapse of Israel as a nation as something final and definitive and he expressed no hope for the future, not even in the very modest and simple form of an expectation that the deported and dispersed people would be gathered together.[5]

---

[4] Noth, *Überlieferungsgeschichtliche Studien: Die sammelnden und bearbeitenden Geschichtswerke im Alten Testament* (2nd ed.; Darmstadt: Wissenschaftliche Buchgesellschaft, 1957), 3–110.

[5] Noth, *The Deuteronomistic History* (trans. J. Doull et al.; 2nd ed.; JSOTSup 15; Sheffield: Sheffield Academic Press, 1991), 142–43. The original reads: "Endlich wäre an Dtr noch die Frage zu richten, was er über den von ihm aus gesehen *künftigen Fortgang der Geschichte* gedacht hat. Zwar war sein Thema ja die vergangene und für ihn abgeschlossen vorliegende Geschichte seines Volkes. Aber wenn man bedenkt, daß die vorexilischen Propheten die von ihnen angekündigte Katastrophe nicht als ein letztes Ende, sondern als den Ausgangspunkt einer neuen Zeit betrachtet hatten, so hätte immerhin auch Dtr in dem Endpunkt seiner Geschichtsdarstellung wohl den

Contrary to Noth's view, Gerhard von Rad favors a quite optimistic reading in his *Theologie des Alten Testaments I* (1st ed., 1957).⁶ He sees DtrH as a "comprehensive confession of Israel's guilt" and as a "doxology of judgment."⁷ "Yet, closing as it does with the note about the favour shown to Jehoiachin (II Kings xxv. 27ff.), it points to a possibility with which Jahweh can resume."⁸

Hans Walter Wolff challenged both Noth's and von Rad's interpretations in "Das Kerygma des deuteronomistischen Geschichtswerks," a paper presented at the University of Göttingen in 1960.⁹ Wolff convincingly pointed out that several aspects of DtrH convey a message of repentance. Solomon's prayer at the dedication of the temple explicitly envisions Israel praying in the situation of exile and converting to YHWH (1 Kgs 8:46–53).¹⁰ Moreover, this message is most explicit in Moses' speeches in Deut 4:29–31; 30:1–10, which Wolff attributes to a "second hand of the deuteronomistic circle."¹¹ Although he points out an important trace in DtrH that contradicts Noth's pessimistic view of the work's end and aim, Wolff himself does not return to the problem of the ending of the story. If the kerygma of DtrH really is repentance, why is there no trace of this message at its very end?¹²

Abschluß eines geschlossenen Geschichtsverlaufs sehen können, ohne doch damit den Weg seines Volkes an ein letztes Ziel gelangt sein zu lassen, und er hätte in den von ihm beigesteuerten deutenden Zusammenfassungen die Möglichkeit gehabt, auf die naheliegende Frage zu antworten, ob denn der Sinn der von ihm dargestellten Geschichte nicht in der Zukunft, in Dingen, die aus dem Zusammenbruch des alten Bestandes erst noch erwachsen sollten, liege, und dies um so mehr, als in seiner Zeit die Erwartung einer aus den geschehenen Katastrophen hervorgehenden künftigen neuen Ordnung der Dinge durchaus lebendig war. Wenn Dtr jene Frage *nicht* aufgegriffen und die vorhandenen Gelegenheiten, etwas über ein zukünftiges Ziel der Geschichte zu sagen, *nicht* genutzt hat, so ist dieses Schweigen vielsagend genug. Er hat in dem göttlichen Gericht, das sich in dem von ihm dargestellten äußeren Zusammenbruch des Volkes Israel vollzog, offenbar etwas Endgültiges und Abschließendes gesehen und eine Zukunftshoffnung nicht einmal in der bescheidensten und einfachsten Form einer Erwartung der künftigen Sammlung der zerstreuten Deportierten zum Ausdruck gebracht" (Noth, *Überlieferungsgeschichtliche Studien*, 107–8).

⁶ Von Rad, *Theologie des Alten Testaments I: Die Theologie der geschichtlichen Überlieferungen Israels* (Munich: Kaiser, 1957), 332–44.

⁷ Von Rad, *Old Testament Theology I: The Theology of Israel's Historical Traditions* (trans. D. M. G. Stalker; 2nd ed.; OTL; Louisville: Westminster John Knox, 2001), 337, 343.

⁸ Ibid., 343.

⁹ Wolff, "Das Kerygma des deuteronomistischen Geschichtswerks," in idem, *Gesammelte Studien zum Alten Testament* (2nd ed.; Theologische Bücherei 22; Munich: Kaiser, 1973), 308–24; repr. from *ZAW* 73 (1961): 171–86; von Rad integrated Wolff's suggestion into the second edition of his *Theologie*. Compare von Rad, *Theology*, 346.

¹⁰ Wolff, "Kerygma," 316–17.

¹¹ Ibid., 320.

¹² J. Gordon McConville ("Narrative and Meaning in the Books of Kings," *Bib* 70 [1989]: 31–49) touches on our question: "What kind of hope, then, does the narrator offer to his readers?" (p. 47). "In Kings," he claims, "the land is lost, but some measure of restoration is a possibility" (p. 48). Following Wolff, McConville refers to 1 Kgs 8:46–51, which shows that "the people's

Thomas Römer suggests a creative view of the pessimistic end of Kings in his article "Transformations in Deuteronomistic and Biblical Historiography: On 'Book Finding' and Other Literary Strategies" (1997).[13] He adduces a theory of Armin Steil according to which "crisis literature" adopts three types of literary attitudes: the attitude of the "prophet," the "priest," and the "mandarin."[14] The "'prophet' offers an eschatological interpretation of the crisis." The "'priest' puts forward a pathological analysis of the crisis and claims for a return to traditional institutions which are legitimated by divine will," whereas the "'mandarin' cannot find 'direct' meaning in the crisis, so the only possibility left to him is to adopt a more distant attitude and so to objectivize the crisis with its integration into a historiographical project."[15] Römer understands the pessimistic end of DtrH as the expression of a negative and distant attitude of a historiographer according to the type of the "mandarin." While Römer's suggestion certainly is heuristically valuable (and we shall return to it at the end of this article), it still fails to explain why the end of DtrH, which is perfectly understandable as crisis literature, was not transformed into a work promoting restoration.

This brief survey of a few interpretations of the ending of Kings cannot claim to be in any way comprehensive. It does not venture to reconstruct the elaborate debate about possible redactional layers in DtrH, which would involve especially the followers of Frank Moore Cross and Rudolf Smend on either side of the Atlantic.[16] This, however, would not help to answer the question that is the main concern

---

repentance is clearly an important precondition of salvation" (ibid.). McConville then points out that Deuteronomy 30 has more to say than does Kings about the restoration of exiles from Judah to their land as well as the manner in which repentance would happen as an act of God's grace (Deut 30:6). "The question why the author of Kings does not adopt the solution offered by Deuteronomy" (ibid.) is left open by McConville and will be a major point of interest in the present article. Similarly, the present contribution will suggest an answer to the question asked by Yair Hoffman: "Why have the restorative passages been supplemented mainly to the book of Jeremiah, none of them to the Former Prophets, and only one to Deuteronomy (30:1–10)?" ("The Deuteronomist and the Exile," in *Pomegranates and Golden Bells: Studies in Biblical, Jewish, and Near Eastern Ritual, Law, and Literature in Honor of Jacob Milgrom* [Winona Lake, IN: Eisenbrauns, 1995] 675).

[13] Römer, "Transformations," 4–5; see also idem, *So-Called Deuteronomistic History*, 111–12.

[14] Armin Steil, *Krisensemantik: Wissenssoziologische Untersuchungen zu einem Topos moderner Zeiterfahrung* (Opladen: Leske & Budrich, 1993).

[15] Römer, "Transformations," 4–5.

[16] For an overview of the history of research, see Römer, *So-Called Deuteronomistic History*, 13–43; Lewis Vale Alexander, "The Origin and Development of the Deuteronomistic History Theory and Its Significance for Biblical Interpretation" (Ph.D. thesis, Southwestern Baptist Theological Seminary, 1993); Norbert Lohfink, "Recent Discussion on 2 Kings 22–23: The State of the Question," in *A Song of Power and the Power of Song: Essays on the Book of Deuteronomy* (ed. Duane L. Christensen; Sources for Biblical and Theological Study 3; Winona Lake, IN: Eisenbrauns, 1993), 36–61; Helga Weippert, "Das deuteronomistische Geschichtswerk: Sein Ziel und Ende in der neueren Forschung," *TRu* 50 (1985): 213–49.

of this article: why even the latest redactions allowed the ending of Kings to leave their readers in a situation of collective trauma. To answer this question, we will look at the scene where the end of the story begins.

II. References to Deuteronomy in 2 Kings 22–23

It is the finding of the "book of the torah" (2 Kgs 22:8) that marks the beginning of the end of the history of Judah according to Kings. The content of the book of the torah makes Josiah tear his clothes (22:11) and become aware of the great wrath of Yhwh against Judah (22:13). Huldah's oracle confirms that God indeed is going to bring divine wrath upon Judah (22:15–20).

Leaving aside the historical question whether the book that is claimed to be found in 2 Kings 22 refers to an early stage of Deuteronomy during the times of Josiah,[17] I will discuss this question on a literary level.[18] Commentators since antiquity have identified the book found (22:9) as (some version or part of) Deuteronomy.[19] Indeed, the narrative employs specific expressions that can easily be identified as metatextual references to Deuteronomy.

The first reference to the book in 2 Kgs 22:8 is decisive: "The high priest Hilkiah said to the scribe Shaphan 'I found the book of the torah in the house of Yhwh.'" The expression "book of the torah" (ספר התורה) is used three times in Deuteronomy 28–30 (28:61; 29:20; 30:10)[20] referring to the book that Moses writes down in Deut 31:9, which Jean-Pierre Sonnet meticulously analyzed as the "book

---

[17] This question has haunted biblical scholars especially since W. M. L. de Wette's *dissertatio critica*, which, however, "does not offer the compelling argument that scholars have commonly taken it to do in presuming an identification of Deuteronomy with 'the book of the Torah' found by Josiah's men in 622 BCE, nor was de Wette the first to argue that identification" (Paul B. Harvey and Baruch Halpern, "W. M. L. de Wette's 'Dissertatio Critica…': Context and Translation," *ZABR* 14 [2008]: 48).

[18] For this approach, see David A. Glatt-Gilad, "Revealed and Concealed: The Status of the Law (Book) of Moses within the Deuteronomistic History," in *Mishneh Todah: Studies in Deuteronomy and Its Cultural Environment. In Honor of Jeffrey H. Tigay* (ed. Nili Sacher Fox, David A. Glatt-Gilad, and Michael J. Williams; Winona Lake, IN: Eisenbrauns, 2009), 185–99. There are good reasons to assume that the story of the finding of the book is a literary construction; see Nadav Na'aman, "The 'Discovered Book' and the Legitimation of Josiah's Reform," *JBL* 130 (2011): 47–62; Römer, *So-Called Deuteronomistic History*, 49–56; Wolfgang Speyer, "Bücherfunde in der Glaubenswerbung der Antike: Mit einem Ausblick auf Mittelalter und Neuzeit," *Hypomnemata* 24 (1970): 43–124.

[19] Cornelius a Lapide, in his early-seventeenth-century commentary, quotes church fathers such as Chrysostom and Athanasius for this opinion (Cornelius a Lapide, *Commentarius in Iosue, Iudicum, Ruth, IV. libros Regum et II. Paralipomenon* [Antwerp, 1664]; see the more commonly available edition of J. M. Peronne [Paris: L. Vivés, 1866], 4:81).

[20] In 31:26, the book additionally includes the Song of Moses (32:1–43), which is added to the torah according to 31:19, 22, 24.

within the book" in Deuteronomy.[21] The remaining three occurrences of the expression in Josh 1:8; 8:34; Neh 8:3 all refer to Deuteronomy.[22] The expression "book of the torah," used twice at the beginning of the narrative of the finding of the book in 2 Kgs 22:8, 11, leaves no doubt, therefore, that readers should be reminded of Deuteronomy.

The book is a leitmotif in the narrative on King Josiah (which ends in 2 Kgs 23:30).[23] Although subsequent references to the book do not consistently use the expression ספר התורה, it is clear that it is always the same book, the one discovered, to which the narrative refers. Several times it is briefly called "the book" (22:13, 16; 23:2–3, 24). Huldah refers to the "words that you have heard" (22:18). In the context of the covenant ceremony it is called "book of the covenant" (23:21), and a last reference to the text terms it "the torah of Moses" (2 Kgs 23:25). These frequent references to the book structure the narrative on Josiah and dominate its dynamics.

In addition to the strong connections to Deuteronomy via metatextual references, readers will even more easily recognize other intertextual allusions to Deuteronomy in the narrative.[24] The table on the following pages lists a selection of intertextual connections between 2 Kings 22–23 and Deuteronomy, which I will then discuss.[25]

Josiah expresses his shock after hearing the words of the book: "Great is the wrath of Yhwh that is kindled against us, because our ancestors did not listen to the words of this book, to act according to all that is written

---

[21] Sonnet, *The Book within the Book: Writing in Deuteronomy* (BibInt 14; Leiden: Brill, 1997).

[22] The usage of the expression in 2 Chr 34:15 is parallel to 2 Kgs 22:8, whereas 2 Chr 34:14 adds a narrative note, how Hilkiah found "the book of the torah of Yhwh through the hand of Moses" (ספר תורת־יהוה ביד־משה).

[23] For a classical commentary on the passage, see Mordechai Cogan and Hayim Tadmor, *II Kings: A New Translation with Introduction and Commentary* (AB 11; Garden City, NY: Doubleday, 1988), 277–302; some of the intertextual connections with Deuteronomy are noted by Geert J. Venema, *Reading Scripture in the Old Testament: Deuteronomy 9–10; 31; 2 Kings 22–23; Jeremiah 36; Nehemiah 8* (OtSt 48; Leiden: Brill, 2004), 52–94.

[24] On criteria to be used in identifying intertextual allusion, see Geoffrey D. Miller, "Intertextuality in Old Testament Research," *CurBR* 9 (2011): 283–309, esp. 294–98; Serge Frolov and Allen Wright, "Homeric and Ancient Near Eastern Intertextuality in 1 Samuel 17," *JBL* 130 (2011): 451–71, esp. 452; or the criteria of Manfred Pfister that I summarized in my "Hab 3 in intertextueller und kontextueller Sicht," *Bib* 85 (2004): 99–108, esp. 99–100. The preceding analysis shows that both qualitative and quantitative criteria (distinctiveness, selectivity, and density) establish extraordinarily strong intertextual relationships between 2 Kings 22–23 and Deuteronomy—in addition to the metatextual reference to the "book of the torah."

[25] The remark "exclusive" in the right-hand column of the table notes that the specific expression occurs only in the passages mentioned (in Deuteronomy, Kings, and eventually in a parallel in Chronicles). If the expression occurs once more in the Hebrew Bible, it is indicated in parentheses (+ reference).

2 Kings	2 Chronicles		Deuteronomy
22:13	34:21	"not listen/keep to act according to words written in this book" לא + לעשות + דברי + כל + כתוב + הספר הזה	28:58 (exclusive)
22:16		"come/bring upon all words" כל דברים + בוא על	30:1
22:17	34:25	"abandon me" (עזב + suffix ני-)	28:20; 31:16
22:17	34:25	"provoke him/me with the deeds of your/their hands" כעס + במעשה ידים	31:29[26]
22:19		"to become a desolation" היה לשמה	28:37
23:3	34:31	"to follow Yhwh and to keep his commandments" הלך אחר[י] יהוה + שמר מצותיו	13:5 (exclusive)
23:3	34:31	"the words of this torah/covenant, written in this book" דברי + הכתבים + הספר הזה	28:58 (exclusive)
23:21		"to make a passover for Yhwh your god" עשה פסח ליהוה אלהים	16:1 (exclusive)[27]
23:24		"detestable things and idols" שקוץ + גלול	29:16[28]
23:24		"torah + written in the book" כתב + ספר + תורה	29:20
23:24		"words of the torah" דברי התורה	17:9; 27:3, 8, 26; 28:58; 29:28; 31:12, 24; 32:46
23:25		"to turn with all one's heart and all one's being" שוב בכל-לבב ובכל-נפש	30:2, 10 (+ 1 Kgs 8:48)

[26] This expression occurs also in 1 Kgs 16:7; Jer 25:6–7; 32:30; 44:8. Jeremiah frequently adopts expressions from Deuteronomy 26–34; see Georg Fischer, "Das Ende von Deuteronomium (Dtn 26–34) im Spiegel des Jeremiabuches," in *"Gerechtigkeit und Recht zu üben" (Gen 18,19): Studien zur altorientalischen und biblischen Rechtsgeschichte, zur Religionsgeschichte Israels und zur Religionssoziologie. Festschrift für Eckart Otto zum 65. Geburtstag* (ed. Reinhard Achenbach and Martin Arneth; Beihefte zur ZABR 13; Wiesbaden: Harrassowitz, 2009), 281–92.

[27] Deuteronomy 16:1 (ועשית פסח ליהוה אלהיך) and 2 Kgs 23:21 (עשו פסח ליהוה אלהיכם) provide the closest parallel to this expression in the Hebrew Bible. 2 Chronicles 30:1 and 5 read לעשות פסח ליהוה אלהי ישראל.

[28] These two expressions occur combined also in Ezek 20:7–8; 37:23.

2 Kings	2 Chronicles		Deuteronomy
23:25		"with all one's heart and being and intensity" בכל־לבב ובכל־נפש ובכל־מאד	6:4 (exclusive)
23:26		"Yhwh turns from the burning of his anger" שוב יהוה מחרון אפו	13:18 (+ Josh 7:26)
23:27		Yhwh "chooses" a place for his "name" to be "there" בחר + "name" שם + "there" שם	12:5, 11, 21; 14:23, 24; 16:2, 6, 11; 26:2

concerning us" (2 Kgs 22:13). This alludes to a specific formulation from Moses' curses in Deut 28:58, "if you do not observe to act according to all the words of this law that are written in this book...."[29] These words introduce the final section of Moses' curses, which announces exile (Deut 28:63–64)[30] and the return to Egypt (28:68).[31] This allusion prepares readers who are familiar with Deuteronomy 28 for the destructive ending of the narrative of Kings—exile (2 Kgs 25:11) and the flight to Egypt (25:26).[32] Deuteronomy 28:58 is also alluded to in a second decisive passage, when Josiah makes the covenant in 2 Kgs 23:3, "to fulfill the words of this covenant that were written in this book."

Two more possible allusions to Deuteronomy 28 can be seen in Huldah's oracle in 2 Kgs 22:17, 19.[33] "Because they have abandoned me" (תחת אשר עזבוני) is the

---

[29] See Glatt-Gilad, "Revealed and Concealed," 193–94.

[30] Norbert Lohfink argues that the final verses of Moses' curses (Deut 28:64–68) reinterpret the meaning of שמד (28:63) from annihilation to dispersion into exile and therefore prepare the theological interpretation of Israel's history, which is presented at the end of Kings ("Der Zorn Gottes und das Exil," in idem, *Studien zum Deuteronomium und zur deuteronomistischen Literatur V* [SBAB 31; Stuttgart: Katholisches Bibelwerk, 2005], 37–55, esp. 52–54; repr. from *Liebe und Gebot: Studien zum Deuteronomium* [ed. Reinhard G. Kratz and Hermann Spieckermann; FRLANT 190; Göttingen: Vandenhoeck & Ruprecht, 2000], 137–55).

[31] On the connection of Deut 28:68 with Deut 17:16 and the motif of the anti-exodus in general, see Thomas Römer, "Exode et anti-Exode: La nostalgie de l'Egypte dans les traditions du désert," in *Lectio difficilior probabilior? L'exégèse comme expérience de décloisonnement. Mélanges offerts à Françoise Smyth-Florentin* (ed. Thomas Römer; Dielheimer Blätter zum Alten Testament und seiner Rezeption in der Alten Kirche 12; Heidelberg: Wissenschaftliche Theol. Seminar, 1991), 155–72.

[32] One of the few commentaries to emphasize this connection is Richard Elliott Friedman, *Commentary on the Torah, With a New English Translation* (San Francisco: HarperSanFrancisco, 2001), 653. Compare also Jer 42:1–43:7: Garrett Galvin, *Egypt as a Place of Refuge* (FAT 2/51; Tübingen: Mohr Siebeck, 2011), 136–37.

[33] Lowell K. Handy explains Huldah's role as a "double-check on the will of the deity" from parallels with texts from Esarhaddon and Nabonidus ("The Role of Huldah in Josiah's Cult Reform," *ZAW* 106 [1994]: 52). While these parallels are interesting, the conclusion that Huldah's

first reason given in the oracle for God's wrath. A very similar expression occurs in Deut 28:20, "because you have abandoned me" (אשר עזבתני), where God's voice bursts through Moses' curses. The same idea reappears in the theophany in Deut 31:16 "and they will abandon me" (ועזבני). Although the expression is very brief, its decisive content and the powerful literary device of the change of voices employed in Deut 28:20 make it a catchword and an easily recognizable allusion. In addition, "to provoke me with all the deeds of their hands" recalls Deut 31:29, Moses' final announcement of his knowledge of Israel's future sin.

Furthermore, Huldah's oracle refers to the words that the king had heard, saying that Jerusalem and its inhabitants would become "a desolation and a curse" (2 Kgs 22:19), which may well echo Moses' words "you shall be a desolation, a proverb, and a byword" (Deut 28:37) and may, through the term "curse," comprehensively refer to the Mosaic curses.

Finally, even the introduction to Huldah's oracle may recall Deuteronomy 28 via Deut 30:1. The beginning of God's word in 2 Kgs 22:16 reads, "I will indeed bring disaster upon this place and on its inhabitants—all the words of the book that the king of Judah has read." The expression "bring upon" (בוא על *hiphil*) in combination with "words" (דברים) may evoke Deut 30:1, "when all these words have come upon you [בוא על *qal*]—the blessing and the curse," which clearly refers to the curses of Deuteronomy 28.

It is commonly acknowledged that Josiah's reform (2 Kings 23) converges with concerns of Deuteronomy.[34] Intertextual connections can be seen, for example, in Josiah's command to celebrate a Passover (2 Kgs 23:21; cf. Deut 16:1) and in the narrator's concluding summary in 2 Kgs 23:24. Josiah is depicted as putting away "detestable things and idols," a rare expression from Moses' Moab covenant speech (Deut 29:16), to establish "the words of the torah written upon the book," which employs typical phraseology from Deuteronomy but may again especially recall the Moab covenant (Deut 29:20).

We find further particularly significant allusions to Deuteronomy in the

---

"prophecy is a very bland stereotypical couple of phrases which could have been found anywhere in the ancient Near East" (p. 51) is imprecise. As shown above, the prophecy specifically refers to formulations in Deuteronomy. Thus, Huldah's prophecy reveals some of the content of the discovered book to the readers of Kings and confirms the continuity of the divine will with the prophecies of Moses. On the function of Huldah's oracle as a *vaticinium ex eventu*, see Michael Pietsch, "Prophetess of Doom: Hermeneutical Reflections on the Huldah Oracle (2 Kings 22)," in *Soundings in Kings: Perspectives and Methods in Contemporary Scholarship* (ed. Mark Leuchter and Klaus-Peter Adam; Minneapolis: Fortress, 2010), 71–80, esp. 72–78.

[34] Recently, Lauren A. S. Monroe argued that Josiah's reform in 2 Kgs 23:4–20 shows connections with concerns expressed in the Holiness Code (*Josiah's Reform and the Dynamics of Defilement: Israelite Rites of Violence and the Making of a Biblical Text* [Oxford: Oxford University Press, 2011], 23–43). Yet she also sees a Deuteronomistic redaction in 2 Kings 22–23 (pp. 77–119) and does not doubt that the exilic (or, as she calls it, "postmonarchic") form of the text refers to Deuteronomy (p. 133).

evaluation of Josiah's reign in 2 Kgs 23:25–27. "Before him there was no king like him, who turned to Yhwh with all his heart, with all his soul, and with all his might" (v. 25) combines easily recognizable expressions from Deut 6:4 and Deut 30:2, 10. According to Deuteronomy 30, this sort of repentance will come along with God's conversion to compassion (30:3, 9), but only after "all these things have come upon you" (30:1). However, 2 Kgs 23:26 is quick to add that "Yhwh did not turn from the fierceness of his great wrath," which again evokes a decisive passage, Deut 13:18. There Moses demands that a town where idolatry had been committed must be totally eradicated "so that Yhwh may turn from his fierce anger."

In the light of this, Deuteronomy 13 seems to serve as an explanation of why Jerusalem could not be saved despite Josiah's wholehearted and active repentance. It seems that only a total eradication of Jerusalem, and any other town where idolatry had been committed, could have spared Judah from external destruction. This intertextual allusion to Deut 13:18, therefore, explains why God declares, "I will remove Judah also out of my sight, as I have removed Israel; I will reject this city that I have chosen, Jerusalem, and the house of which I said, My name shall be there" (2 Kgs 23:27). Needless to say, the wording is again deeply rooted in, and reminiscent of, Deuteronomy.[35]

The complex intertextual relationship between 2 Kings 22–23 and Deuteronomy should be analyzed in greater detail, and, indeed, there are numerous additional connections with Deuteronomy in earlier chapters of Kings. For the purpose of the present argument, however, it has become sufficiently evident that readers of 2 Kings 22–23 are emphatically referred to Deuteronomy: first through the metatextual reference to the "book of the torah," and then through several intertextual allusions that are concentrated in Josiah's reaction to hearing the words of the book (2 Kgs 22:13), Huldah's oracle concerning the future of Judah (2 Kgs 22:16–19), and the framing passages of Josiah's reform (2 Kgs 23:3 and 24–27).

The allusions refer especially to passages that are related to the disastrous end that awaits Israel in the case of its disobedience (Deuteronomy 28–31). Besides the curses in ch. 28, the issue of repentance in ch. 30 is also addressed, precisely to explain why Josiah's conversion could not rescue Judah and Jerusalem. Although there are clear allusions to Deut 30:1–10, the actual possibility of the restoration of God's people that is unfolded in these verses is completely missing from 2 Kings 22–23. At this point, readers of Kings, who have been left in suspense regarding the concrete content of the discovered book,[36] are supposed to remember and take to heart what Moses envisions for their future in Deuteronomy.

---

[35] Moreover, this formulation draws on 1 Kgs 9:6–9, which plays on Deut 29:21–27.
[36] See Burke O. Long, *2 Kings* (FOTL 10; Grand Rapids: Eerdmans, 1991), 262: "Obviously the account does not divulge the exact contents of the 'book.' Emphasis falls instead on dramatizing the responses to it." The dramatic responses to the reading of the book even heighten readers' curiosity regarding its content. See also Venema, *Reading Scripture*, 72, who suggests that the lack

III. The Chance of the Moab Covenant (Deuteronomy 29–30)

Readers of Kings will remember that Moses refers to Israel's more distant future especially in three extended passages of his farewell speeches in Deuteronomy: 4:25–31; 28:15–68; 29:17–30:10.[37] But in these passages exile is explicitly presented as the ultimate consequence in the case of Israel's faithlessness. The full scheme of Deuteronomy's view of Israel's future leads from sin to exile, repentance, and restoration. However, Moses discusses only those elements of the scheme that fit the rhetorical purpose of the respective stage of his speeches:

Deuteronomy	Sin	→ Exile	→ Repentance	→ Restoration
4:25–31	4:25 (idolatry)	4:26–28	4:29–31	–
28:15–68	28:15, 58 (disobedience)	28:64–68	–	–
29:17–30:10	29:18, 25–26 (faithlessness)	29:28	30:1–2	30:3–10

In his first glimpse into the future, which circles around the theme of idolatry as a decisive reason for a disaster, Moses already mentions the repentance in exile (4:25–31). Yet the curse section of Deuteronomy 28 elaborates on the aspects of disobedience and its disastrous consequences, and it does not seem to leave room for any hope. Deuteronomy 30:1–10 is the only passage in which Moses presents a prospect of restoration. Readers who wish to know how possible restoration may happen are bound to remember the context of this passage, which is the Moab covenant speech, chs. 29–30.

Deuteronomy 29–30 is the rhetorical culmination of the entire sequence of speeches in chs. 1–30, which aims at the decision for life, that is, the decision for Yhwh, Yhwh's torah, and Yhwh's covenant in 30:15–20.[38] Moses starts with a usual rhetorical figure, reminding Israel of Yhwh's deeds for them in the desert,

---

of detail regarding the circumstances of the finding of the book in 2 Kings 22 refers readers to a known book.

[37] I am not discussing here the special case of the Song of Moses (Deut 32:1–43), which is introduced as an additional revelation through the theophany in 31:16–21. This Song refers to the crisis in Israel's future (32:19–33) and God's final defeat of Israel's enemies (32:34–43). However, there is no direct reference to Israel's return from exile. See Dominik Markl, *Gottes Volk im Deuteronomium* (BZABR 18; Wiesbaden: Harrassowitz, 2012), 232–42.

[38] For a more elaborate argument on this reading of chs. 29–30, see Markl, *Gottes Volk*, 88–125; for a detailed rhetorical analysis, see Timothy A. Lenchak, *"Choose Life!" A Rhetorical-Critical Investigation of Deuteronomy 28,69–30,20* (AnBib 129; Rome: Pontificio Istituto Biblico, 1993).

for which the people shall obey the stipulations of the covenant (29:1–8). He then addresses all the people, those present and even absent members of the people (that is, most probably future generations, 29:9–14).

Moses then reminds Israel of the idols they have seen among other nations (29:15–16) and begins to unfold the disastrous consequences of possible hidden false oaths among the people (29:17–27). In an imaginary future dialogue, Moses quotes "all nations," asking why this calamity has come upon the land (29:23), to which the answer is given: "Because they forsook the covenant of Yhwh … the anger of Yhwh was kindled against that land, bringing on it every curse written in this book. Yhwh uprooted them from their land in anger, fury, and great wrath, and cast them into another land, as is the case today" (29:24–27).

The final two verses employ two special features of "direct" communication with addressees of the text: the reference to the book (which is part of the book of Deuteronomy that addressees are reading, 29:26) and the "today" of exile. The speech of Moses, although suited to its context within the narrated world of Deuteronomy, is designed unmistakably to perforate the thin screen that separates it from the world of addressees who are experiencing (or have experienced) the reality of exile.

This strategy of reader communication is further developed in a subtle trick of Deut 30:1:[39] "And it will happen, when all these things have come upon you, the blessing and the curse …" Again, this sentence not only addresses Moses' audience within Deuteronomy, but it must be felt to be a direct address also to readers who understand that the curse has in fact come upon them. This virtually immediate address to readers continues as they are told of their possible (or actual) experience of repentance and return to their home country (30:1–10).[40] The same address, "you" (singular), is continued until the end of Moses' speech, in which addressees finally are urged to make a decision between life and death:[41] "I call heaven and earth to witness against you today that I have set before you life and death, blessings and curses. Choose life so that you and your descendants may live, loving Yhwh your God, obeying him" (30:19–20).

Despite this forceful rhetorical demand, we are not told in Deuteronomy

---

[39] For this and other strategies of reader communication in Deuteronomy, see Markl, *Gottes Volk*, 70–81.

[40] For a detailed analysis of Deut 30:1–10 that is skillfully developed around the leitmotif "to turn" (שוב), see Gottfried Vanoni, "Geist und Buchstabe: Überlegungen zum Verhältnis der beiden Testamente und Beobachtungen zu Dtn 30,1–10," *BN* 14 (1981): 65–98. The root שוב appears seven times in this passage; see Georg Braulik, "Die Funktion von Siebenergruppierungen im Endtext des Deuteronomiums," in idem, *Studien zum Buch Deuteronomium* (SBAB 24; Stuttgart: Katholisches Bibelwerk, 1997), 63–79, esp. 65.

[41] "Life/to live" occurs six times in Deut 30:15–20 (and a seventh time in 30:6), highlighting life as the aim of torah; see Jeffrey H. Tigay, *Deuteronomy* דברים: *The Traditional Hebrew Text with the New JPS Translation* (JPS Torah Commentary; Philadelphia: Jewish Publication Society, 1996), 287.

about Israel's response.⁴² This response is expected from exilic (or postexilic) readers. Though there is no indication of this response in the narrative, there seems to be a response suggested to readers implied in the text at its turning point: "The hidden things belong to Yhwh our God, but the revealed things belong to us and to our children forever, to observe all the words of this law" (29:28).⁴³

Deuteronomy 29–30 constructs its implicit audience as a community that is supposed to identify with experiencing a situation of exile at the turning point to restoration (29:24–30:10). These chapters encourage the people to commit themselves to the Moab covenant and the torah of Deuteronomy. While the decisive turn to their obedience is seen as an act of divine grace, the circumcision of the heart (30:6),⁴⁴ they are also urged with the greatest rhetorical intensity to make a deliberate decision for God and God's torah (30:15–20).

IV. No Future without Moses: The Pragmatic Function of 2 Kings 22–25

Against the backdrop of the foregoing observations, I suggest an interpretation of the pragmatic function of the end of Kings. 2 Kings 22–23 is decisive in DtrH's "account before the tribunal of divine justice,"⁴⁵ since the law book at this tribunal is Deuteronomy. 2 Kings 22–23 explains both why the disaster *had to happen* and why it had to happen *despite* the efforts of the uniquely just king Josiah.⁴⁶

---

⁴²In fact, there could be an indirect indication of Israel's decision in Deut 34:9, which reports Israel's actual obedience. See Sonnet, "Redefining the Plot."

⁴³The "revealed things" (הנגלת) are obviously equated with the torah, while the meaning of "hidden things" (הנסתרת) is more difficult to determine. For a thorough treatment of the verse, see Alan Lenzi, *Secrecy and the Gods: Secret Knowledge in Ancient Mesopotamia and Biblical Israel* (SAAS 19; Helsinki: Neo-Assyrian Text Corpus Project, 2008), 322–39, with a convincing analysis of the meaning of הנסתרת based on a comparison of the usages of the word in Sir 3:22; 42:19; 48:24–25 (pp. 328–33). Lenzi emphasizes the opposition between the hidden and the revealed things and their possible implications. My understanding of the verse, however, proposes that it aims at the self-commitment of a we-group to obey the torah; therefore, the verse may have a function for the making of the Moab covenant that is comparable to the consent and ratification of Israel in the making of the Sinai covenant (Exod 19:8; 24:3, 7); see Markl, *Gottes Volk*, 104–7.

⁴⁴On the theologically decisive meaning of this motif at the end of the Pentateuch, see Ernst Ehrenreich, *Wähle das Leben! Deuteronomium 30 als hermeneutischer Schlüssel zur Tora* (BZABR 14; Wiesbaden: Harrassowitz, 2011), 183 and 196–97.

⁴⁵Jan Assmann calls DtrH a "Rechenschaft vor dem Tribunal der göttlichen Gerechtigkeit" ("Die Erzählbarkeit der Geschichte: Bedingungen für die Entstehung von Geschichte im alten Orient," in *Die Vielfalt der Kulturen* [ed. Jörn Rüsen, Michael Gottlob, and Achim Mittag; Erinnerung, Geschichte, Identität 4; Frankfurt am Main: Suhrkamp, 1998], 392).

⁴⁶The story makes every effort to depict a consistent image of God and history and not to subvert the idea in "Deut 30 that repentance must precede return" (contra Janzen, *Violent Gift*, 204–5).

It has long been recognized that the final passage, 2 Kgs 23:31–25:26, is marked by a dry and even laconic style.[47] It merely tells what *had* to happen. Jehoahaz, Jehoiakim, Jehoiachin, and Zedekiah are portrayed as supernumeraries, preparing the scene for Nebuchadnezzar. 2 Kings 24:20 resumes the central motif of divine wrath[48] and leads to the account of the destruction of Jerusalem. Chapter 25 leaves the Judeans exiled in Babylon or having fled to Egypt; the latter can be seen as the fulfillment of the metaphorically hyperbolized final curse of Deut 28:68: "Yhwh will bring you back in ships to Egypt, by a route that I promised you would never see again."

If the real purpose of the DtrH was, as Noth suggested, to explain the disaster of the exile as divine judgment, this aim would have indeed been achieved. Yet what sort of reader could be imagined who could have been satisfied with this explanation? Who could be that theoretical theologian who would be happy if God was finally justified and a blind, former king got his daily food supply? Any readers who were personally affected by this story or empathized with the figures involved must have asked themselves: What about the future? What about the people? What about *us*?

Whoever may seriously ask this question is not given any answer at the end of Kings. Yet this question may remind readers that precisely the disaster presented at the end of Kings proves the accuracy of a lost and rediscovered book, the book of the torah of Moses. Therefore, the metatextual references and intertextual allusions in 2 Kings 22–23 and the subsequent unsatisfying end of 2 Kings 24–25 together are seen as implicitly urging readers to reread Deuteronomy. Whoever wants to know an answer to the question of what chance there may be for the future will find it in Moses' speech in Deuteronomy 29–30.[49]

There is no happy ending that can be gained cheaply. Whoever wants to be consoled by a message of hope is forced to turn to Moses' rhetoric of blessing and curse and heaven and earth as witnesses as they make their decision between life

---

[47] See Weippert, "Das deuteronomistische Geschichtswerk," 238–39. Richard D. Nelson refers to "the wooden phrases which evaluate the last four kings" (*The Double Redaction of the Deuteronomistic History* [JSOTSup 18; Sheffield: JSOT Press, 1981], 37). It should not be overlooked that one of the last theological reasons given in 2 Kgs 24:4, that Yhwh did "not want to forgive," forms an exclusive intertextual connection with Deut 29:19. The combination of the two verbs (אבה + סלח) occurs only in these two verses in the canon. 2 Kings 24:2 therefore again alludes to the Moab covenant speech, precisely where Moses begins to speak about the disastrous consequences of breaking the covenant. The connection between Deut 29:19 and 2 Kgs 24:4 is thus much stronger than even Vanoni's thorough analysis of deuteronomistic terminology suggests: compare, e.g., G. Vanoni, "Beobachtungen zur deuteronomistischen Terminologie in 2 Kön 23,25–25,30," in *Das Deuteronomium: Entstehung, Gestalt und Botschaft* (ed. N. Lohfink; BETL 68; Leuven: Leuven University Press, 1985), 357–62, esp. 361.

[48] See Lohfink, "Zorn Gottes."

[49] Within the narrative complex from Genesis to Kings, the answer can be found only in Deuteronomy 29–30.

and death. This ingenious metatextual and literary-pragmatic function of the ending of Kings is the reason why this ending was preserved and why no happy ending was added. The reconstitution of "Israel" as the people of God depended on the constant memory of the catastrophe and its moral impact that is rhetorically condensed in Deuteronomy 29–30. Moses, and not the narrator of Israel's history, has the "last word" regarding Israel's future.[50] The DtrH does not serve the purpose of amusement, but it is meant to remain a thorn in the side of its readers. Even at the end of Kings, the Deuteronomistic narrator serves the purpose of enhancing Mosaic authority.

V. Hermeneutical Perspectives: The Torah Book and the Composition of the Canon

As a postlude, these final reflections will just hint at a few points that have, because of my concentration on the issue at stake, not been discussed in this article but which still seem to be of hermeneutical significance.

I have not addressed the complex questions concerning the literary history in which the texts concerned evolved.[51] However, it should be noted that there are many good reasons to assume that several passages in Deuteronomy 30–34 were deliberately composed to conclude the Pentateuch,[52] which gained its special

---

[50] Thus, the whole narrative arc from Deuteronomy to Kings must be taken into consideration if one is to analyze the relationship of authority between the narrator and Moses—an undertaking begun by Robert Polzin, *Moses and the Deuteronomist: A Literary Study of the Deuteronomic History*, part 1, *Deuteronomy, Joshua, Judges* (New York: Seabury, 1980), esp. 25–36.

[51] See, e.g., *The Pentateuch: International Perspectives on Current Research* (ed. Thomas B. Dozeman, Konrad Schmid, and Baruch J. Schwartz; FAT 78; Tübingen: Mohr Siebeck, 2011); Hermann-Josef Stipp, *Das deuteronomistische Geschichtswerk* (ÖBS 39; Frankfurt a. M.: Lang, 2011); *Die deuteronomistischen Geschichtswerke: Redaktions- und religionsgeschichtliche Perspektiven zur "Deuteronomismus": Diskussion in Tora und Vorderen Propheten* (ed. Markus Witte et al.; BZAW 365; Berlin: de Gruyter, 2006); Konrad Schmid, "Das Deuteronomium innerhalb der 'deuteronomistischen Geschichtswerke' in Gen–2 Kön," in *Das Deuteronomium zwischen Pentateuch und Deuteronomistischem Geschichtswerk* (ed. Eckart Otto and Reinhard Achenbach; FRLANT 206; Göttingen: Vandenhoeck & Ruprecht, 2004), 193–211; *The Future of the Deuteronomistic History* (ed. Thomas Römer; BETL 147; Leuven: Leuven University Press, 2000); *Israel Constructs Its History: Deuteronomistic Historiography in Recent Research* (ed. Albert de Pury, Thomas Römer, and Jean-Daniel Macchi; JSOTSup 306; Sheffield: Sheffield Academic Press, 2000).

[52] See, e.g., Eckart Otto, "Das postdeuteronomistische Deuteronomium als integrierender Schlußstein der Tora," in idem, *Die Tora: Studien zum Pentateuch: Gesammelte Aufsätze* (BZABR 9; Wiesbaden: Harrassowitz, 2009), 421–46; reprinted from Witte et al., *Die deuteronomistischen Geschichtswerke*, 71–102. See also Markl, *Gottes Volk*, 282–85, with references to further literature.

hermeneutical role during Persian times.[53] Although this literary process meant to some degree a separation of the Pentateuch from the books of the Former Prophets, it seems that, at this late stage, the Former Prophets were not meant to be read in isolation from their prehistory presented in the Pentateuch, nor without their theological foundation, which Deuteronomy provides. It is therefore not necessary to presuppose a theory of DtrH or the Enneateuch to accept the argument presented here.

Moses' "book of the torah" provides a narrative motif that connects especially Joshua and Kings with Deuteronomy.[54] If one reads the narratives from Genesis to Kings as a unified historical work, Deuteronomy 30 appears at the center of the narrative plot. It is the most prominent passage of this narrative complex, in which a future beyond Kings (beyond exile) is envisioned.[55] Readers witness the writing of the "book of the torah" in Deuteronomy immediately after Moses' solemn predictions regarding Israel's future (Deut 31:9), while they see it resurfacing just before the "end of history" (2 Kgs 22:9). Israel's foundation, which is coming to an end with Moses' writing of his testament, becomes the anchor for any possible hope at the end of the narrative complex. While Israel is doomed to dispersion, the new emergence of the book becomes the foundation for the future.[56] Viewed in this light, the "word" of Deuteronomy is for postexilic "Israel" nothing less than "your life, and through this word you may live long in the land" (Deut 32:47).[57]

From a canonical perspective, Konrad Schmid emphasized that Genesis to Kings "in the arrangement of the MT … segues into the account of the *corpus propheticum*, where we encounter decisive statements about Israel's future."[58] Thus, Israel's future, which is left unclear by the open end of 2 Kgs 25:27–30, "is the subject of extensive theological discussion and exploration in the subsequent

---

[53] See James W. Watts, "Using Ezra's Time as a Methodological Pivot for Understanding the Rhetoric and Functions of the Pentateuch," in Dozeman et al., *Pentateuch: International Perspectives*, 489–506.

[54] Compare Venema, *Reading Scripture*, 47–52; Glatt-Gilad, "Revealed and Concealed." On further implications of this intertextual game, exemplified in 1 Kings 8, see David A. Bergen, "The Heart of the (Deuteronomic) Matter: Solomon and the Book of the Law," *SR* 35 (2006): 213–30.

[55] Although Lev 26:42–45 implies the possibility of restoration, only Deut 30:1–10 explicitly speaks about the return to the land.

[56] Römer, *So-Called Deuteronomistic History*, 51: "The 'cleansing' of the temple was indeed of not much use, since it was destroyed a few decades later. But the discovery of the book offered the possibility to *understand* this destruction, and to worship Yahweh *without any temple*" (emphasis original).

[57] On the significance of these concluding "words" of Moses (cf. Deut 32:45), see my "This Word Is Your Life: The Theology of 'Life' in Deuteronomy," in *Gottes Wort im Menschenwort: Festschrift für Georg Fischer SJ zum 60. Geburtstag* (ed. Dominik Markl, Claudia Paganini, and Simone Paganini; ÖBS 43; Frankfurt am Main: Lang, 2014), 71–96, esp. 88–89, 92–93.

[58] Schmid, *Genesis and the Moses Story: Israel's Dual Origins in the Hebrew Bible* (trans. James D. Nogalski; Siphrut 3; Winona Lake, IN: Eisenbrauns, 2010), 44.

prophetic books."[59] This hermeneutical perspective gains strength mainly through the intertextual connections between the end of Kings and especially Isaiah and Jeremiah.[60] Isaiah 36–39, the structural center of the book,[61] renders and expands 2 Kgs 18:13–20:19, while Jeremiah 52 reuses and expands 2 Kgs 24:18–25:30.[62] These extensive intertextual references emphasize that both Isaiah and Jeremiah are strongly concerned with the fate of Judah and Jerusalem.

Important though these observations are, they must not obscure the fact that 2 Kings 25 *really is* an end. It is the end of the most extensive narrative complex of the Bible. One cannot overestimate the audaciousness of the authors and redactors who have shaped and preserved this drastic ending—who did not fall into the nearly universal psychological trap of self-admiring historiography. Both Chronicles and the Gospel of Mark give textual evidence of how unbearable a traumatic and open ending was perceived to be in biblical times[63] (which probably has not changed among recipients today).

Maybe the original author(s) of 2 Kings 25 really did have the attitude of a "mandarin," as in Römer's application of Steil's typology. Yet the latest redactor(s) of Kings shifted this attitude. By preserving the laconic end, the narrator seems to hide in the mantle of a "mandarin," while blinking both eyes back and forth: one eye of a "priest" blinks back to Moses in Deuteronomy, the other eye of a "prophet" twinkles forward to Isaiah and Jeremiah. It is perhaps the ambivalence of simultaneously preserving real seriousness and sublimely conveying irony, which marks great literature and maybe even profound theology.

---

[59] Ibid.

[60] The canonical sequence as such may well have been more pluralistic than Schmid suggests; compare Norbert Lohfink, "Moses Tod, die Tora und die alttestamentliche Sonntagslesung," *TP* 71 (1996): 481–94.

[61] See Ulrich Berges, *The Book of Isaiah: Its Composition and Final Form* (trans. Millard C. Lind; Hebrew Bible Monographs 46; Sheffield: Sheffield Phoenix, 2012), esp. 505: "The suppression of the exile events, which appear as already overcome only in the hindsight of history (40.1–11), displays the pragmatics of chaps. 36–39 with perfect clarity. In the book of Isaiah, Zion cannot fall, the temple cannot burn.... The entire book takes its direction from this thematic center."

[62] Georg Fischer, *Jeremia: Der Stand der theologischen Diskussion* (Darmstadt: Wissenschaftliche Buchgesellschaft, 2007), 27–31; idem, "Jeremiah 52: A Test Case for Jer LXX," in *X. Congress of the International Organisation for Septuagint and Cognate Studies, Oslo, 1998* (ed. Bernard A. Taylor; SCS 51; Atlanta: Society of Biblical Literature, 2001), 37–48.

[63] 2 Chronicles 36:22–23 adds to the end of the plot of 2 Kings 25 Cyrus's edict and announcement of the rebuilding of the temple in Jerusalem and thus ends on a glorious note of restoration. Mark 16:9–20 is most probably a secondary addition to an earlier, shorter ending of the Gospel. See, e.g., Joel Marcus, *Mark 8–16: A New Translation with Introduction and Commentary* (Anchor Yale Bible 27A; New Haven: Yale University Press, 2009), 1088–89.

The Levite of Judges 17–18

DAVID Z. MOSTER
DavidMoster@gmail.com
3201 Oxford Avenue, Bronx, NY 10463

Surprisingly little attention has been paid to the Levite of Judges 17–18, perhaps because he is unnamed and not listed in the standard biblical encyclopedias. This study examines Judges 17–18 in order better to understand how the Levite is characterized in the narrative. By means of close textual analysis, the Levite is shown to be a complex and somewhat contradictory figure, being passive but ambitious, meek but confident, a thief as well as a servant of Yhwh, and a "father" with no sense of familial obligation. He is a type figure who still has a number of well-developed traits. For example, he is a wanderer with no destination, speaks when spoken to, and is a sojourner who is recognizably out of place. He is valued for his priestly capabilities but is nevertheless subservient to the men who seek his services. He is persuadable, self-serving, and ultimately disloyal. Therefore, even though his name is not known, the Levite of Judges 17–18 can still be considered one of the more richly drawn characters in the book of Judges and perhaps in the Hebrew Bible as a whole.

In Judges 17–18, a man named Micah establishes a temple and hires a Levite as his priest. Unbeknownst to Micah, the Levite is approached by the tribesmen of Dan and asked to work for them instead. The Levite obliges and walks off with the sacred objects of Micah's temple. Try as he might, Micah cannot prevent the Danites from taking the Levite or the temple objects. Although two recent books have been devoted to this episode, surprisingly little attention has been paid to the Levite as a character, perhaps because he is unnamed and not listed in the standard biblical encyclopedias.[1] This investigation, which is informed by a number of literary studies of the Hebrew Bible, examines Judges 17–18 in order to better understand how

---

[1] See Jason S. Bray, *Sacred Dan: Religious Tradition and Cultic Practice in Judges 17–18* (LHBOTS 449; New York: T&T Clark, 2006); E. Aydeet Mueller, *The Micah Story: A Morality Tale in the Book of Judges* (StBibLit 34; New York: Lang, 2001). Because the Levite is unnamed, a brief but insightful character analysis appears in Adele Reinhartz, *Why Ask My Name? Anonymity and Identity in Biblical Narrative* (New York: Oxford University Press, 1998), 77–79.

the Levite is characterized in the story as it sits before us.² The verses pertaining to the Levite will be treated one by one and a summary character analysis will be provided at the conclusion.

²I have found the following studies particularly helpful: Adele Berlin, *Poetics and Interpretation of Biblical Narrative* (Bible and Literature Series 9; Sheffield: Almond, 1983), 23–107; Jean Louis Ska, *"Our Fathers Have Told Us": Introduction to the Analysis of Hebrew Narratives* (SubBi 13; Rome: Pontificio Istituto Biblico, 1990), 83–94; Meir Sternberg, *The Poetics of Biblical Narrative: Ideological Literature and the Drama of Reading* (Indiana Literary Biblical Series; Bloomington: Indiana University Press, 1985), 321–64.

Although it is not the subject of this study, the composition history of Judges 17–18 should be addressed. There are a number of scholars who suggest that the narrative was originally composed of two or even three original stories. For example, George F. Moore argues that the "narrative is not all from one hand" but comes from a combination of the J and E sources (*A Critical and Exegetical Commentary on Judges* [ICC 7; New York: Charles Scribner's Sons, 1910], 367–69). He lists five reasons for dissecting the narrative: (1) the inventory of Micah's objects "in various permutations is confusing"; (2) at first the Levite is said to come from Bethlehem (17:8–11) but later is said to live in the vicinity of Micah (18:15); (3) there is a "manifest plethora" of direct speech in 18:2, 7, 8–10; (4) there is "redundancy," "conflicting representations," and "confusion" in 18:13–21; (5) the two summary statements about the duration of the Danite temple "cannot both come from the same source."

According to this approach, a study of the Levite would require an analysis of the two or even three "original" stories one by one. The problem, however, is that there is simply not enough evidence to isolate the "original" stories with any confidence. Furthermore, a number of scholars argue that the story that sits before us is in fact an original composition; that is, there are no "original" stories to be isolated. For example, see Martin Noth, "The Background of Judges 17–18," in *Israel's Prophetic Heritage: Essays in Honor of James Muilenburg* (ed. Bernhard W. Anderson and Walter Harrelson; New York: Harper, 1962), 69. Noth sees the story as originally unified, though "this is not to deny that the original story was later distorted somewhat by a few alterations and additions." None of these "alterations and additions" pertains to the Levite: "To me it seems doubtful that the antecedent history of the 'Levite,' which is briefly reported in 17:7–9, has its own special basis in tradition. It is reasonable to suppose that here we have only a typical picture of 'Levite' such as was common in ancient Israel. In support of this judgment is the fact that Jg. 19:1ff. gives a picture of a 'Levite' that is similar in some respects, although it is not to be assumed that one story depends on the other in a traditio-historical or even in a literary way."

In light of this debate and the inherent difficulties of isolating underlying texts, I avoid a historical reconstruction of Judges 17–18. Rather, I follow recent scholars such as Mueller by treating the story as unified, even if the unity is secondary. Mueller, who is open to the idea that Judges 17–18 is composed of two or perhaps three original stories, writes: "That scholars have not been able to solve the problem of what may constitute originally separate narratives underscores the skill of the final author" (*Micah Story*, 14). She concludes that "it is plausible that the final author preserved and updated earlier narratives," but she acknowledges that form critics "disagree about the nature, authorship, and the date of origin of such materials" (p. 125). Accordingly, the Levite is analyzed in this study as he appears in the final form of the text.

I. Textual Analysis

The Levite is not introduced with a proper name. While many exegetes identify him as Jonathan the son of Gershom the son of Manasseh, a priest mentioned at the end of the story in 18:30, the text does not explicitly make this connection.[3] Even if this identification is correct, however, the Levite's proper name is revealed only *after* the story comes to a close. This is highly peculiar for biblical narrative and suggests that the Levite's proper name is not necessary for understanding the story, at least not until the very end. I now consider the reasons for this anonymity, whether it be initial or throughout.

Adele Reinhartz points to a number of "richly drawn" characters without proper names in the Hebrew Bible, for example, the servant of Abraham (Genesis 24), the wife of Manoah (Judges 13), the wife of Potiphar (Genesis 39), the queen of Sheba (1 Kings 10), and the quarreling harlots of Solomon's reign (1 Kings 3).[4] Anonymity for these characters, she contends, suggests that they are to be understood as types, what Chris Baldick defines as "a fictional character who stands as a representative of some identifiable class or group of people."[5] Just as the servant of Abraham represents the general category "servant," and the wife of Manoah represents the general category "wife," the Levite of Judges 17–18 represents the general category "Levite." In other words, it is the Levite's "Leviteness" that makes him integral to the narrative of these two chapters.

The Levite's introduction begins in 17:7, "There was a נער." The title נער, which

---

[3] This connection was made explicit as early as the talmudic period, e.g., *b. B. Bat.* 109b. Some modern scholars also take this approach, e.g., Yaira Amit, *Judges: Introduction and Commentary* (in Hebrew; Mikra le-Yisraʾel; Tel Aviv: Am Oved, 1999), 277.

[4] Though Reinhartz focuses on anonymity, she notes that a proper name can develop characterization in four ways (*"Why Ask My Name?"* 6). First, it can convey meaning by means of its etymology. Whereas the interpretation of names is today a scholarly endeavor, the biblical authors sometimes provide explanations of their own, for example, those for Noah (Gen 5:29, זה ינחמנו, "this one will relieve us"), Moses (Exod 2:10, מן המים משיתהו, "I drew him out of the water"), and that of Gershom mentioned above (Exod 2:22; 18:3, גר הייתי בארץ נכריה, "I have been a stranger in a foreign land"). Second, a proper name unifies the disparate information provided about a character. It is the name "Moses" that ties together the killing of an Egyptian, the marrying of a Midianite, the speaking at the burning bush, and the splitting of the sea. Conversely, when characters such as Jacob/Israel, Jethro/Reuel/Hobab, and Gideon/Jerubaal have two proper names, the unity of a story can be called into question. Third, a proper name provides the narrator with a convenient way of referring to a character. This is related to the fourth aspect, that a proper name distinguishes one character from another. Without a proper name, pronouns such as "he" and "she" are often confusing, especially when two characters have similar traits.

[5] Chris Baldick, *The Oxford Dictionary of Literary Terms* (3rd ed.; Oxford: Oxford University Press, 2008), 343.

appears also in 18:3 and 18:15, usually means "youth" or "servant" but is ambiguous here.⁶ On the one hand, we are not told that the Levite is a servant to another person, suggesting that he is a youth and not a servant. On the other hand, he is called an איש ("man") in the next verse (17:8), suggesting that he is a servant and not a youth. Perhaps there is no contradiction and the term נער is meant to convey that the Levite is either unmarried,⁷ a servant to the temple, a servant to Micah, a grown man but still younger than Micah,⁸ or all of the above. Whatever the case may be, the introductory term נער signifies that the Levite is in some way not fully developed, either physically as a "youth" or socially as a "servant" or "unmarried man."

The second piece of introductory information is geographical: the נער comes from "Bethlehem of Judah" (Judg 17:7). There were two Bethlehems, one nine miles south of Jerusalem in Judah (Judg 19:1, 2, 18; Ruth 1:1–2; 1 Sam 17:12) and the other in the northern territory of Zebulun (Josh 19:15; Judg 12:8–10).⁹ The Levite's birthplace in Judah characterizes him as an Israelite who comes from the heartland of one of the largest and most influential tribes. He is additionally said to come "from the *family* of Judah" (ממשפחת יהודה). This is contradicted by the next phrase in 17:7, "and he is a Levite" (והוא לוי), a title repeated eight times in the story (17:9–13; 18:3, 15). Ostensibly, one person cannot belong to two tribes; the נער is either a Judahite or a Levite. While some solve the contradiction by suggesting that the Levite's parents belonged to two different tribes or that the early Levites were a professional class and not a tribe, it will now be shown that the very next phrase, "and he sojourned there" (והוא גר שם), which uses the root גור ("to sojourn") suggests that the Levite did not actually belong to the tribe of Judah at all.¹⁰

As D. Kellerman points out, the root גור appears more than one hundred times in the Hebrew Bible and is used for a person "who lives among people who are not his blood relatives, and thus he lacks the protection and the privileges which usually come from blood relationship and place of birth."¹¹ This explains why the Levite,

---

⁶ For a detailed discussion, see H. F. Fuhs, "Naʿar," *TDOT* 9:480–83. The two general meanings are both found in Judges. The title "youth" is applied to the newborn Samson (13:5, 7–8, 12, 24) as well as to Gideon's son who has not yet reached manhood (8:20), and the title "servant" is applied to the servants of Abimelech, Gideon, and Samson (7:10–11; 9:54; 16:26).

⁷ According to Lawrence E. Stager, the primary meaning of נער is not "a youth" but an "unmarried male who has not yet become a 'head of household.' He is in some sort of dependent status, hence the frequent translation 'servant'" ("The Archaeology of the Family in Ancient Israel," *BASOR* 260 [1985]: 25). Although this definition could easily be applied to the Levite here, Stager surprisingly translates נער in Judg 17:7 as "youth" (p. 27).

⁸ Reinhartz, "Why Ask My Name?" 77.

⁹ See Henri Cazelles, "Bethlehem (Place)," *ABD* 1:712–15. It is not clear why the biblical authors felt the need to explain the Judean city ("Bethlehem of Judah") as opposed to the Zebulunite one (simply "Bethlehem").

¹⁰ For examples of the two solutions cited, see *b. B. Bat.* 109b; and Moore, *Critical and Exegetical Commentary*, 383.

¹¹ Kellerman, "Gûr," *TDOT* 2:443.

who comes from the area of Judah, introduces himself as a "Levite" and not as a "Judahite" in 17:9: "I am a Levite from Bethlehem of Judah." The root גור takes on more significance in light of the story's conclusion, which mentions "Jonathan son of Gershom son of Manasseh" (יהונתן בן גרשם בן מנשה), an important priest from the temple of Dan (Judg 18:30).[12] As many point out, the Levitic name "Gershom" (גרשם) is spelled with the same consonants as the words "he sojourned there" (גר שם), which introduce the Levite in 17:7. Moreover, these very words are applied to the Levites in Deut 18:6, and the name Gershom is even said, according to Exod 2:22 and 18:3, to derive from the root גור. Thus, the heavy emphasis on the root גור suggests that the Levite is to be understood as a sojourner (גר) who once lived among the Judahites, not as a tribesman of Judah himself. In accordance with Jason S. Bray, the phrase ממשפחת יהודה should therefore be translated as "from the *clansland* of Judah" as opposed to the more common "from the *family* of Judah."[13]

In the next statement, the Levite is portrayed as a wanderer without a destination: "the man left Bethlehem of Judah to sojourn wherever he could find" (17:8). Notice that, when the Levite arrives, it is Micah who initiates the conversation: "'Where do you come from?' Micah asked him. He replied, 'I am a Levite from Bethlehem of Judah and I am traveling to sojourn wherever I can find'" (17:9). The order of this conversation is significant because the Levite is continually presented as a passive figure, one who speaks when spoken to. This characteristic is continued when it is Micah and not the Levite who dictates the terms of their agreement: "Micah said to him, 'Stay with me and be a father and a priest to me, and I will pay you ten [shekels] of silver a year, an allowance of clothing, and your living'" (17:10). As one might expect from a passive figure, the Levite accepts Micah's terms without qualms: "The Levite went, agreeing to stay with the man, and the נער became like one of his own sons" (17:10–11).[14]

The Levite is called a "father" (אב) by Micah, and, for comparison, many point to Joseph, who is called a "father to Pharaoh" (אב לפרעה) even though he is only the viceroy of Egypt (Gen 45:8). Similarly, Eliakim, the head of Hezekiah's palace, is called a "father [אב] for those who live in Jerusalem and the house of Judah" (Isa 22:21) even though he is not the king. Thus, the term "father" conveys an important status but not the highest status. The Levite's relative inferiority can be seen in Micah's payment, which is "ten [shekels] of silver a year, an allowance of clothing, and your living" (17:10). Ten shekels is a paltry 0.9 percent of the money that Micah took from his mother earlier in the story (eleven hundred shekels in 17:2). Micah,

---

[12] The LXX manuscripts have "Moses" (משה) instead of "Manasseh" (מנשה). This makes sense in light of Exod 2:22 and 1 Chr 23:15; 26:24, which identify Gershom as the son of the Levite Moses.

[13] Bray, *Sacred Dan*, 20–21.

[14] The word נער is ambiguous here. The sentence could mean either that Micah became a father figure to the Levite נער or that the Levite became a father figure to Micah's son, mentioned in 17:5 though not called a נער.

who provides the Levite with money, clothing, and food (lit., מחיה, "living"), is similar to other characters with power and authority in the Hebrew Bible. A slave-master must provide food and clothing to his female slave (Exod 21:10) and King Evil-Merodach of Babylon provides prison garments and regular rations to Jehoiachin, the captured king of Judah (2 Kgs 25:9). Gehazi, the servant of Elisha, gets leprosy when he asks Naaman the Aramean for "a talent of silver and two changes of clothing" (2 Kgs 5:22). The punishment comes because, at least in Elisha's eyes, Gehazi's acceptance of money and clothing is an acknowledgment of Naaman's superiority.

The Levite's characterization as the weaker partner is continued in 17:12: "Micah consecrated the Levite [וימלא מיכה את יד הלוי], and the young man became his priest and remained in Micah's temple." There are only three other instances in the Hebrew Bible of a person "consecrating" (מלא + יד) someone else, and in all three it is the consecrator who has the position of power. First, it is Moses, the unequivocal leader of the Israelites, who consecrates (מלא + יד) Aaron and his sons (Exod 29:33, 35). Second, it is Jeroboam, the king of the north, who consecrates (מלא + יד) new priests at Dan and Bethel (1 Kgs 13:33; 2 Chr 13:9). Third, it is Micah who consecrates his own son at the beginning of our story (17:5). Like Moses, Jeroboam, and Micah vis-à-vis his son, Micah is the more powerful party in relation to the Levite.

We are next told Micah's, and not the Levite's, feelings about the deal: "Now I know that Yhwh will prosper me because I have a Levite as my priest" (17:13). Micah's statement indicates that the anonymous Levite, who is presented here as a type, is valuable because of his Leviteness. Indeed, Micah replaces his very own son with the Levite as his priest. Micah's statement also marks a turning point in the narrative, for the consecrated Levite is now called "the priest" (הכהן) in the scenes that involve the tribesmen of Dan.

The five Danite scouts reach the hills of Ephraim and hear the Levite's voice in 18:3: "they recognized the voice of the Levite נער." Even though the Levite's voice is heard, we are not told what he says. The Danites somehow discern that the Levite is out of place and ask him a threefold question: "Who brought you here? What are you doing in this place? What is your business here?" (18:3). Three- or even fourfold questions are quite rare in the Hebrew Bible and are seemingly used for emphasis. In the midst of a terrible storm the sailors ask Jonah, "What is your business? Where have you come from? What is your country? Of what people are you?" (Jonah 1:8). Faced with the imminent death of his brother Benjamin, Judah pleads to the viceroy of Egypt, "What can we say to my lord? How can we plead? How can we prove our innocence?" (Gen 44:16). David asks Jonathan, "What have I done? What is my crime? What is my guilt against your father, that he seeks my life?" (1 Sam 20:1).[15] The threefold question of our story serves two purposes. First, it reveals that the

---

[15] For other examples, see 1 Sam 1:8; Job 9:12; Prov 30:4; and Lam 2:13.

Danites are curious about the Levite, perhaps because he has a southern accent like them. Second, the repetition emphasizes that the Levite, like the tribe of Dan itself, is recognizably out of place.

The Levite responds to the Danites in 18:4: "Micah did such and such for me, he hired me, and I became a priest for him." Three points can be made about this response. First, it continues the Levite's passive characterization because the action is attributed to Micah and not the Levite. Second, because the Levite introduces himself as a "priest," the Danites immediately ask him for an oracle (vv. 3–5). This indicates that the Levite's typified status as priest, and not just his Leviteness, is what makes him an efficacious oracle giver. Third, the Levite says that he is Micah's "priest," though Micah actually hired him as both "a father and a priest" (לאב ולכהן). This sly omission of "father," which recasts the bonds of kinship[16] as being strictly financial, makes it easier for the Levite to betray his master, Micah, in the next scene. Similarly, unlike Micah in 17:10, the Levite uses the root שכר ("to hire for wages"), suggesting that he views the deal as strictly financial.

The sole exception to the Levite's passive characterization occurs when he reveals Yhwh's disposition to the Danites: "Go in peace; before Yhwh is the mission you are going on" (18:5–6). Here the Levite sounds confident when he gives the unequivocal command, "go" (לכו), and his prediction is shown to be accurate when the Danites march on to victory (18:27–31). Perhaps this assertive and effectual characterization is due to the fact that, at least in the author's eyes, the Levite is fulfilling his typified role as a temple priest. Indeed, if it were not for his priestly capabilities, the Levite would be of little importance to either Micah or the Danites.

In a later scene, when the entire Danite tribe meets the Levite for the first time, the narrator contrasts the Danites' might with the Levite's meekness. While the Danite scouts were originally introduced as "mighty men" (אנשים בני חיל) in 18:2, the Levite is again called a נער in 18:15, which indicates either physical or social underdevelopment. The narrator paints a vivid picture of the scene: "[The Danites] greeted him peacefully; the six hundred Danite men, girt with their weapons of war, stood at the entrance of the gate…. The priest was standing at the entrance of the gate with the six hundred men girt with their weapons of war" (18:15–17). Both the Danites and the Levite are said to be standing at the entrance of the gate, but the Danites are twice depicted as six hundred strong and dressed for war, while the Levite is but one person and apparently not dressed for war. When the Levite sees that the temple's objects are being taken, he asks the six hundred men, "What are you doing?" (18:18). This is important because of what he does not say; that is, he does not tell them to stop. This again signifies the Levite's meekness relative to the

---

[16] Micah hired the Levite with the formulation היה לי לאב ולכהן, "be for me a father and a priest" (17:10). This type of היה + ל + ל formulation is usually used for familial and covenantal agreements. For example, Abraham acquires Sarah as his wife (Gen 20:12, ותהי לי לאשה); the daughter of Pharaoh adopts Moses as her son (Exod 2:10, ויהי לה לבן); and Yhwh and David become a father and son to each other (2 Sam 7:14, אני אהיה לו לאב והוא יהיה לי לבן).

Danites' strength. Yet, as Mueller correctly points out, the Levite is not necessarily being criticized, for "it would have been both heroic and suicidal for him to resist the robbery."[17]

The stronger Danites respond with four forceful commands: "Be quiet, put your hand on your mouth, come with us, be our father and priest" (18:19). The second command, "Put your hand on your mouth" (שים ידך על פיך), is worthy of attention. This phrase only appears four other times in the Hebrew Bible and always involves the limiting of power: the once strong nations will dread Yhwh (ישימו יד על פה, Mic 7:16); the haughty observers will dread Job (ושימו יד על פה, Job 21:5); the once argumentative Job gives up his case (ידי שמתי למו פי, Job 40:4); and the arrogant man clasps his mouth in shock, apparently because of his own demise (יד לפה, Prov 30:32). In light of these parallels, it appears that the narrator is yet again highlighting the Danites' position over and above that of the Levite.

It is significant that the Danites' fourth command employs the same language that Micah used in 17:10: "Be our father and priest" (והיה לנו לאב ולכהן). By repeating Micah's offer almost verbatim, the narrator evokes the original deal and thus portrays the Levite as duplicitous. The Danites convince the Levite by appealing to his personal ambitions: "Would you rather be priest to one man's household or be priest to a tribe and clan in Israel?" (18:19). The Levite's ambitious double-dealing is also seen in 18:20, the only verse that reveals his feelings: "The priest's heart was made merry" (וייטב לב הכהן). This joy, more than anything else, is what characterizes the Levite as disloyal to Micah. It is now understandable that, without being told what to do, "[the Levite] took the ephod, the household gods, and the sculptured image, and he came in the midst of the [Danite] people" (18:20). Here the Levite assists in the robbery, repaying his master with betrayal. This is the last we hear of the Levite in the narrative, unless 18:30 refers to him: "Jonathan son of Gershom son of Manasseh, and his descendants, served as priests to the Danite tribe until the land went into exile."

II. Conclusion

This analysis has portrayed the Levite as a character with a number of well-developed traits. He is a נער who speaks when spoken to, a wanderer with no destination, and a sojourner who is recognizably out of place. He is valued as a "father" and as a priest who speaks in the name of Yhwh, but he is not in charge of the men who seek his services. He is ambitious, persuadable, self-serving, and ultimately disloyal. Although he is portrayed as passive and meek, he joins the Danites and actively assists in the robbery of Micah's temple. He is not criticized by the narrator explicitly, perhaps because he is a weak character as opposed to an evil

---

[17] Mueller, *Micah Story*, 71.

one. It is ultimately up to the reader to decide just how negatively the Levite is portrayed.[18]

Though the Levite's anonymity suggests that he is to be understood as a type, he is by no means flat, superficial, or defined by a single trait. He changes over time, going from homeless to homed and Levite to priest. He is a complex and somewhat contradictory figure, being passive but ambitious, meek but confident, a נער as well as a man, a thief as well as a servant of Yhwh, and a "father" with no sense of familial obligation. Aside from the "inside view" of 18:20 ("The priest's heart was made merry"), we are not informed of his emotions, thoughts, or motivations. This is not altogether surprising, for, as Jean Louis Ska notes, "the predominance of action and the lack of interest in the psychological processes of the characters are two of the main characteristics of Biblical narrative."[19] Therefore, despite the fact that we know neither his name nor the inner workings of his mind and heart, the Levite of Judges 17–18 can be considered one of the more richly drawn characters in the book of Judges and perhaps in the Hebrew Bible as a whole.

---

[18] Both ancient and modern commentators tend to view the Levite in a negative light. For example, according to *b. B. Bat.* 109b, the name of the Levite's grandfather, Moses (משה), was changed by means of a superlineal *nun* (נ) to Manasseh (מנשה) in 18:30 in order to dissociate the idolatrous Levite from the righteous Moses. Similarly, Yaira Amit writes that the Levite is "portrayed in a negative light" (*Hidden Polemics in Biblical Narrative* [BibInt 25; Leiden: Brill, 2000], 106), and Reinhartz observes that the Levite has a "negative portrayal" (*"Why Ask My Name?"* 79). Although there is no indication that the statement "In those days there was no king in Israel; every man did as he pleased" (17:6; also see 18:1; 19:1; 21:25) specifically applies to the Levite, it may very well add to a negative portrayal. Yet it is not clear what this phrase refers to or even if it is negative. For a detailed discussion and bibliography, see Mueller, *Micah Story*, 103–7.

[19] Ska, *"Our Fathers Have Told Us,"* 83.

New in Biblical Studies
WJK WESTMINSTER JOHN KNOX PRESS
PUBLISHING EXCELLENCE SINCE 1858

DANIEL
THE OLD TESTAMENT LIBRARY
CAROL A. NEWSOM
with Brennan W. Breed
9780664220808
Hardback • $50.00

FAITH AND FEMINISM
Ecumenical Essays
B. DIANE LIPSETT AND PHYLLIS TRIBLE, EDS.
9780664239695
Paperback • $35.00

READING THE PARABLES
INTERPRETATION: RESOURCES FOR THE USE OF SCRIPTURE IN THE CHURCH
RICHARD LISCHER
9780664231651
Hardback • $35.00

BIBLICAL PROPHECY
Perspectives for Christian Theology, Discipleship, and Ministry
INTERPRETATION: RESOURCES FOR THE USE OF SCRIPTURE IN THE CHURCH
ELLEN F. DAVIS
9780664235383
Hardback • $40.00

WWW.WJKBOOKS.COM • 1.800.523.1631

JBL 133, no. 4 (2014): 739-749

The Value of a Curious Translation: Revisiting Proverbs 2:5

ZOLTÁN SCHWÁB
zoltan.schwab@dunelm.org.uk
2E Old Dryburn Way, Durham DH1 5SE, United Kingdom

The tradition of the spiritual senses has been an inspiration for major recent theological endeavors (such as those of Karl Rahner, Hans Urs von Balthasar, and Sarah Coakley). Many consider Origen as the "founding father" of this theological tradition. He found substantial biblical evidence for the existence of a spiritual sensation in Prov 2:5, which, according to him, speaks of a divine sense (*sensus divinus*, αἴσθησις θεία). However, this rendering differs significantly from both the MT (דעת אלהים) and the LXX (ἐπίγνωσις θεοῦ). Therefore, a venerable theological tradition seems to stem from a rather "idiosyncratic" reading of the biblical text. This article investigates how the translator of Origen's text might have arrived at his/her translation. My conclusion is that, although it cannot be accepted as a good translation of the Hebrew, Origen's text grasps important elements of the deeper theological structure of Proverbs 2; thus, it represents a possible interpretation of the text.

I. Proverbs 2:5 and the Theological Tradition of the Spiritual Senses

Tasting an exotic fruit for the first time can be disappointing. Its taste is seldom as rich as expected. But tasting it the second time often brings greater satisfaction, because tastes need to be learned. Can, however, human senses also be trained to see, taste, smell, touch, and hear the divine in physical phenomena? After all, Paul teaches that God's power and divine nature are visible "through the things he has made" (Rom 1:20), and Psalm 34 encourages its readers to "taste and see that the Lord is good" (Ps 34:9[8]).

The experience of sensation can be just as vivid in dreams as in wakefulness. A dreamed exotic fruit can be tastier than anything. Origen suggested that this realistic dream-sensation is comparable to what the prophets and apostles experienced in their God-given visions (*Cels.* 1.48). This leads to a question similar

739

to the previous one: can the *inner* sensation faculties be trained to be more open to the inspiration of the Holy Spirit?

The spiritual senses tradition discusses these and similar questions. This tradition comprises diverse positions. Some speak about how to develop the physical senses so that they become spiritual; others speak about the spiritual senses as separate from the physical ones. Some speak about a fivefold experience of God; others discuss a generic spiritual sense or mention only one or two spiritual senses. Hence, the history of theology does not present a unified doctrine of the spiritual senses; it is rather a tradition of manifold teachings with family resemblances.[1]

Nonetheless, it is an influential tradition. Karl Rahner, in the beginning of his academic career, wrote extensively about it.[2] It was probably one of his main inspirations for developing the idea of the pre-apprehension (*Vorgriff*) of God, which is a precognitive knowledge of God's presence.[3] Hans Urs von Balthasar, another giant of twentieth-century Catholic theology, also wrote about the spiritual senses tradition and used it for articulating his influential thoughts about the unity of corporeal and spiritual perception.[4] The Anglican philosophical theologian Sarah Coakley is working on a major four-volume systematic theology, the second volume of which will focus on epistemology and the spiritual senses.[5] These examples show that the tradition is alive and well even in contemporary theological thinking.

Balthasar called Origen the "inventor" of the "doctrine" of the five spiritual senses.[6] Here I would like to draw attention to only one element of Origen's complex thought, namely, that when he wanted to demonstrate the existence of a spiritual sensation he consistently turned to a special textual variant of Prov 2:5b:

> We speak of the soul as being able to use teeth.... In a similar way we speak of it as using all the other bodily organs, which are transferred from their corporeal significance and applied to the faculties of the soul; as Solomon says, "You will find a divine sense" [*sensum divinum invenies*]. (*Princ.* 1.1.9.)[7]

---

[1] Paul L. Gavrilyuk and Sarah Coakley, "Introduction," in *The Spiritual Senses: Perceiving God in Western Christianity* (ed. Paul L. Gavrilyuk and Sarah Coakley; Cambridge: Cambridge University Press, 2012), 18.

[2] Rahner, "The 'Spiritual Senses' according to Origen," in Rahner, *Theological Investigations*, vol. 16, *Experience of the Spirit: Source of Theology* (trans. David Morland; London: Darton, Longman & Todd, 1979), 81–103; and, in the same volume, "The Doctrine of the 'Spiritual Senses' in the Middle Ages," 104–34.

[3] Mark J. McInroy, "Karl Rahner and Hans Urs von Balthasar," in Gavrilyuk and Coakley, *Spiritual Senses*, 263–68.

[4] Balthasar, *The Glory of the Lord: A Theological Aesthetics*, vol. 1, *Seeing the Form* (trans. Erasmo Leiva-Merikakis; Edinburgh: T&T Clark, 1982), 365–425; McInroy, "Karl Rahner and Hans Urs von Balthasar," 268–73.

[5] Coakley, *God, Sexuality, and the Self: An Essay 'On the Trinity'* (Cambridge: Cambridge University Press, 2013), xiv–xv.

[6] Balthasar, *Seeing the Form*, 367.

[7] G. W. Butterworth, *Origen on First Principles: Being Koetschau's Text of De Principiis Translated into English, together with an Introduction and Notes* (London: SPCK, 1936), 327–28.

Anyone who looks into this subject more deeply will say that there is, as the scripture calls it, a certain generic divine sense which only the man who is blessed finds on this earth. Thus Solomon says: "Thou shalt find a divine sense" [αἴσθησιν θείαν εὑρήσεις]. (*Cels.* 1.48.)[8]

And if you wish to learn from the sacred Scriptures about the superior and incorporeal sense, listen to Solomon's words in Proverbs, "Thou shalt find a divine sense." (*Cels.* 7.34.)[9]

Despite the far-reaching influence of Origen's reading of Prov 2:5, modern biblical scholarship remains silent about it. Commentaries and monographs on Proverbs, to my best knowledge, do not even mention Origen's reading.[10] This silence may partly be explained by a certain divide between biblical scholarship and philosophical theology; that is, many biblical scholars simply might not be aware of the spiritual senses tradition. Another explanation can be that Origen's reading appears to

---

[8] Origen, *Contra Celsum* (trans. Henry Chadwick; Cambridge: Cambridge University Press, 1953), 44.

[9] Ibid., 422. See also Origen, *Comm. Rom.* 4.5; *Comm. Matt., Comm. ser.* 63 (Matt 25:1–5; besides the Latin, see also *Catena* no. 273); *Princ.* 4.4.10; *Hom. Exod.* 1.4; *Cant.* 1.4.

[10] I have checked the following works: Kenneth T. Aitken, *Proverbs* (Daily Study Bible; Louisville: Westminster, 1986); Richard J. Clifford, *Proverbs: A Commentary* (OTL; Louisville: Westminster John Knox, 1999); Ellen F. Davis, *Proverbs, Ecclesiastes, and the Song of Songs* (Westminster Bible Companion; Louisville: Westminster John Knox, 2000); Daniel J. Estes, *Hear, My Son: Teaching and Learning in Proverbs 1–9* (New Studies in Biblical Theology; Leicester: Apollos, 1997); Michael V. Fox, *Proverbs 1–9: A New Translation with Introduction and Commentary* (AB 18A; New York: Doubleday, 2000); Charles T. Fritsch and Rolland W. Schloerb, "Proverbs," in *IB* 4:767–957; Berend Gemser, *Sprüche Salomos* (HAT 1/18; Tübingen: Mohr Siebeck, 1937); Edgar Jones, *Proverbs and Ecclesiastes: Introduction and Commentary* (Torch Bible Commentaries; London: SCM, 1961); Derek Kidner, *The Proverbs: An Introduction and Commentary* (TOTC; London: Tyndale, 1964); Tremper Longman III, *Proverbs* (Baker Commentary on the Old Testament Wisdom and Psalms; Grand Rapids: Baker Academic, 2006); William McKane, *Proverbs: A New Approach* (OTL; London: SCM, 1970); Arndt Meinhold, *Die Sprüche: Kapitel 1–15* (ZBK; Zurich: Theologischer Verlag, 1991); Roland E. Murphy, *Proverbs* (WBC 22; Nashville: Thomas Nelson, 1998); W. O. E. Oesterley, *The Book of Proverbs: With Introduction and Notes* (WC; London: Methuen, 1929); Leo G. Perdue, *Proverbs* (IBC; Louisville: John Knox, 2000); Otto Plöger, *Sprüche Salomos* (BKAT 17; Neukirchen-Vluyn: Neukirchener Verlag, 1984); Gerhard von Rad, *Wisdom in Israel* (trans. James D. Martin; Harrisburg, PA: Trinity Press International, 1972); Helmer Ringgren and Walther Zimmerli, *Sprüche/Prediger* (ATD 16.1; Göttingen: Vandenhoeck & Ruprecht, 1962); Allen P. Ross, *Proverbs*, in *The Expositor's Bible Commentary*, vol. 6 (Grand Rapids: Zondervan, 2008); Magne Saebø, *Sprüche* (ATD 16.1; Göttingen: Vandenhoeck & Ruprecht, 2012); R. B. Y. Scott, *Proverbs, Ecclesiastes: Introduction, Translation, and Notes* (AB 18; Garden City, NY: Doubleday, 1965); Crawford H. Toy, *A Critical and Exegetical Commentary on the Book of Proverbs* (ICC; Edinburgh: T&T Clark, 1899); Daniel J. Treier, *Proverbs & Ecclesiastes* (Brazos Theological Commentary on the Bible; Grand Rapids: Brazos, 2011); Raymond C. Van Leeuwen, "Proverbs," in *NIB* 5:17–264; Bruce K. Waltke, *The Book of Proverbs: Chapters 1–15* (NICOT; Grand Rapids: Eerdmans, 2004); Stuart Weeks, *Instruction and Imagery in Proverbs 1–9* (Oxford: Oxford University Press, 2007).

be so capricious to biblical scholars that they do not consider it a likely candidate for contributing to the interpretation of the biblical text. Paul Gavrilyuk and Coakley probably echo the initial impression of biblical scholars, too, when they call Origen's version an "idiosyncratic rendering of Proverbs 2:5."[11] John M. Dillon uses even stronger language:

> We may note the bizarre nature of this reference.... It is a Greek version ... of Proverbs 2:5: "Then you will understand the fear of the Lord / and find the knowledge of God." The LXX has for this latter phrase, "καὶ ἐπίγνωσιν θεοῦ εὑρήσεις," which is an accurate rendering of the Hebrew, *daʿat ʾĕlohîm timṣāʾ*, and would never have given occasion to such an exegesis as that which Origen gives it. Presumably Origen's authority took *elohim* as a descriptive, or subjective, rather than an objective, genitive (which, I am assured by those who know Hebrew better than I do, is *not* a possible interpretation here, and thus must be the work of someone who knew Hebrew imperfectly), and it is this that Origen can creatively misinterpret.... We have here, therefore, a good example of a piece of Origenist doctrine hatched from the wind-egg of a false translation.[12]

Despite its unpromising appearance as a translation, however, Origen's reading (which is identical to the earlier reading of Clement of Alexandria) might deserve some attention from biblical scholars, at least because of its theological influence, if nothing else.[13] Thus, in the following I am going to consider how the "divine sense" translation might have been born and especially how it relates to the Hebrew text.

II. Αἴσθησις Θεία Fits the Greek Text

Origen's translation is explicable in its Greek context. First, αἴσθησις is a usual rendition of דעת, especially in (other verses of) the LXX version of Proverbs.[14] Thus, in a sense, Origen's text is just more consistent in its translation.

Furthermore, Origen's "divine sense" suggests that it is not only a sense for the divine but also a sensation with divine origin or nature (*Cels.* 7.34).[15] Hebrew

---

[11] Gavrilyuk and Coakley, "Introduction," 2–3.

[12] Dillon, "Aisthêsis Noêtê: A Doctrine of Spiritual Senses in Origen and in Plotinus," in *Hellenica et Judaica: Hommage à Valentin Nikiprowetzky* (ed. A. Caquot, M. Hadas-Lebel, and J. Riaud; Collection de la Revue des études juives 3; Leuven: Peeters, 1986), 444 n. 3.

[13] The reading first appears in Clement of Alexandria's writings in *Strom.* 1.4.27.

[14] Outside of Proverbs, αἴσθησις occurs in the LXX in Exod 28:3; Ezra 1:22; Judg 16:17; Sir 22:19; Ep Jer 1:41. דעת is more commonly translated by other words, mainly by γνῶσις (G. Johannes Botterweck and J. Bergman, "יָדַע Yādaʿ," *TDOT* 5:448–81). In Proverbs, however, αἴσθησις is by far the most common translation of דעת: it translates דעת twenty-one times, while the second most common translation, γνῶσις, stands only eight times for דעת; Prov 2:5 is the only place where ἐπίγνωσις translates דעת.

[15] Gregory of Nyssa grasps Origen's thought well when he writes, "There is in us a dual

genitival constructions, in our case "knowledge of God," can express the same nuance. For example, when Job 15:2a writes, "Should the wise answer with דעת רוח?," most translators agree that דעת רוח means something like "windy knowledge."[16] Thus, purely on the basis of Hebrew grammar, it is possible that "God" in the "knowledge of God" should be translated as an adjective: divine (*pace* the acquaintances of Dillon who are knowledgeable about Hebrew).

Finally, the wider Greek context makes Origen's reading especially attractive. Most LXX manuscripts contain an extra, third line in v. 3:

> ³ For if you call upon Wisdom,
> and give your voice to understanding,
> and seek discernment [αἴσθησιν] with loud voice,[17]
> ⁴ and if you seek her like silver
> and search for her like [hidden] treasures,
> ⁵ then you will understand the fear of the Lord,
> and discover knowledge of God [or, in Origen, "divine sense" (αἴσθησιν θείαν)].
> (LXX Prov 2:3–5)[18]

Αἴσθησις, which is introduced in the extra LXX line of v. 3, can be easily understood as the direct object throughout v. 4. Thus, after this long search for αἴσθησις, discovering a *divine* αἴσθησις in v. 5 makes a seamless reading.[19]

Therefore, the text used by Origen follows the LXX tradition of translating דעת with αἴσθησις. It is grammatically possible, and, rather than being "idiosyncratic," it provides an especially smooth reading in its Greek context. Whether it

---

activity of perception, the one bodily, the other more divine [θειοτέρα]—just as the Word says somewhere in Proverbs, 'You will find a divine sense'" (Gregory of Nyssa, *Homilies on the Song of Songs* [trans. Richard A. Norris Jr.; WGRW; Atlanta: Society of Biblical Literature, 2012], 34–37). I have slightly revised the translation of the biblical quotation.

[16] "Vain knowledge" (KJV); "empty notions" (NIV); "windy knowledge" (NRSV); etc. Similarly, when אלהים is the *nomen rectum*, it is often translated adjectively; for instance, Isa 35:4 (גמול אלהים)—TNIV [Today's New International Version]: "divine retribution"); Exod 31:3 (רוח אלהים—NRSV: "divine spirit"); Gen 23:6 (נשיא אלהים—KJV, NIV, NRSV: "mighty prince"). For the different types of Hebrew genitival constructions, see *IBHS*, 143–54.

[17] This extra line might be the result of the double translation of Hebrew Prov 2:3b. The line is present in most manuscripts but missing from some important ones. It is debated how and why it got into the text. See Johann Cook, *The Septuagint of Proverbs: Jewish and/or Hellenistic Proverbs? Concerning the Hellenistic Colouring of LXX Proverbs* (VTSup 69; Leiden: Brill, 1997), 114–16.

[18] Translation is that of Nicholas King, *The Old Testament: A Translation of the Septuagint*, vol. 3, *The Wisdom Literature* (Buxhall: Kevin Mayhew, 2008), 201.

[19] Herwig Görgemanns and Heinrich Karpp also suggest that αἴσθησις might have entered v. 5 under the influence of v. 3 (*Origenes, Vier Bücher von Den Prinzipien* [2nd ed.; Texte zur Forschung 24; Darmstadt: Wissenschaftliche Buchgesellschaft, 1985], 121 n. 26). In fact, the issue might be somewhat more complicated. Clement of Alexandria, whom Origen might follow in his translation of Prov 2:5b, quoted the whole of Prov 2:3–5, and his v. 3 is significantly different from the LXX version (*Strom.* 1.4.27). Nevertheless, his version also contains αἴσθησις in v. 3, so the above argument, even if with some adjustments, would also apply to his reading.

represented an existing textual tradition or the invention of some patristic authors, it would have seemed natural to a Greek reader.

III. Αἴσθησις Θεία as a Wrong Translation

There are other considerations, however, that suggest that Origen's text alters the meaning of the Hebrew significantly. First of all, differently from the Greek αἴσθησις, the Hebrew דעת never refers to the bodily organs of perception.[20] In addition, it is unlikely that דעת אלהים, knowledge of God, could be understood adjectively. This is primarily because the parallel expression in Prov 2:5a is "fear of the Lord" where "Lord" seems to be the object of fear. One could easily argue that because "fear of the Lord" is a set phrase and simply means "piety," it actually goes very well with having a "divine sense" (or sense for the divine). Indeed, Clement of Alexandria, whom Origen might follow in his quotation of Prov 2:5, apparently understood the verse along these lines and translated fear of the Lord as "piety" (νοήσεις θεοσέβειαν καὶ αἴσθησιν θείαν εὑρήσεις [Strom. 1.4.27]).

However, the mistake made by the translator of αἴσθησις θεία as "divine sense" is exactly that he/she did not recognize that just as "fear of the Lord" is a set phrase, so is "knowledge of God," which takes God as the object of knowledge. There are many verses outside Proverbs that clarify the expression דעת אלהים. For instance, the book of Hosea not only uses the exact phrase, דעת אלהים, but also refers to the knowledge of God in many different ways.[21] We find "Let us seek, let us pursue to know the Lord" (Hos 6:3: נדעה נרדפה לדעת את יהוה), where the object marker את makes it clear that the Lord is the object of knowledge.[22] In the light of this and similar verses, it is probable that the "knowledge of God/Lord" is a religious *terminus technicus*, in which God is the object, and therefore אלהים should not be translated as "divine."[23] Thus, the problem is not necessarily with the Hebrew knowledge of the translator responsible for αἴσθησις θεία, but with him/her not taking into account how the idea and terminology of the knowledge of God appear outside Prov 2:5.

Therefore, even if Origen's Greek translation makes perfect sense in its immediate Greek context, it is, nevertheless, a mistranslation.

---

[20] Botterweck and Bergman, "יָדַע Yādaʿ," 448–81; David J. A. Clines, ed., "דַּעַת," DCH 2:457–59.

[21] See Hos 2:10, 22; 4:1, 6; 5:4; 6:3, 6; 8:2; 10:12 (LXX); 11:3; 13:4.

[22] Biblical quotations, unless noted otherwise, are my translations.

[23] See Judg 2:10; 1 Sam 2:12; 3:7; Prov 3:6; Isa 11:9; Jer 31:34; Hos 2:22. For other biblical passages that suggest that God is the object of knowledge, see Botterweck and Bergman, "יָדַע Yādaʿ," 469–79.

IV. Αἴσθησις Θεία as a Feasible Interpretation

Even if "divine sense" is not a good *translation* of דעת אלהים, it may be, accidentally or not, a feasible *interpretation* of it. This statement is based on three observations: (1) דעת can refer to perception; (2) דעת אלהים can refer to the perception of God; and (3) knowledge in Proverbs 1–9 has a divine nature. Let us see these points in more detail.

First, the semantic field of ידע and דעת, similarly to αἴσθησις, is rather broad, and, besides "knowing" and "knowledge," includes perception. For example, when in Lev 5:3 someone touches an impure object without knowing it and later he ידע this, this means that he "recognizes" what the situation is. This broad semantic field is suggested also by the way these words are used together with expressions of seeing or hearing:

Ps 31:8b(7b)   ראית את עניי ידעת בצרות נפשי
You have **seen** my affliction, you **knew** the distress of my soul.

Jer 2:19b   דעי וראי כי רע ומר עזבך את יהוה
Know and see that it is evil and bitter for you to leave the LORD.

(Job 5:27b)   שמענה ואתה דע לך
Hear and perceive for yourself.[24]

Although ידע and דעת do not refer directly to the physical organs of perception, in some verses they are closely related. When in 2 Samuel 19 the old Barzillai rejects David's invitation to the royal court, his rhetorical question "Do I know what is good and bad?" probably refers not to the lack of his mental capacities but to his blunt physical sensation: "Today I am eighty years old; do I know what is good and bad [האדע בין טוב לרע]? Does your servant taste what he eats and what he drinks? Do I still listen to the voice of singing men and singing women?" (2 Sam 19:36[35]).[25] Even more straightforward is Ben Sira 3:25, which draws a parallel between the eye and דעת: "without a pupil, there is no light; without דעת (knowledge/right perception?), there is not wisdom."[26]

---

[24] See also Exod 2:25; 3:7; 6:3; Num 24:16; Deut 4:35; 11:2; 29:3; 1 Sam 12:17; 14:38; 18:28; 23:22, 23; 24:12; 25:17; 26:12; 2 Sam 19:36; 24:13; 1 Kgs 20:7, 22; 2 Kgs 5:7; Neh 4:5; Job 28:7; Ps 138:6; Isa 5:19; 29:15; 33:13; 40:21, 28; 41:20, 23; 44:9, 18; 48:8; 58:3; Jer 2:23; 5:1; 6:18; Ezek 38:23.

[25] P. Kyle McCarter Jr.'s suggestion that the phrase refers to the ability to enjoy sexual pleasure would not be irreconcilable with my argument (*II Samuel: A New Translation with Introduction, Notes, and Commentary* [AB 9; Garden City, NY: Doubleday, 1984], 422). However, his exposition is rather speculative. At any rate, the phrase repeatedly occurs in the context of tasting food (e.g., Gen 3:4–6; Isa 7:15). A. A. Anderson also takes it as a reference to the proper functioning of physical senses (*2 Samuel* [WBC 11; Dallas: Thomas Nelson, 1989], 239).

[26] Hebrew: באין אישון יחסר אור באין דעת תחסר חכמה. The Hebrew text is from Pancratius C.

Thus, Michael V. Fox can describe דעת as "broader … than English 'knowledge', insofar as it includes minimal acts of awareness and innate intellectual capacities apart from learned information and skills."[27] Given this broad meaning of דעת, which includes awareness, perception, and an innate capacity to perceive rightly, the Greek αἴσθησις seems to be a fitting general choice for translating the word.

Second, דעת אלהים can refer to the perception of God. This is admittedly not how most biblical scholars explain the phrase. They say either that it is rooted in marital language and expresses an intimate relationship with God, that it is rooted in treaty language and expresses obedience to God's commandments, or that it is rooted in creedal confessions and expresses knowledge about the characteristics of God.[28] I do not wish to argue, however, with these (not mutually exclusive) understandings by offering another one, I only suggest that the connotation of perceiving the divine can *also* be present.

Isaiah connects the lack of the knowledge of God with a failure to perceive God's activity: "they do not *look* at the deeds of the Lord, or *see* the work of his hands. Therefore my people go into exile for the lack of recognition/knowledge [מבלי דעת] (of me)" (Isa 5:12b–13a).[29] Similarly, knowing God and perceiving God's activity and presence are hardly differentiable in some verses of Hosea: "She did not know/perceive [לא ידעה] that it was I who gave her the grain, the wine, the oil" (Hos 2:10a[8a]);[30] "It was I who taught Ephraim to walk, I took them up in my arms, but they did not recognize/know [לא ידעו] that I healed them" (Hos 11:3). In 1 Samuel 3 the young Samuel cannot identify the Lord's voice because he "did not yet know the Lord" (1 Sam 3:7). In all of these examples, the issue is not knowledge about God or obedience to God but an inability to see, hear, or recognize God.

Although Prov 2:5b does not necessarily warrant this "perception of God" interpretation of the knowledge of God, its context is open to it. This is most

---

Beentjes, *The Book of Ben Sira in Hebrew: A Text Edition of All Extant Hebrew Manuscripts and a Synopsis of All Parallel Hebrew Ben Sira Texts* (VTSup 68; Leiden: Brill, 1997), 24.

[27] Fox, *Proverbs 1–9*, 31.

[28] Botterweck and Bergman, "יָדַע Yādaʿ," 477–79.

[29] Hans Wildberger thinks that "knowledge" does not refer to the "knowledge of God" (*Isaiah 1–12: A Continental Commentary* [trans. Thomas H. Trapp; Minneapolis: Fortress, 1991], 202). However, the theme of the knowledge of God, as in Hosea, runs through these chapters (see 1:3; 11:2). As Brevard S. Childs writes, "The … oracle (vv. 11ff.) is directed against … a wealthy class … [who] have no regard for God's activity in the world, not perceiving his work as creator. This lack of knowledge … introduced the book in 1:3 [The ox knows his owner, the ass his master's crib, but Israel does not know, my people do not consider.] (cf. Hos. 4:1) [4:1b: There is no faithfulness and no knowledge of God in the land.]" (*Isaiah* [OTL; Louisville: Westminster John Knox, 2001], 47). See also John Goldingay, *Old Testament Theology*, vol. 3, *Israel's Life* (Downers Grove, IL: InterVarsity, 2009), 491–92.

[30] Cf. Hos 2:22[20], which makes clear that the knowledge of God is what is at issue: "And I will betroth you in faithfulness, and you shall know the Lord [וידעת את יהוה]."

obvious if we compare the immediately following vv. 6–8 with their parallel verses in 2:10–12:

⁵Then you will understand the fear
of the Lord
and knowledge of God you will find;
⁶Because the Lord gives wisdom,
from his mouth
[come] knowledge and understanding.
⁷He hides prudence for the upright—
(he is) a shield for those who walk
in integrity,³¹
⁸Guarding the paths of justice
he safeguards the way of
his faithful ones.

¹⁰Because wisdom will come into
your heart
and knowledge will be pleasant to your soul.
¹¹Shrewdness will safeguard you,
understanding will guard you:
¹²Saving you from the evil way,
from the man who speaks perversions.³²

In v. 10, *wisdom* comes into the heart, though in v. 6 Yhwh gives it. In vv. 11–12 *wisdom* defends the student, but in vv. 7–8 Yhwh defends him. It is as if vv. 6–8 tell the same story as vv. 10–12, but allowing a glimpse backstage, which is not visible to every observer: Yhwh is the real provider of wisdom and safety. Thus, it would be natural to understand vv. 5–8 as suggesting that those who have the knowledge of God can experience and perceive this background activity of God.

Third, knowledge in Proverbs 1–9, including knowledge of God, has a divine origin and nature. God uses three special tools in Prov 3:19–20 in creating the world: wisdom (חכמה), understanding (תבונה), and knowledge (דעת).³³ God gives precisely these three instruments to human beings in Prov 2:6. The special relation-

---

³¹ Grammatically "shield" can be in apposition both to Yhwh and to prudence. As God is clearly the subject of 2:7a and 2:8b, to suppose that God is the subject throughout vv. 7–8 seems to me the most natural reading.

³² The parallelism between 2:6–8 and the following verses is recognized by many, e.g., Carole R. Fontaine, "Proverbs," in *Harper's Bible Commentary* (ed. James L. Mays; San Francisco: Harper & Row, 1988), 447–65; Michael V. Fox, "The Pedagogy of Proverbs 2," *JBL* 113 (1994): 233–43; Weeks, *Instruction*, 61; Hans F. Fuhs, *Das Buch der Sprichwörter: Ein Kommentar* (FB 95; Würzburg: Echter, 2001), 59–67; Waltke, *Proverbs*, 216–19. Many commentators concentrate only on the parallelism between vv. 6–8 and vv. 10–11 because v. 12 starts a new section. However, the "way" metaphor connects v. 8 to v. 12. For our purposes it is not necessary to go into further details concerning the complex structure of the whole chapter and the possible historical development of it (i.e., whether vv. 5–8 are later insertions). On these issues, see, e.g., Diethelm Michel, "Proverbia 2: Ein Dokument der Geschichte der Weisheit," in *Alttestamentlicher Glaube und Biblische Theologie: Festschrift für Horst Dietrich Preuss zum 65. Geburtstag* (ed. Jutta Hausmann and Hans-Jürgen Zobel; Stuttgart: Kohlhammer, 1992), 233–43; Rolf Schäfer, *Die Poesie der Weisen: Dichotomie als Grundstruktur der Lehr- und Weisheitsgeschichte in Proverbien 1–9* (WMANT 77; Neukirchen-Vluyn: Neukirchener Verlag, 1999), 66–74; R. N. Whybray, "Some Literary Problems in Proverbs I–IX," *VT* 16 (1966): 482–96.

³³ For the significance of the triad wisdom–understanding–knowledge, see Raymond C. Van Leeuwen, "Cosmos, Temple, House: Building and Wisdom in Mesopotamia and Israel," in

ship between God and knowledge is also underlined in this verse by saying that knowledge (דעת) comes "from the Lord's mouth" (Prov 2:6; LXX: "from his face"). Therefore, this knowledge could appropriately be described as "divine."

The biblical text does not say explicitly that this "divine" knowledge, given in v. 6, is identical to the knowledge of God that is mentioned in the previous verse. Nevertheless, it would be a reasonable interpretation to identify these two "knowledges"—and not just because only a few words separate them. There are many biblical verses in which only the word "knowledge" is mentioned, but, as is made clear by the context, knowledge of God should be understood. When Hosea writes "My people are destroyed for lack of knowledge [דעת]; because you have rejected knowledge [דעת], I reject you from being a priest to me" (Hos 4:6), he is probably referring to the knowledge of God, as is clear from the context of Hos 4:1. Similarly, Isa 5:13 and 11:2 mention only "knowledge," but knowledge of God should be understood.[34] That Prov 2:6 is a similar case is confirmed not much earlier by Prov 1:29, which mentions knowledge (דעת) in parallel with fear of the Lord, just as knowledge of God is parallel to fear of the Lord in Prov 2:5.

Therefore, we could summarize the above as follows: God has a special knowledge (Prov 3:19–20), which is given to human beings (Prov 2:6), and this knowledge is nothing else than the knowledge (perception) of God (Prov 2:5). Undoubtedly, it sounds somewhat odd that God has the knowledge of God. However, this is not such a bizarre statement, if we understand divine knowledge as the full comprehension of reality, which, of course, incorporates the comprehension of spiritual reality. In this case, the two statements—(1) "God has a full vision of reality" and (2) "This full, godly vision is manifested in human beings in the form of comprehending God"—stand easily next to each other.

To conclude, although the Hebrew phrase "knowledge of God" does not explicitly express its own divine nature, its wider context makes clear that it comes from God and is comparable to God's full vision of reality. Accordingly, even if "divine sense" is not a precise translation of the Hebrew phrase itself, it grasps important elements of its wider theological context.

V. Conclusions

Origen's "divine sense" is not an entirely capricious translation, because the Hebrew genitival construction in itself allows it, because αἴσθησις is a regular rendering of דעת, and because it makes good sense in the Greek context. Nevertheless, it is still not a good translation. "Knowledge of God," as we know from its other

---

Wisdom Literature in Mesopotamia and Israel (ed. Richard J. Clifford; SBLSymS 36; Atlanta: Society of Biblical Literature, 2007), 67–90.

[34] See n. 29 above.

occurrences, does not in itself refer to the divine nature of the knowledge. Furthermore, Origen uses the expression "divine sense" to put an exclusive emphasis on perceiving the divine, whereas דעת אלהים has other nuances (intimate relationship with God, obeying God's commands, knowing things about God). However, the Hebrew phrase can refer to perception too, and the *context* of Prov 2:5 suggests that God is the source of this perception/knowledge. Therefore, although "divine sense" cannot be accepted as a good *translation*, it is, arguably, a feasible *interpretation* of Prov 2:5b.

Admittedly, it is an interpretation that accounts for only selective features of the text. However, the aim of this article was not to provide a comprehensive interpretation of Prov 2:5 and to evaluate the whole theory of Origen in the light of it.[35] More modestly, the aim was to understand how ancient translators might have arrived at the translation αἴσθησις θεία and to scrutinize its relationship to the Hebrew text. On this restricted level Origen's text does not seem as fanciful as some suggest, and it can be perceived as a creative appropriation of some features of the theological structure of Proverbs 2.

---

[35] Proverbs 2 probably would not support such a neat separation between physical and spiritual perception as was stated by Origen, as these supposedly separate types of sensation are not differentiated in it.

The Antipedo Baptists of Georgetown, South Carolina, 1710–2010
Roy Talbert, Jr. and Meggan A. Farish

"This is local history at its best—carefully researched, well written, and filled with texture, color, and interest."—David Shi, tenth president of Furman University and author of *America: A Narrative History*
192 pp., 14 b&w illus., hc, $34.95; eb, $34.95

Ezra and the Law in History and Tradition
Lisbeth S. Fried

"Lisbeth Fried takes the reader on a responsible yet memorable journey into the life and afterlife of Ezra as a key personality in the history, literature, and reflection of religious and scholarly communities over the past 2,500 years. A worthwhile and informative read!"—Mark J. Boda, professor of Old Testament, McMaster Divinity College, professor of theology, McMaster University
248 pp., hc and ebook, $59.95
Studies on Personalities of the Old Testament

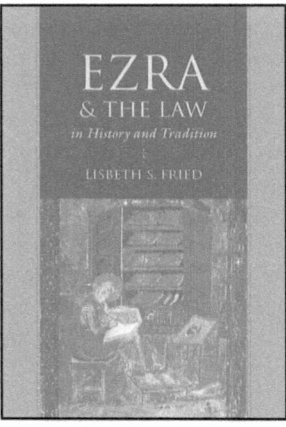

Fundamentalism
Perspectives on a Contested History
Edited by Simon A. Wood and David Harrington Watt

"This marvelous collection has something to provoke every reader who has ever used the word 'fundamentalism' to describe a state of mind other than one's own. Wood and Watt have assembled a fine group of diverse scholarly experts on Christianity, Judaism, and Islam—many of whom disagree vehemently with each other regarding the utility of 'fundamentalism.'"
—Marie Griffith, director, John C. Danforth Center on Religion and Politics, Washington University
216 pp., hc and ebook, $49.95
Studies in Comparative Religion

THE UNIVERSITY OF SOUTH CAROLINA PRESS
Seventy Years of Publishing Excellence

800-768-2500
www.uscpress.com

סַנְסִנָּיו (sansinnāyw; Song of Songs 7:9) and the *Palpal* Noun Pattern

ERAN VIEZEL
eviezel@bgu.ac.il
Ben Gurion University of the Negev, Beer Sheva, 8410501 Israel

The word סַנְסִנָּיו (sansinnāyw; Song 7:9) is a *hapax legomenon*, and there is no scholarly consensus about its meaning. It has been variously identified as denoting the branches of a date palm, clusters of dates, or the blossoms or the fruit of a date palm. The word *sansinnāyw* belongs to the class of noun pattern termed *palpal* (פַּלְפַּל). This article maintains that some of the words of the *palpal* noun pattern share a common semantic characteristic. This characteristic enables one to determine the precise meaning of the word סַנְסִנָּיו: a fruit-laden cluster of dates.

As is well known, Hebrew nouns can be categorized according to classes of patterns (*mišqal*). Some of the classes of noun patterns include words that share a common semantic characteristic, and it is possible to discern groups of meaning within the pattern.[1] The shared semantic characteristic may not appear in every single word in a particular noun pattern,[2] but this fact should not prevent us from recognizing the distinct groups of meaning. Hebrew language textbooks tend to feature instructive tables of noun patterns and their meanings. Thus, for example, words of the *qattelet* pattern relate to diseases and afflictions: יַלֶּפֶת, בַּהֶרֶת, עִוֶּרֶת, and with modified vocalization for guttural letters: סַפַּחַת, קַדַּחַת, קָרַחַת, גַּבַּחַת, צָרַעַת.[3] Even if they are not entirely systematic, the shared semantic aspect of words in noun patterns can help in determining the meanings of doubtful words.

---

[1] See, e.g., Paul Joüon, *A Grammar of Biblical Hebrew* (trans. and ed. T. Muraoka; 2 vols.; SubBi 14; Rome: Pontificio Istituto Biblico, 1996), 2:238.

[2] It must be emphasized that it is necessary to distinguish between the synchronic and diachronic divisions between nominal root types. Thus, for example, the words זרוע (e.g., Exod 6:6) and ברוש (e.g., Isa 41:9) appear to belong to a single noun group, but comparison with other languages demonstrates that זרוע belongs to the *qitāl* type, whereas ברוש is of the *qutāl* type. See, e.g., Yehoshua Blau, *Torat ha-Hegeh ve-ha-Tsurot* (7th ed.; Tel Aviv: Ha-Kibbutz ha-Me'uhad, 1992), 209.

[3] See, e.g., Lev 13:2, 42; 21:20; 22:22; Deut 28:22. As noted, the phenomenon is not fully systematic, and in each pattern there are words that do not share a common semantic attribute.

The word סַנְסִנָּיו (*sansinnāyw*; Song 7:9), from the quadriliteral root סנסן,[4] belongs to the noun pattern known to Hebrew language specialists as *palpal* (פַּלְפַּל). To the best of my knowledge nobody to date has suggested a semantic association connecting the words of this pattern. It appears to me that at least some of the words belonging to the *palpal* pattern share a common semantic characteristic: they refer to something that is round, or roughly circular, that occurs in replicating multiples. In this matter, it appears that we must distinguish between the shared semantic characteristic of *palpal* nouns, גלגל, תלתל, דרדר, סלסל, זלזל and סנסן (which I will discuss below),[5] and the shared semantic characteristic of the verbs of the *palpal* pattern, which is separate and expresses repetition and intensification of the action.[6]

The word גלגל (*galgal*, "wheel") reflects the semantic characteristic noted above for words in the *palpal* pattern: a wheel is round and, significantly, the speed of its revolutions creates an optical illusion of multiple circles. Moreover, the primary function of the wheel is to propel a cart or chariot. Accordingly, the word "wheel" tends not to occur alone but almost always within a group of wheels. This is emphasized in verses such as Jer 47:3, "The rumbling of their wheels [גלגליו]"; Isa 5:28: "Their chariot wheels [גלגליו] like the wind."[7]

The word תלתל (*taltal*, "curl") also clearly expresses the proposed semantic significance of the *palpal* pattern. So, in Song 8:11, "His locks are *taltallîm*." Curls in hair appear as an abundance of replicating circles.

The word דרדר (*dardar*, generally translated as "thistle")[8] occurs twice in the Bible, both times alongside the word קוץ ("thorn"): "Thorns and *dardar* shall it sprout for you" (Gen 3:18); "Thorns and *dardar* shall grow on their altars" (Hos 10:8). A number of scholars have attempted to identify *dardar* with a specific plant.[9] It seems to me, however, that the collocation "thorn and *dardar*" invites us to conclude that, like קוץ, *dardar* has a general meaning that is not restricted to a particular type of plant. It may be that the sense I proposed for words of the *palpal* pattern can clarify the fine distinction between the word "thorn" and the word *dardar*. The seasonal plants in the land of Israel dry out in the summer, and the hills and valleys become covered with vast expanses of yellow vegetation. When the edges of the leaves of the plants dry out, they become sharp, and when the flowers of the plants

---

Cf., e.g., the following nouns of the *qattelet* type: גַּחֶלֶת (Isa 47:14), יַבֶּשֶׁת (Ps 95:5), לֶהֱבֶת (1 Sam 17:7), צַלַּחַת (2 Kgs 21:13).

[4] Cf. also from the root סנסן the city Sansannah (Josh 15:31).

[5] For פרפר and ערער, see n. 15 below.

[6] Cf. פצפץ and פרפר (Job 16:12), קרקר (Num 24:17; Isa 22:5), חרחר (Prov 26:21).

[7] Cf. Ezek 23:24; 26:10. Biblical citations follow the JPS translation.

[8] In modern Hebrew, the word דרדר is used specifically for plants of the genus *Centaurea*. Of course, this does not offer proof concerning the original meaning of the word.

[9] E.g., Immanuel Löw, *Die Flora der Juden* (1924–34; 4 vols.; repr., Hildesheim: Olms, 1967), 1:405–7.

shrink and shed their leaves, what remains are dried balls that hang at the edge of the stem. Perhaps we may distinguish between thorn and *dardar* on the basis of this schematic division: the dried-out, pointy, prickly edges of the leaves are the thorns,[10] and the dried-out flowers—the countless dry balls that cover the hills and fields in summer—are the *dardar*. If this proposal is correct, then *dardar* too bears the shared semantic attribute of the words in the *palpal* pattern.

I would suggest that סלסל (*salsal*) and זלזל (*zalzal*) also reflect the sense I have proposed for the *palpal* pattern, even though their meaning is indeterminate. Jeremiah 6:9 states, "Like a vintager over *salsillôt*." Exegetes remain divided in their opinions. Some associate the word *salsillôt* with "basket" (*sal*). Others understand the word to mean the thin branches of the vine, the tendrils, which they take to be a secondary form of *zalzal*, a word that appears in Isa 18:5, "He will trim away the *zalzallîm* with pruning hooks."[11] If *salsillôt* is in fact the baskets in which the vintager places his grapes during the grape harvest, then, like other baskets in antiquity, it would have been made of reeds or interwoven threads.[12] The appearance of multiple circles is also applicable if the word *salsal*, like the word *zalzal*, means the tendrils of the grapevine. The tendril is a very thin and atrophied branch that winds around in circles, serving the vine by attaching to nearby bushes and trees. Whether *salsillôt* means basket or tendril, the word *salsal* had acquired, by an early period, a meaning similar to *taltal* and came to signify hair care. Thus, for example, in *b. Roš Haš.* 26b, in the criticism, "How long will you be *měsalsel* with your hair?!"[13] From here, it was a short path to an adaptive usage in the sense of respect, honor, and style in general, without any association with hair: "Acquire wisdom; with all your acquisitions, acquire discernment. *Salsělehā* [= *salsel* her] to you and she will exalt you" (Prov 4:7–8). This is simply the result of assimilation due to the shared semantic attributes of the words in the *palpal* pattern.[14]

The shared semantic characteristic of the nouns in the *palpal* pattern[15] can

---

[10] Cf. "lacerating thorns" (Ezek 28:24).

[11] On the expression of this controversy in the Middle Ages, see the summary in Eliezer Ben Yehuda, *A Complete Dictionary of Ancient and Modern Hebrew* (in Hebrew; 16 vols.; repr., Jerusalem: Makor, 1980), 4078 n. 1; and see, *inter alios*, Gustaf Dalman, *Arbeit und Sitte in Palästina* (1928–39; 7 vols.; repr., Hildesheim: Olms, 1964), 4:301; John Bright, *Jeremiah: Introduction, Translation, and Notes* (AB 21; Garden City, NY: Doubleday, 1965), 44; *HALOT* 2:758, s.v. זלול; Yair Hoffman, *Jeremiah: Introduction and Commentary* (in Hebrew; 2 vols.; Jerusalem: Magnes, 2001), 1:22.

[12] Cf. Gen 40:16: "three openwork (or: wicker) baskets."

[13] For additional examples, see Ben Yehuda, *Complete Dictionary*, 4076–78.

[14] Indeed, in Jewish sources in the Middle Ages, the words *salsal* and *taltal* already appear as a common collocation, and both of them acquire metaphorical meanings of respect and style. In a poetic paraphrase of the verse "His locks are *taltallîm*" (Song 5:11), Immanuel Haromi criticizes those "who *yistalselû* with their *taltallîm*" (Dov Jarden, *Mahberoth Immanuel Haromi* [...][Jerusalem: D. Jarden, 1985], vol. 1, 12:229, line 282).

[15] In 2 Kgs 5:12, the river פַּרְפַּר (*parpar*) is mentioned, but it is impossible to know how it

help us determine the precise meaning of the word סַנְסִנָּיו (sansinnāyw). Song of Songs 7:8–10a reads, "Your stately form is like the palm, your breasts are like clusters. I say: let me climb the palm, let me take hold of its *sansinnāyw*; let your breasts be like clusters of grapes, your breath like the fragrance of apples, and your mouth like choicest wine."[16]

The word סַנְסִנָּיו in 7:9 is a *hapax legomenon,* and there is no consensus about its correct meaning. In Jewish exegesis across the ages, there is broad agreement that סַנְסִנָּיו means the branches of the date palm.[17] Among the moderns, however, there is controversy. There are those who maintain that the meaning really is the branches of a date palm,[18] but others suggest that the word refers to clusters of dates, and generally they specify that the intended meaning is the thin stems of the cluster that hold the dates or the blossoms that precede the fruit, or that it is the fruits themselves.[19]

---

got its name. See Michael C. Astour, "The Origin of the Terms 'Canaan,' 'Phoenician,' and 'Purple,'" *JNES* 24 (1965): 350. In contrast, the animal known in modern Hebrew as *parpar,* that is, butterfly, also reflects the semantic attribute we have identified in the *palpal* pattern. A butterfly has four rounded wings which, when in motion, create an illusion of multiple circles. For the possibility that the tree ערער (Jer 17:6) is *Juniperus phoenicea* and for illustration of its multiple rounded fruits, see Jehuda Feliks, *Plant World of the Bible* (in Hebrew; Ramat Gan: Massada, 1968), 82–83.

[16] Verse 9 should be read in accordance with the LXX, εἶπα ἀναβήσομαι ἐν τῷ φοίνικι (אמרתי אעלה בתמר), with the definite article, and not following the MT בתמר. The continuation of v. 10 is in the words of the beloved woman: "Let it flow to my beloved as new wine gliding over the lips of sleepers."

[17] Thus the medieval exegetes, for example, Rashi, Rashbam, Ibn Ezra, Isaiah Di-Trani, Gersonides; see Sara Japhet, "The Anonymous Commentary on the Song of Songs in Ms. Prague: A Critical Edition and Introduction," in *"To Settle the Plain Meaning of the Verse": Studies in Biblical Exegesis* (ed. Sara Japhet and Eran Viezel; Jerusalem: Bialik Institute, 2011), 247. See also Eliezer Halevi Grunhut, *Midrash Shir Hashirim Printed from a Geniza Manuscript* (Jerusalem: Ktav Yad Vasefer Institute, 1981), 116. Similarly, too, see the medieval lexicons, e.g., Angel Sáenz-Badillos, *Měnahem Ben Saruq Mahberet: Edición crítica e introducción* (Granada: Universidad de Granada, 1986), 66*; Wilhelm Bacher, *Sepher Haschoraschim [...] von Abulwalîd Merwân Ibn Ǧanâh (R. Jona)* (Berlin: H. Itzkowski, 1896), 348.

[18] Thus in some biblical translations, e.g., RSV(1952), NKJV (1982), JPS Tanakh (1985). See, *inter alios,* Ben Yehuda, *Complete Dictionary,* 4126; Robert Gordis, *The Song of Songs and Lamentations: A Study, Modern Translation and Commentary* (rev. and augm. ed.; New York: Ktav, 1974), 97; Peter Jay (trans.), *The Song of Songs* (Poetica 6; London: Anvil Press Poetry, 1975), 22; Marvin H. Pope, *Song of Songs: A New Translation with Introduction and Commentary* (AB 7C; Garden City, NY: Doubleday, 1977), 593, 636; Philip S. Alexander, *The Targum of Canticles: Translated, with a Critical Introduction, Apparatus, and Notes* (ArBib 17A; Collegeville, MN: Liturgical Press, 2003), 182. There are those who maintain that the word denotes specifically the base of the palm branch, from which the dates are suspended. See, e.g., Abraham Even-Shoshan, *A New Dictionary* (in Hebrew; Jerusalem: Kiryat Sefer, 1996), 1821; Elie Assis, *The Infinity of Love in the Song of Songs: A Literary Analysis* (in Hebrew; Tel Aviv: Yedioth Ahronot and Chemed Books, 2009), 164.

[19] See, e.g., the following translations, NJB (1990); NASB (1973); NIV (1984); ESV (English Standard Version; 2001). See also, *inter alios,* Löw, *Die Flora der Juden,* 2:336–37; BDB, 703; Duane

The lack of agreement is especially evident in a number of scholarly publications whose authors preferred not to determine the correct meaning of the word.[20] This exegetical controversy is also found in the ancient versions. The LXX seems to take the word סַנְסִנָּיו to mean "branches": "I will take hold of its heights" (ὕψεων αὐτοῦ). In contrast, the Vulgate renders the word as "fruit" (fructus).

Close reading of the text does not help shed light on the meaning of סַנְסִנָּיו. The beloved man compares his beloved woman to a date palm and imagines himself (אמרתי [בלבי])[21] climbing the tree.[22] Two activities are mentioned in v. 9: the beloved ascends ("let me climb the palm," אֶעֱלֶה בְתָמָר), and then he grasps ("let me take hold of its סַנְסִנָּיו," אֹחֲזָה בְּסַנְסִנָּיו). The root עלה ("to climb") calls to mind climbing, as up a ladder, or stairs (e.g., Gen 28:12; Exod 20:23). It is true that climbing up a date palm differs from climbing other trees and somewhat resembles climbing up a ladder: the trunk of the tree is encircled with stumps that have withered or were removed by the owner of the tree in order to grant access to the fruit. These stumps serve as a ladder and make the climb much easier. As some scholars have emphasized, אחז + ב (generally translated as "[take] hold of") is a verb that denotes a decisive and directed action. Its occurrences in the biblical text indicate strenuous effort.[23] It thus seems that we ought to distinguish between the stage of climbing up the tree, which is simple and easy, like ascending a ladder, and the stage of grasping the סַנְסִנָּיו, which demands considerable effort, and to determine that this grasping occurred after the ascent, that is, at the top portion of the tree. The context allows us to determine the location of סַנְסִנָּיו, but it does not allow us to determine if it is the branches that the beloved grasps or, rather, the fruit.

A number of scholars base their opinion concerning the correct meaning of the word סַנְסִנָּיו on the Akkadian *sissinnu*.[24] However, the meaning of this word too is subject to dispute, essentially the same dispute that exists regarding the word סַנְסִנָּיו: there are those who maintain that the meaning of *sissinnu* is a branch of a

---

Garrett, *Song of Songs* (WBC 23B; Nashville: Thomas Nelson, 2004), 245; *HALOT* 2:761; Menahem Zevi Kaddari, *A Dictionary of Biblical Hebrew* (in Hebrew; Jerusalem: Bar-Ilan University Press, 2006), 759.

[20] See Roland E. Murphy, *The Song of Songs: A Commentary on the Book of Canticles or the Song of Songs* (Hermeneia; Minneapolis: Fortress, 1990), 183; J. Cheryl Exum, *Song of Songs: A Commentary* (OTL; Louisville: Westminster John Knox, 2005), 238.

[21] Thus many commentators. Cf. the paraphrase of Moshe Ibn Tibbon, "I say if only it were so..." (*Perush al Shir ha-Shirim* [Lyck: M'kize Nirdamim, 1874], 21b).

[22] On the date palm in the world of images in the biblical period, see Joan Goodnick Westenholz, "The Seven Species, the First Fruits of the Land," in *Sacred Bounty Sacred Land: The Seven Species of the Land of Israel* (ed. Joan Goodnick Westenholz; Jerusalem: Bible Lands Museum, 1998), 44–50.

[23] See Yair Zakovitch, *The Song of Songs: Introduction and Commentary* (in Hebrew; Jerusalem: Magnes, 1992), 125; Garrett, *Song of Songs*, 245; e.g. Gen 22:13; 25:26; Exod 4:4.

[24] This is the case, even though they are not perfect etymological parallels. See Benno Landsberger, *The Date Palm and Its By-products according to the Cuneiform Sources* (AfOB 17; Graz: Im Selbstverlage des Herausgebers, 1967), 18 n. 55.

palm, and others who say that the meaning is a cluster of dates, or date blossoms. More recently, opinion has shifted toward the definition of blossoms, and not branches.[25]

My proposal that words of the noun pattern *palpal* share a distinct meaning—a circle or circular appearance that is replicated many times—is a helpful argument in support of taking סַנְסִנָּיו to mean a cluster of the fruit of the date palm, and not the blossoms, and certainly not the branches. The date clusters that grow among the high branches of the date palm are composed of dozens of thin delicate branches, intertwined with one another. The dates are suspended from them, first the flowers of the date, and in the next stage, the fruit. The shape of the fruit, in all its different species and variations, is round, sometimes a near-perfect circle and sometimes a long ellipsis. The appearance of a cluster of dates somewhat resembles a cascade of curly hair. The date thus shares the semantic characteristic identified in other words of the *palpal* pattern. It seems, then, that the beloved in Song 7:9 who grasps the סַנְסִנָּיו of the tree, is not grasping the branches, nor a cluster of dates at the time of their blossoming but rather a cluster laden with fruit.

In light of this, the word "clusters" (אשכולות) in v. 8 ("your breasts are like clusters") are the clusters of the fruit of the date palm, and they are to be distinguished from the "clusters of grapes" (אֶשְׁכְּלוֹת הַגֶּפֶן) that appear in the subsequent verse. If this is the case, then it would indicate the following verse division. In vv. 8–9a, the beloved is compared to a date palm: "Your stately form is like the palm, your breasts are like clusters. I say: let me climb the palm, let me take hold of its סַנְסִנָּיו." Then, in vv. 9b–10a, the woman is compared to other fruits: "let your breasts be like clusters of grapes, your breath like the fragrance of apples, and your mouth like choicest wine." The word "clusters" (אשכולות) effects the association between the two groups of similes. If my analysis is correct, then the Masoretic division of the verses does not suit the content of the poem.

---

[25] See esp. Landsberger, *Date Palm*, 18–19; Harold R. Cohen, *Biblical Hapax Legomena in the Light of Akkadian and Ugaritic* (SBLDS 37; Missoula, MT: Scholars Press, 1978), 125; *CAD* 15:325–28, and the bibliography cited there. Another meaning of *sissinnu* is "broom." Note that in postbiblical Hebrew, the word *makbēd* (מַכְבֵּד) is similarly used for both a cluster of blossoms and a broom (e.g., *Midrash Tanḥ. Maseʿei* 13). Accordingly, *sissinnu* may also be a flowering cluster rather than a branch. For the Syriac *sīsnā* in the sense of a flowering cluster, see Immanuel Löw, *Aramäische Pflanzennamen* (Leipzig: Engelmann, 1881), 119; R. Payne Smith, *Thesaurus Syriacus* (2 vols.; Oxford: Clarendon, 1879–1901), 2617. On the Aramaic סִינְסְנָא, סַנְסְנָא in the sense of the fruits of the date palm or a cluster of blossoms, see, e.g., Gustaf Dalman, *Aramäisch-Neuhebräisches Handwörterbuch zu Targum, Talmud und Midrasch* (Göttingen: Pfeiffer, 1938), 296; Michael Sokoloff, *A Dictionary of Jewish Palestinian Aramaic of the Byzantine Period* (Ramat-Gan: Bar Ilan University Press, 1992), 384. On *ssn* in Ugaritic in the sense of a date palm or branch, see Gregorio del Olmo Lete and Joaquín Sanmartín, *A Dictionary of the Ugaritic Language in the Alphabetic Tradition* (trans. Wilfred G. E. Watson; 2 vols.; HO, Section 1: The Near and Middle East 67; Leiden: Brill, 2003), 2:772.

JBL 133, no. 4 (2014): 757–775

"How can you say, 'I am not defiled ...'?" (Jeremiah 2:20–25): Allusions to Priestly Legal Traditions in the Poetry of Jeremiah

DALIT ROM-SHILONI
dromshil@post.tau.ac.il
Tel Aviv University, Tel Aviv 6997801, Israel

In diametric opposition to the marital love of Jer 2:2, vv. 20–25 accuse the people את צעה זנה, "you recline as a whore" (v. 20b), and the following verses elaborate on this adulterous behavior. The goal of this study is to present the intrinsic role of the literary allusions to pentateuchal Priestly and Deuteronomic traditions in this prophecy, to acknowledge the variety of sources evoked, and to suggest a specific allusion to a Priestly legal tradition (or even text) that seems to give Jeremiah's prophecy special force. Three markers point to the *sôṭâ* trial of Num 5:11–31 as the evoked legal tradition (or text). Focusing on one specific poetic passage, commonly taken as "Jeremianic," a portion of the prophet's words in his early career, the article calls attention to Priestly allusions in Jeremiah and raises some of the intriguing questions about Jeremiah's acquaintance with Priestly materials, questions that should be addressed in the study of both the prophetic literature of Jeremiah and in pentateuchal studies.

I

Jeremiah 2:20–25 is set within the first oracle collection in Jeremiah (2:1–4:4), which is generally considered "an early collection of oracles and other utterances by the prophet."[1] Following a double accusation that the people have deserted God

---

This study was written with the help of the Israel Science Foundation (grant 148/09). A short version of this paper was introduced at the International Conference "Convergence and Divergence in Pentateuchal Theory: Bridging the Academic Cultures of Israel, North America and Europe," held at the Israel Institute of Advanced Studies, Jerusalem, May 2013. I thank Dr. Ruth Clements for her ever-insightful comments, and Professor Christophe Nihan for his thoughtful notes on an earlier version of this paper. Responsibility for this article is fully mine.

[1] So Jack R. Lundbom, *Jeremiah 1–20: A New Translation with Introduction and Commentary* (AB 21A; New York: Doubleday, 1999), 249. Lundbom dated 2:1–3, 4–9, 10–13, 20–22, 23–25,

(עָזְבֵךְ אֶת יְהוָה אֱלֹהָיִךְ, vv. 17, 19), vv. 20–25 open the second part of the chapter (vv. 20–37).[2] They elaborate on disobedience, which is exemplified through three quotations.[3] Verses 20–22 present God's surprise and disappointment at the people's ungratefulness, conveyed in the words: לֹא אֶעֱבֹד ("I will not serve!," v. 23; the Qere, לֹא אֶעֱבוֹר, will be discussed below); vv. 23–25 shatter the people's claims of innocence with a rhetorical question that brings the quotation: לֹא נִטְמֵאתִי אַחֲרֵי הַבְּעָלִים לֹא הָלָכְתִּי ("I am not defiled, I have not gone after the Baalim," v. 23a). Finally, the prophecy arrives at the people's confession: נוֹאָשׁ לוֹא כִּי אָהַבְתִּי זָרִים וְאַחֲרֵיהֶם אֵלֵךְ ("It is no use. No, I love the strangers, and after them I must go," v. 25b). Hence, while scholars tend to divide vv. 20–25 into two independent oracles (vv. 20–22, 23–25), I want to emphasize the thematic continuity between the two.[4]

31–32 to "the reform years of 622 BCE" (see pp. 254, 263, 268, 278, 282, 293); vv. 14–19 to the years between 611–609 (p. 274); vv. 33–37 "just prior to Josiah's death" (p. 297); and vv. 27–28, 29–30 "closer to 597" (pp. 288, 290). A relatively early dating and presumably authentic authorship for Jeremiah 2 had already been suggested by Bernhard Duhm (*Das Buch Jeremia* [KHC 11; Tübingen: Mohr Siebeck, 1901], 15) and Wilhelm Rudolph (*Jeremia* [3rd ed.; HAT 12; Tübingen: Mohr Siebeck, 1968], 13–14), among others. Yair Hoffman argues that the bulk of chs. 2–10 may be assumed to belong to the first scroll, as portrayed in Jer 36:1–2, 3, 7, 29, and thus as prior to 605 B.C.E. (*Jeremiah 1–25* [in Hebrew; Mikra LeIsrael; Jerusalem: Magnes Press, Hebrew University; Tel Aviv: Am Oved, 2004], 122–23, although he notes post-605 passages within these chapters, including 2:14–15, 28–30 [p. 127]). Jacob Milgrom suggests the time span of 627–616 B.C.E., with a clear preference for a date close to 622 ("The Date of Jeremiah, Chapter 2," *JNES* 14 [1955]: 65–69). A different approach, that of redaction criticism, has perceived Jer 2:1–4:2 as a composite admixture of passages, the product of generations of transformations by tradents and redactors; for a thorough history of scholarship on this unit, see Mark E. Biddle, *A Redaction History of Jeremiah 2:1–4:2* (ATANT 77; Zurich: Theologischer Verlag, 1990), 1–32. While following Siegfried Herrmann ("Jeremia – der Prophet und die Verfasser des Buches Jeremia," in *Le livre de Jérémie: Le prophète et son milieu. Les oracles et leur transmission* [ed. P. M. Bogaert; BETL 54; Leuven: Peeters, 1997], 197–214), Biddle distinguishes between what he considered to be the kernel of ch. 2, the second feminine singular addressee (vv. 20–25, 33–37, and already in vv. 16–20, all in response to the question posed in v. 14), and the "generations structure," which he considers to have elaborated on it (pp. 34–38, 48–49, 206–28).

[2] Commentators debate the internal division of the prophetic passages in ch. 2. Lundbom (*Jeremiah 1–20*, 254, 270) divides vv. 1–19 into four passages: vv. 1–3, 4–9, 10–13, 14–19; and vv. 20–37 into five: vv. 20–22, 23–25, 26–28, 29–32, 33–37. Hoffman (*Jeremiah 1–25*, 126) divides the entire chapter to ten passages: vv. 1–3, 4–9, 10–13, 14–18, 19–22, 23–25, 26–28, 29–30, 31–32, 33–37. See further Georg Fischer, *Jeremiah 1–25* (HTKAT; Stuttgart: Herder, 2005), 152–53.

[3] On the formal and rhetorical roles of the quotations in this chapter, exemplary of the entire book, see Thomas W. Overholt, "Jeremiah 2 and the Problem of 'Audience Reaction,'" *CBQ* 41 (1979): 262–73. Compare Lundbom (*Jeremiah 1–20*, 275–76), who divides vv. 20–28 into four oracles based on the repeated rhetorical feature of four quoted sayings (vv. 20b, 23a, 25b, 27c). I consider this division unsound, as v. 27c does not seem to belong to this complex (and it certainly has no second person feminine singular characteristics, pace Herrmann, "Jeremia – der Prophet und die Verfasser," 203–8; and Biddle, *Redaction History*, 46–47). I will argue that vv. 23–25 are structured as an *inclusio*; see p. 766 below.

[4] Commentaries tend to distinguish the two segments, vv. 20–22, 23–25, as separate literary units; see Robert P. Carroll, *Jeremiah: A Commentary* (OTL; Philadelphia: Westminster, 1986),

As I will show here, the pentateuchal allusions in vv. 20–25 tie these verses together. Each of these allusions reinforces the exhortation in several ways, within the boundaries of the marital metaphor.

The goal of this study is to present the intrinsic role of the literary allusions to pentateuchal Priestly and Deuteronomic traditions within this prophecy, to acknowledge the variety of sources evoked, and to suggest a specific allusion to a Priestly law that seems to give Jeremiah's prophecy special force.

II

Jeremiah 2:20

כי מעולם שברתי עלך נתקתי מוסרותיך ותאמרי לא אעבד [ק: אעבור], כי על־כל־
גבעה גבהה ותחת כל עץ רענן את צעה זנה

For long ago you broke your yoke, tore off your yoke-bands, and said, "I will not work!" [Qere: "I will not transgress!"] On every high hill and under every verdant tree, you recline as a whore.

Jeremiah 2:20 stands as a superscription to the entire passage, but its blurred rhetorical (syntactic) structure had caused textual divergences, and quite different points of departure that await clarification.

As presented by Barbara A. Bozak, two major issues cut across the MT and the versions.[5] First, there is one textual conflict in the MT that concerns the people's response: Is this meant to be a rebellious response (לא אעבד, following the Ketiv), or an obedient acceptance of God's sovereignty (לא אעבור, as suggested by the Qere)?[6] Yet, prior to this textual difficulty stand the different readings of the MT and the LXX concerning the agent of the two verbs שברתי and נתקתי. While the MT (as well as the Targum) casts the two verbs as first person singular (שברתי, נתקתי), the LXX (and likewise the Vulgate and the Peshitta) reads them as second person feminine singular: ὅτι ἀπ' αἰῶνος συνέτριψας τὸν ζυγόν σου, διέσπασας τοὺς δεσμούς σου (reflecting second person readings of שברת, נתקת). Was this God or the people? The two readings each suggest a different understanding of the verse, and they thus deserve independent attention.[7]

132; compare Fischer (*Jeremiah 1–25*, 153, 166–69), who indeed understands vv. 20–25 as a single unit.

[5] Bozak, "Heeding the Received Text: Jer 2,20a, A Case in Point," *Bib* 77 (1996): 524–37.

[6] The Targum, Rashi, and Qara follow the Qere tradition. Qimhi suggests that the same meaning stands behind the Ketiv as well ("I will not worship [other gods anymore]"). According to William McKane (*A Critical and Exegetical Commentary on Jeremiah* [2 vols.; ICC; Edinburgh: T&T Clark, 1986], 1:40), this seems to be reflected also in the reading of the Peshitta לא אפלוח (standing for the Ketiv לא אעבד).

[7] Compare William L. Holladay (*Jeremiah 1: A Commentary on the Book of the Prophet Jeremiah, Chapters 1–25* [Hermeneia; Philadelphia: Fortress, 1986], 52), who prefers the LXX version, arguing that "the context clearly demands that the consonantal text be taken as

Reading the verbs (and the possessive pronouns) as second person feminine singular, LXX 2:20 seems to be pursuing a one-dimensional (even trivial) track of the people's rebellion against God: "For from of old (from eternity) you broke your yoke and tore your bonds, and said: I will not serve you, rather I will go on every high hill and under every shady tree, there I will be spread out in my fornication."[8]

Thematically, this metaphor of breaking the yoke is used elsewhere by Jeremiah, in his admonition of the people in Jerusalem (5:1–5). In both 5:5 and LXX 2:20, these metaphors of rebellion (שבר על, ניתק מוסרות) are taken from the political arena. Elsewhere in Jeremiah, "the yoke" denotes subjugation to Nebuchadnezzar, king of Babylon (27:11, 12; 28:2, 4, 11–14). LXX Jer 2:20, like 5:5, transforms this political metaphor to characterize the people's long-acknowledged disobedience against God, an issue that has already been central in 2:4–9, 10–13, 14–19. In addition, this LXX version fits perfectly with the immediate context: the rebellious quotation לא אעבד (in v. 20a), exemplified by worshiping other gods "upon every high hill and under every shady tree" (v. 20b).

Nevertheless, MT Jer 2:20 seems to put forward a much more forceful prophetic proclamation.[9] Jeremiah indeed often uses political metaphors in reference to the relationship between God and the people, but the MT suggests that the metaphors שבר על and ניתק מוסרות, denoting release from subjugation with God as agent and reflecting on a long-past occasion (מעולם), depend on an altogether different historical framework. These two phrases appear in two other distinct contexts, where they both refer back to the release from Egyptian bondage: Lev 26:13: ואשבר מטת עלכם; Ps 107:13–14: ומוסרותיהם ינתק. It is difficult (and unnecessary) to establish any actual literary dependence among these three occurrences; a more cautious suggestion would be to argue for a shared conceptual heritage. Nevertheless, the two latter passages seem relevant to Jeremiah 2, as they suggest the possibility that in the words כי מעולם שברתי עלך נתקתי מוסרותיך the prophet recalls the paradigmatic salvation from Egypt. Thus, just as Jeremiah had previously evoked that distant and positively remembered period in 2:2, 6–7, so here in 2:20, he once again harks back to the constitutive period in the relationship between God and the people.[10] This time, however, the memory of the past emphasizes the people's ungratefulness in the present. Leading up to the people's forceful exclamation,

---

representing the archaic second singular feminine." This unanimous preference for the LXX unites most of the critical commentators on Jeremiah; see Bozak, "Heeding the Received Text," 525 n. 8.

[8] The Vulgate and the Peshitta accept the LXX reading of the second feminine singular but then transform the second feminine singular possessive pronouns עלך and מוסרותיך into the first person singular: עלי and מוסרותי ("my yoke" and "my yoke-bands"); and see McKane, *Jeremiah*, 1:40.

[9] Bozak had already argued in favor of the MT version. She carefully discusses five points that have been raised against it and concluded that "MT of Jer 2,20 makes sense as it stands," and she further contended that the MT is thematically preferable ("Heeding the Received Text," 537).

[10] The identification of the exodus as the past event of salvation is supported by מעולם, aptly translated by Holladay (*Jeremiah 1*, 52, 97) as "a long time ago" (based on Josh 24:2); see also Fischer, *Jeremiah 1–25*, 166.

לא אעבד, the political language in MT Jer 2:20 points up the extreme contradiction between the divine past salvation and the people's present rebellion.

Nevertheless, syntactically and logically, MT Jer 2:20 remains a challenge, as there seems to be a missing link between the two components (divine salvation in the past and the people's rebellion in the present). Contrary to Bozak, I argue that the people's response (ותאמרי לא אעבד) is not simply an antithetic parallelism to the divine promise of salvation.[11] I suggest, rather, that the two proclamations are based on a thematic ellipsis.

As a literary and rhetoric device, ellipsis entails excluding words, phrases, and at times full clauses that are understood to be part of the semantic and conceptual fields of the saying and are easily supplied by the listener/reader.[12] T. V. F. Brogan explained that "in ellipsis the thought is complete; it is only that a word or words ordinarily called for in the full construction but not strictly necessary are omitted (since obvious)."[13] The ellipsis may be recognized by the fact that the saying in its current state is syntactically or thematically deficient, in which case supplying the omitted component is intentionally left to the listener/reader. David Yellin called this technique one of the brilliant "poetic ornaments" of biblical poetry, a rhetorical device that can be present in prose, at some times unintentional but at others a purposeful way for authors to arouse their audience's attention, by the surprise, the wit, and the need to solve the riddle of the missing element.[14]

Indeed, MT Jer 2:20a seems to suggest an ellipsis, as it brings together only two out of three components of the God–people covenant relationships. It opens with God's past salvific deeds on behalf of the people and then jumps to the people's rebellious response, represented by לא אעבד. Jeremiah 2:20 lacks the central (and obvious) narrative midpoint between these two episodes—the institution of a covenant relationship in which God became sovereign of the people and obligated them to obedience. This omission in Jer 2:20 might be intentional, as it has a functional-thematic role. Through its elliptical presentation, v. 20 causes a syntactical-thematic crux, portraying the people's disobedience as a direct response to divine deliverance. The passage emphasizes that not only did the people betray God's covenant, but they have acted ungratefully *ad absurdum*, repaying God's caring acts with disobedience. This line of argument accords with the amazement already expressed in 2:4–9, 10–13.

---

[11] See Bozak, "Heeding the Received Text," 536.

[12] For ellipsis as a literary technique, see Frank Polak, *Biblical Narrative: Aspects of Art and Design* (in Hebrew; Biblical Encyclopedia Library 11; Jerusalem: Bialik, 1994), 30–31.

[13] Brogan, "Ellipsis," in *The New Princeton Encyclopedia of Poetry and Poetics* (ed. A. Preminger and T. V. F. Brogan; Princeton: Princeton University Press, 1993), 326.

[14] Yellin, *Studies in the Bible* (in Hebrew; ed. E. Z. Melamed; Kitve David Yelin 6; Jerusalem: Mas, 1983), 241–50. Yellin opens his discussion by referring to acknowledgments of this phenomenon as early as the tannaitic composition *Baraita of the Thirty-Two Ways of Rabbi Eliezer Son of Rabbi Joseph the Galilean*, no. 9, called דרך קצרה ("The Short Way"); and in medieval exegesis by Menachem Ibn Saruq, Jonah Ibn Janach, and Ibn Ezra (p. 241).

While the ellipsis of this central component has caused the above-mentioned textual and interpretive difficulties, I find Jer 2:20 (MT) to be beautifully constructed. All the seemingly problematic components of the MT's text may be accounted for in this rhetorical structure: שבר על (as also ניתק מוסרות) together with עבד. The obvious ellipsis may be supplied with the aid of Jeremiah's consolation prophecy in 30:8–9:[15]

⁸והיה ביום ההוא נאם יהוה צבאות אשבר עלו מעל צוארך ומוסרותיך אנתק ולא יעבדו בו עוד זרים. ⁹ועבדו את יהוה אלהיהם ואת דוד מלכם אשר אקים להם.

⁸In that day—declares the LORD of Hosts—<u>I will break the yoke from off your neck and I will rip off your bonds. Strangers shall no longer make slaves of them</u>; ⁹<u>instead, they shall serve the LORD their God</u> and David, the king whom I will raise up for them.

The "missing" element in 2:20 is the mention of the commitment to serve God, ועבדו את יהוה אלהיהם (in place of the rulers from whose servitude they have been set free).[16] This ellipsis intrigues me in what it assumes as "obvious"—the constitution of the covenant relationships back to Egypt and through the exodus traditions. Jeremiah 2:20 relies on well-known non-Priestly and Priestly conceptions of the God–people relationship used in the Pentateuch and known also from the psalmodic literature. Both non-Priestly and Priestly exodus narratives and legal materials relate not only the divine deliverance but the transference from Pharaoh's rulership to acceptance of God's sovereignty, service, and commandments (Exod 7:16, 26; 8:16; 9:1, 13; 10:3; etc).[17] Jeremiah seems to know that conception, phrased so clearly by the Holiness Legislation (HL), Lev 25:55:[18]

---

[15] To my mind, there is no need to detach Jer 30:8–9 from the prophet (or his Judean tradents); the date may indeed be preexilic or immediately following the Destruction. For the earlier dating, see Marvin A. Sweeney, "Jeremiah 30–31 and King Josiah's Program of National Restoration and Religious Reform," *ZAW* 108 (1996): 569–83; for the latter option, see Jack R. Lundbom (*Jeremiah 21–36: A New Translation with Introduction and Commentary* [AB 21B; New York: Doubleday, 2004], 369–76, 393), who dates vv. 8–9 after the fall of Jerusalem, composed during Jeremiah's "Mitzpah sojourn" and thus prior to 582 B.C.E. Compare Holladay (*Jeremiah 2: A Commentary on the Book of the Prophet Jeremiah, Chapters 26–52* [Hermeneia; Minneapolis: Fortress, 1989], 173), who considers this passage postexilic. For a discussion of the layers within the consolation prophecies in Jeremiah, see Dalit Rom-Shiloni, "Group-Identities in Jeremiah: Is It the Persian Period Conflict?" in *A Palimpsest: Rhetoric, Ideology, Stylistics, and Language Relating to Persian Israel* (ed. Ehud Ben-Zvi, Diana V. Edelman, and Frank Polak; Perspectives on Hebrew Scriptures and Its Contexts 5; Piscataway, NJ: Gorgias, 2009), 11–46, esp. 25–26.

[16] Holladay (*Jeremiah 1*, 97) suggests Hos 10:11 as an early example of the metaphoric use of "yoke" for "Yahweh's covenant," and he is fascinated by this use of "the same expression for Israel's servitude to Yahweh as for her servitude to Pharaoh or Babylon" (Holladay further mentions Jer 31:17 and Deut 32:15, in which this metaphor serves as the background).

[17] Another and different opposition is set by (את) עבד, and it concerns the worship of God versus other gods; see Exod 23:25; Deut 10:12, 20; Ps 2:11; etc.

[18] For the Holiness Legislation's emphasis on God's deeds in history, and most of all God's salvation in Egypt and the exodus as the basis for God's "ownership" of Israel, see Israel Knohl,

כִּי לִי בְנֵי יִשְׂרָאֵל עֲבָדִים עֲבָדַי הֵם אֲשֶׁר הוֹצֵאתִי אוֹתָם מֵאֶרֶץ מִצְרַיִם אֲנִי יְהוָה אֱלֹהֵיכֶם

For it is to me that the Israelites are servants: they are my servants, whom I freed from the land of Egypt, I the LORD your God.

But here is where I am afraid our knowledge reaches its limit. I do not see any clear literary dependence between this passage (or concept) in Jeremiah and any of the non-Priestly or HL references that we have in front of us. Jeremiah 2:20 (MT) seems to belong to that group of passages in Jeremiah where the most that can be said is that the prophet relies on earlier national-historical traditions known to us from the Pentateuch. But I do not think we have a way to prove the existence of any of those inherited traditions in writing, or to identify particular literary segments of the developing pentateuchal corpus ("sources," "traditions," or however labeled) that might be presumed to be in Jeremiah's possession. This, however, is only one dimension of the allusive qualities of Jer 2:20–25, to which I will shortly turn.

Understanding v. 20 as an ellipsis validates two major points. First, on the textual level, MT Jer 2:20 may be seen as perfectly acceptable, and the versions (LXX, Vulgate, Peshitta) stand as secondary, harmonistic, and interpretive suggestions meant to cope with the syntactical-thematic crux of the MT version. In this category I would also include the Qere לֹא אֶעֱבוֹר. This Qere tradition suggests that a declaration of obedience is the appropriate theological response to the divine promise of salvation. However, if the text is seen as elliptical, the Ketiv, לֹא אֶעֱבֹד, may be seen as the more plausible response; this is further validated by the frequent occurrences of the phrases שָׁבַר עַל and עָבַד לֹא to convey political subjugation (Jer 30:8–9; likewise the demand to serve Nebuchadnezzar, Jer 27:6–8, 11–13; 28:14).[19] Hence, this Qere correction seems to be a hypercorrection, and clearly an unnecessary one.

Second, on the thematic level, the entire proclamation, though elliptical, emphasizes the great contrast between God's beneficent treatment of the people and the people's ungrateful rejection of God's sovereignty. The two elliptical sentences that constitute v. 20a are crucial for formally demonstrating the breach of the God–people relationship. Furthermore, this disjunction between God's commitments to the people and the people's disregard of God's care stands behind the prophet's choice to utilize the marital metaphor in this passage.[20] The political

---

The Sanctuary of Silence: A Study of the Priestly Strata in the Pentateuch (Minneapolis: Fortress, 1995), 164–65, 175. A similar reasoning serves in Lev 25:42 to prohibit Israelite slavery; see Jacob Milgrom, *Leviticus 23–27: A New Translation with Introduction and Commentary* (AB 3B; New York: Doubleday, 2000), 2240–41.

[19] So also Bozak, "Heeding the Received Text," 532. The term עָבַר does not appear in this context of subjugation, and thus the reading may result from simple scribal confusion of ר and ד, or may reflect a scribal *correction* of *dalet* to *reš* (as suggested orally by Dr. Ruth Clements).

[20] A similar disjunction also operates in the marital metaphor of Hos 2:4–15 and Ezek 16:1–15. It therefore seems to be one of the basic elements of this metaphor. See Dalit Rom-Shiloni, "The Covenant in the Book of Jeremiah: On the Employment of Marital and Political

imagery of breach of servitude (v. 20a) paves the way for the inversion of the marital metaphor that began the first section of this chapter (2:2) and its transformation into the imagery of the disloyal adulteress (20b), which governs the second section: את צעה זנה ("You recline like a whore," v. 20b).[21]

Verse 20, thus, builds a clear thematic progression, illustrated in the closing phrases of each of its two parts:

| ותאמרי לא אעבד | נתקתי מוסרתיך | כי מעולם שברתי עלך |
| את צעה זנה | ותחת כל עץ רענן | כי על כל גבעה גבהה |

ותאמרי לא אעבד responds to God's salvific actions with a refusal to obey; and את צעה זנה comprises the concluding divine accusation with the categorical designation of Israel as a whore, a definition that will have an important rhetorical function in the following verses.[22]

In line with the preceding analysis, I will argue in the remainder of this article that vv. 21–25 elaborate, exemplify, and intensify the opening statement of v. 20 (in its MT version), illustrating not only the people's disobedience but also the great disloyalty and ungratefulness they show toward God. Thus, the structure of vv. 21–25 serves as additional argument in favor of the MT version of Jer 2:20.

III

Among the great qualities of the book of Jeremiah as a whole, and of the poetic sections in particular, is its allusive language, which too often has been studied only

---

Metaphors," in *Covenant in the Persian Period* (ed. Richard Bautch and Gary N. Knoppers; Winona Lake, IN: Eisenbrauns, forthcoming, 2015).

[21] The term זנה (in 2:20) functions here and elsewhere in Jeremiah (as in 3:1, 6, 8, etc) to depict the unfaithfulness of the people as the behavior of a married and yet adulterous wife, behavior also designated by נאף (as in Jer 3:8; and metaphorically, 3:9). Hence the two verbs (זנה and נאף) seem to be interchangeable, although the substantive זונה does not refer by definition to a *married*, and thus adulterous woman, but rather to an unmarried woman (Gen 38:15; Josh 2:1; Judg 11:1). The word צעה is more difficult. It appears four times in the Hebrew Bible, twice in Jeremiah (2:20; 48:12) and twice in Isaiah 40–66. In all four cases the meaning is doubtful; see Shalom M. Paul, *Isaiah 40–66: Translation and Commentary* (ECC; Grand Rapids: Eerdmans, 2012), 373, 563. Rashi seems to suggest a contextual explanation that draws on the similarity between צעה and מצע (note the *hapax legomenon* מצע in Isa 28:20); so Qara: "lying whore," accepted by McKane, *Jeremiah*, 1:41. Holladay (*Jeremiah 1*, 98) emphasizes the use of the two participles at the end of Jer 2:20 and thus translates: "You are sprawling, whoring." I would concur with the NJPS translation ("you recline as a whore"), which seems to capture the participial forms as defining the people's qualities, rather than repeated behavior. Still, Carroll's comment (*Jeremiah*, 130) seems in place: "the reader's imagination will serve better than a translation."

[22] I would accept Bozak's suggestion that the poetic pattern of MT Jer 2:20 is constructed in the pattern A/A'/B || C/C'/B' ("Heeding the Received Text," 536), but I argue, further, that B and B' function in the indicative as parallel proclamations, and each has a separate function in this verse.

in discussions of authorship.²³ The current investigation recognizes the importance of these literary allusions for understanding the prophetic message.

Verses 20–25 evoke several pentateuchal traditions. Deuteronomic phrasing has been suggested in v. 20b: כי על כל גבעה גבהה ותחת כל עץ רענן ("upon every high hill and under every shady tree").²⁴ William L. Holladay reconstructed the growth of this phrase and noted its uses in the Hebrew Bible. According to Holladay, Hos 4:13 is the initial occurrence of a three segment phraseology containing mountains, hills, and trees; it was adapted in Deut 12:2, which compressed the detailed reference to three specific trees (אלון לבנה ואלה) to the general phrase "every green tree"; and finally, Jer 2:20, according to Holladay, both dropped the first component and extended the כל from the last (כל עץ רענן) to the earlier one (כל גבעה גבהה). Holladay argued that Jeremiah was the one "who 'standardized' the phrase"²⁵ and that Jer 2:20b in turn was the basis for the adaptations of this two-segment phrase into the Deuteronomistic writings (1 Kgs 4:23; 2 Kgs 17:10; and later on into Deutero-Isaiah and later writings, Isa 57:5, 7; and 30:25).²⁶ Holladay thus reconstructed reciprocal literary connections between the poetry of Jeremiah and Deuteronomistic writings, which later found their way back into the prose sections of Jeremiah (Jer 3:6, 13; 17:2).²⁷ Though this might have occurred in theory, the present example seems weak. Holladay specified three arguments for the genuineness of this phrase in Jer 2:20b: (1) it fits the context; (2) the assonance גבעה גבהה is in line with Jeremiah's style of wordplays; (3) there are other similar examples of what Holladay considered a broader phenomenon, that is, phrases in prose passages in Jeremiah and in "the Deuteronomic revision of Kings" that draw upon "genuine poetic oracles of Jeremiah."²⁸ Be that as it may, for the sake of the current study, two major points may be gleaned: (1) the reliance of Jer 2:20 on Deut

---

²³ Allusions to Deuteronomy and Deuteronomistic literature have usually been evaluated as secondary and editorial. See an earlier paper, Dalit Rom-Shiloni, "Actualization of Pentateuchal Legal Traditions in Jeremiah: More on the Riddle of Authorship," *ZABR* 15 (2009): 254–81. Awareness of the multiple literary sources and references in Jeremiah may be found in Fischer's commentary (*Jeremiah 1–25*, 65–74).

²⁴ John Bright, "The Date of the Prose Sermons of Jeremiah," *JBL* 70 (1951): 15–35; see p. 35, Appendix B, no. 2.

²⁵ Holladay, "On Every High Hill and under Every Green Tree," *VT* 11 (1961): 170.

²⁶ Ibid., 170–76; idem, *Jeremiah 1*, 98. Moshe Weinfeld (*Deuteronomy and the Deuteronomic School* [Oxford: Clarendon, 1972], Appendix A, I.15, pp. 322, 366) explains the similarity between Hosea, Deuteronomy, and Jeremiah especially on matters of idolatrous and syncretistic worship as "a current northern thought flowing down to Judah" (p. 366).

²⁷ Holladay discusses this concept of literary dependence more extensively in his commentary (*Jeremiah 2*, 53–63).

²⁸ Holladay, *Jeremiah 1*, 173.

12:2;²⁹ and (2) the freedom of the Jeremian phraseology, which made significant changes in the Deuteronomic wording.³⁰

Two other Deuteronomic/Deuteronomistic phrases occur in vv. 23–25 (אחרי הבעלים לא הלכתי, "I have not gone after the Baals" [v. 23]; and אהבתי זרים ואחריהם אלך, "I have loved strangers, and after them I will go" [v. 25]); they structure these verses as an *inclusio*:³¹

A   23 אֵיךְ תֹּאמְרִי לֹא נִטְמֵאתִי, אַחֲרֵי הַבְּעָלִים לֹא הָלָכְתִּי—

   B   רְאִי דַרְכֵּךְ בַּגַּיְא, דְּעִי מֶה עָשִׂית: בִּכְרָה קַלָּה, מְשָׂרֶכֶת דְּרָכֶיהָ.
             24 פֶּרֶה לִמֻּד מִדְבָּר, בְּאַוַּת נפשו (נַפְשָׁהּ) שָׁאֲפָה רוּחַ--תַּאֲנָתָהּ, מִי יְשִׁיבֶנָּה;

     C/C′   כָּל־מְבַקְשֶׁיהָ לֹא יִיעָפוּ, בְּחָדְשָׁהּ יִמְצָאוּנְהָ.

   B′   25 מִנְעִי רַגְלֵךְ מִיָּחֵף, וגורנך (וּגְרוֹנֵךְ) מִצִּמְאָה;

A′   וַתֹּאמְרִי נוֹאָשׁ—לוֹא, כִּי־אָהַבְתִּי זָרִים וְאַחֲרֵיהֶם אֵלֵךְ.

A   How can you say, "I am not defiled, I have not gone after the Baals"?

   B   Look at your deeds in the valley, consider what you have done! a restive young camel, relentlessly running about, a wild ass at home in the wilderness, in her heat sniffing the wind! Who can restrain her lust?

     C/C′   None who seek her need weary themselves; in her month they will find her.

   B′   Keep your feet from going unshod and your throat from thirst.

A′   But you said, "It is no use. No, I love the strangers, and after them I must go."

---

²⁹ Compare Winfried Thiel, *Die Deuteronomistische Redaktion von Jeremia 1–25* (WMANT 41; Neukirchen-Vluyn: Neukirchener Verlag, 1973), 80–82.

³⁰ On the Jeremian phraseology, see Bright, "Date of the Prose Sermons," 15–35, esp. the Appendix; Helga Weippert, *Die Prosareden des Jeremiabuches* (BZAW 132; Berlin: de Gruyter, 1973); Holladay, *Jeremiah 2*, 53–63; Lundbom, *Jeremiah 1–20*, 63–65, 126, and passim; Konrad Schmid, "Jeremiah," in Jan Christian Gertz, Angelika Berlejung, Konrad Schmid, and Markus Witte, *T&T Clark Handbook of the Old Testament: An Introduction to the Literature, Religion and History of the Old Testament* (London: T&T Clark, 2012), 442–46.

³¹ The two phrases are הלך אחרי אלהים (see Deut 13:5; 1 Kgs 14:8; 2 Kgs 23:3) and the more frequent phrase הלך אחרי אלהים אחרים (Deut 4:3; 6:14; 8:19; 11:28; 28:14) and its derivatives, such as הלך ועבד אלהים אחרים (as in Deut 13:3, 7, 14; 17:3; 29:25; Josh 23:16; 1 Sam 26:19; 1 Kgs 9:6; and so in Jer 7:6, 9; 11:10; 13:10; 16:11; 25:6; 35:15). Similar formulas include those that specify the other gods (as in 1 Kgs 11:5; 18:21). הבעלים and זרים serve in this latter role in Jer 2:23, 25. Weinfeld interprets these phrases as illustrating loyalty (*Deuteronomy and the Deuteronomic School*, Appendix A, V.1, p. 322) or disloyalty (A, I.15, p. 320) to God, following the Akkadian *alāku arki*, which indicates political domination. Hence, this phraseology marks the Deuteronomic transference of political terminology to the theological arena (ibid., 83 n. 2, 332).

The subunit A/A´ introduces the rhetorical question that quotes the people's statement of innocence: "How can you say, 'I am not defiled, I have not gone after the Baalim'?" (v. 23a), and closes with the people's confession of sins: "It is no use. No, I love the strangers, and after them I must go" (v. 25b).³² While this framework seems to be clear, the inner flow of the passage is more enigmatic.³³ The subunit B/B´ presents two sets of imperative clauses that first admonish the people, "Look at your deeds in the valley, consider what you have done!" (v. 23b), and then warn them, "Save your foot from going bare, and your throat from thirst" (v. 25a). Finally, the subunit C/C´ use zoological imagery. The governing image is that of the young she-camel; within the phrase occurs a reference to the פרה, a wild ass (v. 24a; otherwise in the Hebrew Bible פרא, as in Job 6:5; etc).³⁴

As in vv. 20–22, this passage (vv. 23–25) continues the marital metaphor to depict the God–people relationship. Thus, throughout A/A´ and B/B´ (as well as in the imagery of C/C´) the second person feminine singular indicates the people, the adulterous wife.³⁵ Most commentators would probably accept William McKane's summary of the passage:

> Israel is compared in vv. 23–25 to a woman abandoned to passion and impulsive behaviour, subject to a determinism which makes her a slave.... The emphasis falls rather on the feverish activity of the promiscuous woman who like the אשה זרה in the book of Proverbs is wanton and feverish and is never at rest (vii 11, ix 13).³⁶

I suggest, however, that in vv. 23–25 Jeremiah not only calls to mind sexual heat but gives additional force to his prophecy by alluding to the Priestly legal tradition (or even text) of the suspected adulteress in Numbers 5.³⁷

---

³² In Jer 18:12, נואש occurs in another rebellious quotation put in the people's mouth, yet not in a metaphor. Isaiah 57:10 seems to rely on Jer 2:25; and see similarly 1 Sam 27:1; Job 6:26; Eccl 2:20.

³³ McKane, "Jeremiah ii 23–25: Observations on the Versions and History of Exegesis," in *The Witness of Tradition: Papers Read at the Joint British–Dutch Old Testament Conference Held at Woudschoten 1970* (ed. M. A. Beek et al.; OtSt 17; Leiden: Brill, 1972), 73–88.

³⁴ Rudolph (*Jeremiah*, 19, 21) points out the disconnected flow of the imagery in this passage (for Rudolph the passage comprises vv. 20–28). Accordingly, all images are "stock images," taken from the prophet's surrounding world, and they show influences of the prophetic heritage.

³⁵ See McKane, "Jeremiah ii 23–25," 80–81, though McKane is cautious as to whether the imagery of the she-camel alludes to sexual heat (p. 81).

³⁶ Ibid., 82.

³⁷ Compare Holladay (*Jeremiah 1*, 100), who identifies the proclamation לא נטמאתי ("I am not defiled") with "the man with bloodstains in v. 22, and the verb reminds one further of its use in v. 7, where the people 'defiled' the land." Overholt ("Jeremiah 2," 270) suggests that נטמאתי in v. 23 echoes "the apodictic prohibitions against defiling the land (Num 35:34; Deut 21:23)." While defilement of the land in Jer 2:7 and 3:1, 2 seems indeed to reflect on, or echo, the Holiness Legislation's conception of the land (e.g., Lev 18:24) and the Priestly conception of Num 35:34, I understand the context of the *sôṭâ* to be in view in Jer 2:23. See Rom-Shiloni, "Actualization of Pentateuchal Legal Traditions," 264–66.

Numbers 5:11–31 describes an ordeal (a test, or a legal curse) aimed at revealing the truth behind the serious accusation of infidelity (vv. 12b–14).[38] Under circumstances of marital distrust, an entire ritual procedure takes place before God (תורת הקנאת, "the ritual in cases of jealousy," v. 29). The suspicious husband accuses his (silent) suspected wife of infidelity; no witnesses are on hand to testify to the actual commission of the deed (v. 13).[39] To reveal the truth, and thus to alleviate the suspicion, the man and his wife arrive at the sanctuary bringing an offering (מנחת קנאת הוא מנחת זכרון מזכרת עון, "a meal offering of jealousy, a meal offering of remembrance which recalls wrongdoing," v. 15).[40] The priest conducts the ritual ordeal (vv. 17–28): he prepares a potion of המים המאררים ("the cursing waters," v. 18), which contains sacred waters, dust from the sanctuary floor, and the words of a curse, written and then washed off into the water (vv. 17, 23); he then explains the procedure to the woman (vv. 19–20, 22).[41] She takes an oath, thus implicitly claiming that she is innocent (v. 22b). The woman is then forced to drink the "bitter waters," an act that will either reveal her guilt (v. 27) or prove her innocence (v. 28). The law concludes (vv. 29–31) by repeating the circumstances under which it is to be applied, noting that through this ordeal, the husband will be cleansed of guilt (for his jealousy), whereas the woman will bear the consequences of her sin: והאשה ההיא תשא את עונה (v. 31).[42] As argued by Tikva Frymer-Kensky, the ceremony

---

[38] For a discussion of the genre, arguing that the passage represents a test (a trial), and clearly not legislation, see Herbert C. Brichto, "The Case of the *Sota* and a Reconsideration of Biblical 'Law,'" *HUCA* 46 (1975): 55–70, esp. 64–69; for the legal curse, see Tikva Frymer-Kensky, "The Strange Case of the Suspected Sotah (Numbers V 11–31)," *VT* 34 (1984): 11–26. In my discussion of Num 5:11–31, I follow the literary and rhetorical approach of Michael Fishbane, Frymer-Kensky, and Jacob Milgrom (see nn. 61–63 below).

[39] Verse 13 features no fewer than four phrases that repeat the concealment of the suspected infidelity; see Jacob Milgrom, *Numbers* במדבר: *The Traditional Hebrew Text with the New JPS Translation* (JPS Torah Commentary; Philadelphia: Jewish Publication Society, 1990), 349–50.

[40] On the ordeal, see Julian Morgenstern, "Trial by Ordeal among the Semites and in Ancient Israel," *HUCA* 2 (1925): 113–43; Ya'akov Licht, *A Commentary on the Book of Numbers* (in Hebrew; 3 vols.; Jerusalem: Magnes Press, Hebrew University, 1985), 1:67–82; Milgrom, *Numbers*, 346–48.

[41] Numbers 5:21 seems to interrupt the priest's words of vv. 20 and 22; see Licht, *Numbers*, 78–79; Milgrom, *Numbers*, 353.

[42] According to Milgrom, v. 31 states that if the ordeal proves the woman's defilement, she is nevertheless "removed from the jurisdiction of man." Milgrom argues that this ordeal was actually intended "to protect a suspected but unproved adulteress" (*Numbers*, 354). For נשא עון as a divine judgment, see Walther Zimmerli, "Die Eigenart der prophetischen Rede des Ezechiel," *ZAW* 66 (1954): 1–26, esp. 8–12; Frymer-Kensky, "Strange Case," 22–25; Milgrom, *Numbers*, 354, 304 n. 80. In contrast to the death penalty assigned to the adulteress (Exod 20:13; Deut 5:17; and Lev 20:10), Milgrom (*Numbers*, 350) understands the divine punishment of the suspected woman to work by the principle of "measure for measure" punishment: "the adulteress who acquiesced to receive forbidden seed is doomed to sterility for the rest of her life" (p. 350). Compare Sarah Shectman ("Bearing Guilt in Numbers 5:12–31," in *Gazing on the Deep: Ancient Near Eastern and Other Studies in Honor of Tzvi Abusch* [ed. Jeffrey Stackert, Barbara Nevling Porter, and David P. Wright; Bethesda, MD: CDL, 2010], 479–93, esp. 490–91), who understands נשא עון in Num 5:31

finishes when the woman drinks the potion and presumably returns home to her husband. No further legal procedures are applied, and the ordeal is not intended to supply evidence for further legal proceedings in a human court. The ordeal, which according to Frymer-Kensky is better termed a "legal 'curse,'" transfers both investigation and judgment to the divine realm and awaits God's verdict and punishment; in distinction from other ancient ordeals, the results are clearly not immediate.[43] Rather, the consequences of the entire procedure are to be revealed in the longer run—if cleansed and innocent, the woman will bear a child to her husband (v. 28); but if she is defiled and guilty, "her belly with swell and her thigh will fall" (5:21–22, 27), a phrase that probably designates fatal damage to her reproductive organs.[44] One theme (and phrase) governs Num 5:11–31, and it repeats throughout the pericope, which illustrates its importance: the crucial doubt as to whether the woman has or has not actually been defiled: והיא נטמאה or והיא לא נטמאה (vv. 13, 14[2], 20, 27, 28, 29; plus an additional occurrence of טמאה, v. 19).[45]

Jeremiah 2:20–25 features three markers that tie this prophecy to the law of the suspected adulteress. The first is linguistic, consisting in the phrase איך תאמרי לא נטמאתי ("How can you say, 'I am not defiled'?," v. 23). This rare usage of the niphal of טמא occurs only here in Jeremiah and otherwise is found in only twenty-nine of 162 occurrences of טמא in the Hebrew Bible.[46] Seven of these twenty-nine forms occur in the pericope concerning the suspected adulteress. I suggest,

---

as conceptually related to the law concerning vows and oaths in Num 30:16. This suggestion is intriguing indeed for the understanding of Num 5:31 in context; but see the discussion below, where I argue that this does *not* seem to be the way Jeremiah understood עון נשא when he alluded to this law.

[43] See Morgenstern, "Trial by Ordeal," 133–34; Martin Noth, *Numbers: A Commentary* (OTL; London: SCM, 1968), 48–49. Licht (*Numbers*, 68) emphasizes that the ordeal is not in itself the woman's legal conviction of adultery nor does it intersect with the formal judicial procedure in cases of adultery. Thus it has no connection with the laws relating to adultery (such as Lev 20:10); just as it has no connection to the law of divorce in Deut 24:1–4 or to the husband's accusation of ערות דבר ("a lewd thing").

[44] Frymer-Kensky suggests that this means a prolapsed uterus ("Strange Case," 24).

[45] The division of this law into two separate strata was based on the presumed difference between them concerning the guilt of the woman. According to stratum A, the woman was indeed defiled, although the facts were concealed (vv. 12–13, 15, 18, 21–24a, 25–26a, 27b, 29, 31), whereas according to stratum B the woman might not actually have sinned (vv. 14, 16, 17, 19, 20, 24b, 27aα, 28, 30). See Shectman, "Bearing Guilt," 479–87. But the repeated stress on לא נטמאה//נטמאה crosses the two suggested strata. More importantly, the ritual ordeal should supply a yes or no answer to this crucial question. Thus, a stratum that already demonstrates a clear knowledge of the woman's guilt would seem to militate against the entire procedure. This has been pointed out aptly by Morgenstern ("Trial by Ordeal," 129): "Trial by ordeal assumes nothing whatsoever as to the guilt or innocence of the party accused, but leaves it entirely to the ordeal to determine this."

[46] Other occurrences of the *niphal* of טמא are Lev 11:24, 43[2]; 18:24[2], 30; 21:1, 3, 4, 11; Num 6:7 (and note טמא *hotpaal* in Deut 24:4); Ezek 14:11; 20:17, 18, 30, 31, 43; 23:7, 13, 30; and Hos 6:10; 9:4. Jeremiah 2:7 (טמא *piel*) mentions defilement of the land caused by improper cultic behavior.

therefore, that Jeremiah here borrows the central term in the law of the suspected adulteress for his prophecy. The crucial question set by the legal-cultic ordeal והיא נטמאה or והיא לא נטמאה ("Is she defiled?" or "Is she not defiled?") is accordingly transformed by Jeremiah into the claim of innocence placed in the mouth of the accused woman/the people. As in the ordeal of Numbers 5, where the priest starts with the assumption that the woman is not defiled (Num 5:19–20), indicated also by the woman's answer to the priest (v. 22), Jeremiah begins with the woman's denial of her adulterous behavior, saying לא נטמאתי. In the refutation that follows, Jeremiah calls the people (as the woman) to "see" and "know" (ראי דרכך בגיא דעי מה עשית, "look at your deeds in the valley, consider what you have done!," Jer 2:23ab) and thus acknowledge their sins, which they persist in denying.[47] The quotations in vv. 23b and 25b frame the accusation against the people as that against the adulterous wife.

The second marker is thematic and alludes to the major accusation against the suspected adulteress in Num 5:12: איש איש כי תשטה אשתו ("If any man's wife has gone astray"). The verb שטה occurs but six times in the Hebrew Bible, four of them in this passage (Num 5:12, 19, 20, 29; and two in Prov 4:15; 7:25) and is taken to mean "straying from the true path."[48] Thus, while Jeremiah does not invoke this specific verb, he does present the woman's "going astray" by means of the animal imagery (vv. 23b–24) and in the various references to "walking" and "path(s)" repeated in these verses (מנעי, v. 23b; ראי דרכך בגיא, v. 23; אחרי הבעלים לא הלכתי, v. 25; and the closing confession: ואחריהם אלך, v. 25b). Pride of place is given, of course, to the description of the she-camel משרכת דרכיה ("restlessly running about," v. 23b), which is nevertheless sought and found by her lovers (v. 24).[49]

The third marker, the admonition כי אם תכבסי בנתר ותרבי לך ברית נכתם עונך לפני ("Though you wash with nitron and use much lye, your sin [NJPS: guilt] is ingrained before Me," v. 22) draws on the closing sentence of the law of the suspected adulteress, Num 5:31: והאשה ההיא תשא את עונה ("but that woman shall bear her sin").[50] As suggested by Milgrom, this final sentence of the postscript

---

[47] In other passages, Jeremiah quotes similar denials of guilt (e.g., 2:35) or even assertions of obedience (3:4–5a), which he repeatedly and fiercely refutes as additional demonstrations of the people's brazen disobedience (2:33–37; 3:1–5). Taken in the context of poetic sources that proclaim the people's righteousness (as in Pss 44:18–23; 80:19–20; Lam 5:7; etc.), these quotations in Jer 2:35; 3:4–5a, while possibly put into the mouth of the people, should be taken with more than a grain of salt.

[48] So Baruch A. Levine, *Numbers 1–20: A New Translation with Introduction and Commentary* (AB 4A; New York: Doubleday, 1993), 194.

[49] Ancient and modern interpreters still struggle with the phrase משרכת דרכיה in this metaphor. See McKane, "Jeremiah ii 23–25," 77–78.

[50] Compare the NJPS: "shall suffer for her guilt." For this apt reading, see Baruch J. Schwartz, "Between a Term and a Metaphor: נשא עון/פשע/חטא in the Bible" (in Hebrew), *Tarbiz* 63 (1994): 149–71, esp. 163–71; idem, "The Bearing of Sin in the Priestly Literature," in *Pomegranates and Golden Bells : Studies in Biblical, Jewish, and Near Eastern Ritual, Law, and Literature in Honor of*

designates an early interpolation in the text that stands outside of the *inclusio* pattern of Num 5:29–30 (note a similar pattern in Num 6:21).[51]

This is where Jeremiah's utilization of this law is so meticulously thoughtful. Jeremiah 2:22 does not carry on the metaphor used in Num 5:31 (and commonly in P and the HL) of sin as a burden but uses the metaphor of sin as a stain that needs to be cleansed, here with two detergents, נתר (sodium carbonate) and ברית (soda, or herbal alkaline salt).[52] The prophet concludes that these efforts are useless, as the people's iniquity remains visible before God (see Jer 16:17).[53] But, though he transfers the imagery, Jeremiah still holds to the Priestly verdict that stands behind נשא עון. This sin of infidelity is among the sins that cannot be undone, a crime that, if indeed proven, is of the category of נשא עון (Num 5:31).[54] By drawing on the Priestly law of the suspected adulteress, the prophet gives further force to his proclamation—the suspected, but concealed (or denied), sin of defilement is clearly revealed to God; that is, the people's disloyalty is easily perceived by God and is beyond reparation.

Jeremiah 2:20–25 thus presents a reverse ordering of the components of Num 5:11–31. נכתם עונך לפני ("the stain of your guilt is before me") concludes the first subunit of Jer 2:20–22, where it leads to the ensuing refutation of the adulteress's denial of guilt (vv. 23–25). This reversal is of great significance. The transferral of this metaphor to the God–people relationship indeed brings Jerusalem to face a divine extreme indictment (which guarantees subsequent judgment).

Nevertheless, it is just as clear that, in alluding to this Priestly tradition (or text), Jeremiah has gone his own way. First, he has transformed the metaphoric imagery from bearing the burden of sin to perceiving sin as a stain exposed to the

---

Jacob Milgrom (ed. David P. Wright, David Noel Freedman, and Avi Hurvitz; Winona Lake, IN: Eisenbrauns, 1995), 3–21, esp. 8–15; and see Gary A. Anderson (*Sin: A History* [New Haven: Yale University Press, 2009], 15–26), who, following Schwartz, explains נשא עון as "to bear (the weight of one's) sin" and emphasizes that נשא עון stands for the culpability of the offender for his/her crime (pp. 24–25, regarding Lev 5:1).

[51] Milgrom recognizes these verses as one of two interpolations into the original pagan ordeal, added to the text by the Priestly author at an early stage of its evolution (the other being v. 21) (*Numbers*, 353–54).

[52] A discussion of the metaphors concerning sin, in Schwartz, "Between a Term and a Metaphor," 163–71; Anderson, *Sin*, 16. For the metaphor of sin as a stain that needs to be cleansed, see Jer 18:23; Isa 1:18; 59:3; Zech 3:4; Lam 1:8–9. This may be plausibly supported by the fact that, while עון occurs twenty times in Jeremiah, all referring to the people's misconduct against God (Jer 3:13; 5:25; 11:10; 13:22; 14:10; 16:10, 17, 18; 18:23; 25:12; 30:14, 15; 31:30, 34; 32:18; 33:8; 36:3, 31; 50:20; 51:6; and in the communal lamentations, 14:7, 20), there are no occurrences of נשא עון in the book.

[53] For נתר and ברית, see Holladay, *Jeremiah 1*, 99; McKane, *Jeremiah* 1:42; Lundblom, *Jeremiah 1–20*, 278.

[54] Schwartz points out the distinction between sins from which the sinner may be "cleansed" through repentance and reparations (including fast, work cessation, etc.) and those deliberate evil deeds that are inexpiable and are concluded with ונשא עונו/חטאתו (as indeed Num 5:31) ("Bearing of Sin," 21).

sight of God (see Jer 17:16). With this transformation to נכתם עונך לפני, the prophet conveys his understanding of נשא עון in Num 5:31 as acknowledgment of the woman's sin.[55]

Furthermore, in נכתם עונך לפני, Jeremiah coins a *hapax legomenon* that serves within the metaphor of sin as a stain as the opposite of כבס ("cleanse").[56] The latter verb, כבס, is a typical Priestly term connected with the Priestly sphere of purification. In both P and HL, כבס designates washing clothes in order to purify them, in a variety of circumstances (as in Lev 13:6; Num 8:7; 31:24) that are all part of the physical purification procedures.[57] In Jer 2:22 (and in 4:14), כבס is used metaphorically to signify cleansing from sins, and thus purifying. This metaphorical usage of כבס is quite exceptional in the Hebrew Bible and occurs also only in Ps 51:4, 9 and Mal 3:2.[58] This distribution seems to draw a very interesting and independent line between Jeremiah and the two Priestly systems of physical purification and defilement versus sin and its expiation.[59] Jeremiah seems to be aware of the purification procedures that include washing of clothes, and he transfers them from their initial personal, cultic context to the metaphorical realm of the relationship between God and the people. But, in addition to that and in order to enforce his proclamation, the prophet intentionally crosses the lines he seems to recognize between physical impurity and sin. Jeremiah presents the absurd efforts of physical cleansing in expiation of a sin that cannot be undone.

These three markers seem strong enough to suggest that Jeremiah, in his early utilizations of the marital metaphor for his prophecy against Jerusalem, has chosen to allude to the striking "legal curse" pronounced against the wife suspected of adultery of Numbers 5; and he has further combined this allusion with echoes of

---

[55] Anderson, *Sin*, 24–26. Milgrom argued that עון means "crime or punishment but never guilt" (*Numbers*, 43); see Exod 28:43; Lev 5:1, 17 ואשם ונשא עונו, "and then realizes his guilt, he shall be subject to punishment"); 17:16; 20:17, 19, and the parallel phrase ישאו חטאם in v. 20; etc. Compare Schwartz, "Bearing of Sin," 12: "'sin-bearing' is a metaphor for guilt and not punishment"; see his entire discussion on pp. 12–15; and Shectman, "Bearing Guilt," 490–91; see n. 50 above.

[56] See Anderson, *Sin*, 16–17; Holladay, *Jeremiah 1*, 99.

[57] כבס and טהר come together in Lev 13:6, 34, 58; 14:8; 15:8, 13; as also יכבס בגדיו וטמא עד הערב, "he shall wash his clothes and be unclean until the evening," in Lev 11:25, 28, 40[2]; 15:5, 6, 7, 10, 11, 17, 21, 22, 27; Num 19:8, 21; see also Lev 6:20; 14:47[2]; 16:26, 28, where washing the clothes is a part of the purification process, though neither טמא nor טהר occurs. I would not suggest a literary allusion (or an echo) in Jer 2:22 to Exod 19:6, 14, which features כבס with קדש as part of the preparations for the covenant ceremony. I believe that the context of טמא in Jer 2:23 lines up with the aforementioned conception of purification procedures from defilement.

[58] Gunnel André considered this figurative usage "a spiritualization of what was originally understood as cultic purity" ("כבס," *TDOT* 7:41). Nevertheless, I do not see a literary dependence between these different metaphorical usages; each seems to echo independently the Priestly formulae. Compare Holladay, who argued that "Jer has both Psalm 51 and Isa 1:15–20 in mind in offering this passage" (*Jeremiah 1*, 99).

[59] On the two systems and their similarities and distinctions, see Schwartz, "Bearing of Sin," 4–10, 20–21.

the Priestly formulae of defilement and purification. Through the allusions to the legal-cultic trial of the *sôṭâ*, the prophet fleshes out his harsh accusation against the people as צעה זנה (v. 20). This is the first time that Jeremiah has stated this denigrating accusation so directly, in emphatic opposition to the naïve and romantic point of departure he himself sketched out in 2:2 to portray the constitution of the God-people relationship. Jeremiah will carry on this denigrating portrayal of the people in 2:33–37 and in 3:1–5 (and following), but 2:20–25 is the passage where the prophet gives shape to this metaphor. He alludes to the legal tradition of the *sôṭâ* by adducing two of its defining phrases (לא נטמאתי; and the divine verdict: נכתם עונך לפני) and then depicts the progression from the woman's denial of her adulterousness to her clear confession and even choice (or obligation) to carry on with this behavior: נואש לוא כי אהבתי זרים ואחריהם אלך, "It is no use. No, I love the strangers, and after them I must go."

IV

The questions that arise from these observations are, I believe, of great importance to both prophetic and pentateuchal studies in general, and to the study of Jeremiah and the Priestly sources in particular.

In this study of Jer 2:20–25, the one clear conclusion that seems striking to me is that Jeremiah appears to be utilizing Priestly legal traditions early in his prophetic career, just as he is understood to utilize Deuteronomic ones. The prophet invokes phrases and conceptions from both; he places them side by side and even interweaves them, in vv. 20 and 23–25. Jeremiah shows the same freedom in using both sets of pentateuchal traditions, the Deuteronomic and the Priestly, for the ad hoc needs of his prophecy.[60]

Scholars of Numbers have adopted three main approaches to the question of the literary unity of Num 5:11–31. (1) The passage has been understood as a compilation of two separate sources. Ever since Bernhard Stade's study (1895), critical exegetes have discerned literary difficulties in Num 5:11–31, and divided the passage into two independent sources.[61] (2) This cultic instruction has been viewed as an early (even pre-Israelite) unit that was briefly interpolated and elaborated in

---

[60] This freedom in utilizing pentateuchal traditions for the sake of the prophecy characterizes the literary allusions in both Jeremiah and Ezekiel; see Rom-Shiloni, "Actualization of Pentateuchal Legal Traditions in Jeremiah," 254–81; eadem, "Deuteronomic Concepts of Exile Interpreted in Jeremiah and Ezekiel," in *Birkat Shalom: Studies in the Bible, Ancient Near Eastern Literature, and Post-biblical Judaism Presented to Shalom M. Paul on the Occasion of His Seventieth Birthday* (ed. Chaim Cohen, Victor Avigdor Hurowitz, Avi Hurvitz, Yochanan Muffs, Baruch J. Schwartz, and Jeffrey H. Tigay; Winona Lake, IN: Eisenbrauns, 2008), 101–23.

[61] Stade, "Beiträge zur Pentateuchkritik: 3. Die Eiferopferthora," *ZAW* 15 (1895): 166–75. See Morgenstern, who had already denied the probability of such a division ("Trial by Ordeal," 128–29). For a fairly recent discussion of the two strata, see Shectman, "Bearing Guilt," 479–93.

certain places. Martin Noth (1968) argued that the law reflects "a fairly ancient practice" already known to the Priestly authors as "a traditional text," which they only "lightly reworked" (additions in vv. 11–12a, as well as the term "tabernacle," v. 17; so already Morgenstern, and later on, Licht).[62] (3) A literary and rhetorical approach has been preferred by scholars who have argued for the unity of this passage, each suggesting different and powerful arguments (Fishbane, Brichto, Frymer-Kensky, Milgrom).[63]

Jeremiah's allusions to this passage testify to his acquaintance with the entire text (or, according to "the Documentarians," with the latest compiled form of the text). Jeremiah clearly knows the terminology (or at least some of the most crucial terms: נטמאה/לא נטמאה, and עון [נשא], which, I argue, he transformed purposefully into עון נכתם, v. 31),[64] just as he is clearly aware of the two major conceptual characteristics of the suspected adulteress trial (the revelation of truth and the clear-cut divine verdict that, if the charge is proven, there can be no reparation). Jeremiah's allusions to the Priestly materials are of an exegetical nature. In the examples discussed here, and so regularly throughout the book, the references are mostly not a simple matter of shared vocabulary. Rather, they are examples of great prophetic creativity (as echos or literary allusions) in which the evoked traditions are used to construct the prophetic message.

But here we come up against the limits of our knowledge: *Could* Jeremiah have known this tradition in a written form? Could Jeremiah's usage of this tradition substantiate Noth's understanding of Num 5:11–31 as "a traditional text" that had reached the Priestly authors already in writing?[65] Might it even serve as evidence of the early preexilic existence of the Priestly sources?[66] And might it further substantiate the presence of strata within the Priestly writings?[67]

---

[62] Noth, *Numbers*, 49; see also George Buchanan Gray, *A Critical and Exegetical Commentary on Numbers* (1903; ICC; repr., Edinburgh: T&T Clark, 1986), 49–56, specifically 53, 55; Licht, *Numbers*, 1:72–74. The early background of the ordeal was presented by Morgenstern, "Trial by Ordeal," 129–30, 140–42.

[63] Michael Fishbane, "Accusations of Adultery: A Study of Law and Scribal Practice in Numbers 5:11–31," *HUCA* 45 (1974): 25–45; Brichto, "Case of the Sota," 55–70; Frymer-Kensky, "Strange Case," 11–26; and Milgrom, *Numbers*, 350–54. See n. 38 above.

[64] Another reference may be suggested in Jeremiah's use of נקה in 2:35 (see Num 5:19, 28).

[65] Noth, *Numbers*, 49.

[66] The early preexilic dating of Priestly literature, allowing for final compilation and redaction to the exilic and the early postexilic periods, has become the mark of Jewish-Israeli scholarship: see, e.g., Yehezkel Kaufmann, *Toldot Ha'Emunah HaYisraelit* (Jerusalem: Bialik, 1956), 1:61–65, 113–220; Menachem Haran, "Behind the Scenes of History: Determining the History of the Priestly Source," *JBL* 100 (1981): 321–33; Knohl, *Sanctuary of Silence*, 199–224; Jacob Milgrom, *Leviticus 1–16: A New Translation with Introduction and Commentary* (AB 3A; New York: Doubleday, 1991), 3–11; Baruch Schwartz, "The Strata of the Priestly Writings and the Revised Relative Dating of P and H: Introduction," in *The Strata of the Priestly Writings: Contemporary Debate and Future Directions* (ed. Sarah Shectman and Joel S. Baden; ATANT 95; Zurich: Theologischer Verlag Zürich, 2009), 1–12.

[67] The literature is vast and well known. I therefore mention only the recent collection, edited

One thing I believe needs to be recognized. The single prophetic passage dealt with here illustrates an accurate awareness of Priestly legal terminology and conceptions by the close of the seventh century or the early sixth century B.C.E. Nevertheless, the nature of the prophetic proclamation does not allow us to determine whether this awareness stems from Jeremiah's personal knowledge of Priestly oral traditions and familiarity with Priestly procedures, or whether Jeremiah at that point already had access to any Priestly texts.[68] Thus, while I would certainly not claim the existence of a continuous text of the Pentateuch by this time, I would argue that Jeremiah (not only his tradents) had at his disposal—in memory or in actual writing—traditions and even texts that would later become part of the Pentateuch, and they were clearly not limited to Deuteronomy (or Dtr).[69]

---

by Shectman and Baden, *Strata of the Priestly Writings*, cited in the preceding note. It might be of interest to add up the data and check whether other allusions to Priestly sources in Jeremiah shed further light on this issue of strata within Priestly interpolations into the book, and I intend to devote a longer study to this issue.

[68] Marvin A. Sweeney has accentuated Jeremiah's priestly background and suggested several contexts in which he finds the prophet's firsthand acquaintance with Priestly materials; see Sweeney, *Tanak: A Theological and Critical Introduction to the Jewish Bible* (Minneapolis: Fortress, 2012), 294.

[69] Jeremiah's utilization of Priestly materials calls to mind David M. Carr's observations on processes of "transmission of texts by way of memory" already in the creative period of the biblical literature; see Carr, *The Formation of the Hebrew Bible: A New Reconstruction* (New York: Oxford University Press, 2011), 25–34.

New from Mohr Siebeck

Rudolf Bultmann / Günther Bornkamm
Briefwechsel 1926–1976
Herausgegeben von Werner Zager

Der Briefwechsel thematisiert neben vielen zentralen Fragen der Theologie insbesondere die Verhältnisbestimmung von theologischer und kirchlicher Arbeit, speziell in der Zeit des Dritten Reichs.

2014. 530 pages (est.).
ISBN 978-3-16-151708-2
cloth (December)

Reinhard Hillmann
Brautpreis und Mitgift
Gedanken zum Eherecht in Ugarit und seiner Umwelt mit einer Rekonstruktion des im Ritual verankerten »Schlangentext«-Mythos

Reinhard Hillmann untersucht die Ugarittexte CAT 1.24 und CAT 1.100 und zeigt, dass es eine Homogenität des Brautpreises gibt, die von der altbabylonischen und mittelassyrischen Zeit bis in die Eisenzeit des Alten Testaments reicht.

2014. 140 pages (est.) (ORA).
ISBN 978-3-16-153561-1
cloth (December)

Paul-Gerhard Klumbies
Herkunft und Horizont der Theologie des Neuen Testaments

2015. 210 pages (est.).
ISBN 978-3-16-153160-6
sewn paper (January)

Custom made information:
www.mohr.de

Daniela C. Luft
Osiris-Hymnen
Wechselnde Materialisierungen und Kontexte. Untersuchungen anhand der Texte »*C30*« / Tb181,Tb183, »*BM447*« /Tb128, und der »Athribis«-Hymne

Osiris – ein Gott der Toten und ein toter Gott; von den Alten Ägyptern wurde er in zahlreichen Hymnen gepriesen. Aber die Hymnen waren Gebrauchstexte und besaßen Funktionen in ihren Kontexten.

2014. 1060 pages (est.) (ORA).
ISBN 978-3-16-153574-1
cloth (est.) (December)

Christoffer Theis
Magie und Raum
Der magische Schutz auserwählter Räume im alten Ägypten nebst einem Vergleich zu angrenzenden Kulturbereichen

Christoffer Theis bearbeitet und kommentiert das aus dem alten Ägypten vorhandene Material und stellt dieses durch einen Vergleich zu Zeugnissen aus angrenzenden Kulturbereichen in einen transkulturellen wie epochenübergreifenden Rahmen.

2014. 1050 pages (est.) (ORA).
ISBN 978-3-16-153556-7 cloth
(November)

Mohr Siebeck
Tübingen
info@mohr.de
www.mohr.de

The *Testament of Job* as an Example of Profeminine Patience Literature

ROBIN WAUGH
rwaugh@wlu.ca
Wilfrid Laurier University, Waterloo, ON N2L 3C5, Canada

Brent D. Shaw, in his very important and influential article "Body/Power/Identity: Passions of the Martyrs," published in 1996, argues that a new means of self-identification emerges in the late antique period, often denoted by the Greek abstract noun *hypomonē* (ὑπομονή, the "endurance of suffering"). The first-century pseudepigraphic text *Testament of Job* offers evidence for this revaluation of suffering, but Shaw goes on to discover "feminized rhetoric" in this work: a phrase that is too dismissive of the *Testament*'s profeminine content. Feminine rhetoric, despite Shaw's slighting of the idea, is a remarkably precocious feature of the *Testament of Job*; moreover, the events surrounding the inheritance of Job's three daughters at the end of this text, taken together, probably represent the most explicit example in biblical or apocryphal texts of engagement with what can only be described as feminine language. Not coincidentally, this text also directly fuses ideas of patience with feminine language, so that the *Testament of Job* and the early *passios* that feature female protagonists demonstrate the generation of an important tradition (and the generation of a literary genre best called patience literature) in Western culture, where women become famous for patience and endurance just as men can gain honor through exhibiting the traditional manly virtues.

Brent D. Shaw, in his very important and influential article "Body/Power/ Identity: Passions of the Martyrs," published in 1996, argues that a new means of self-identification emerges in the late antique period.[1] Documents, literary compositions, and other kinds of cultural material record a revaluation of the endurance of suffering, often denoted by the Greek abstract noun *hypomonē* (ὑπομονή),

---

[1] Shaw, "Body/Power/Identity: Passions of the Martyrs," *JECS* 4 (1996): 279; see also 278. Subsequent references to this article will be given in the text in parentheses.

as a new "subjectivity," to use Judith Perkins's term.[2] For example, Ignatius of Antioch (ca. 108 C.E.) announces, "I desire (or 'love') to suffer," a phrase almost inconceivable in works written just a few years before, and "nobility through patience" becomes possible and desirable, as many late antique compositions concerning martyrs and similar protagonists attest ("Body," 289 and n. 65, 309).[3] Perkins then identifies Shaw's idea of a civic body as the prototype for "the Christian community," which is defined and strengthened by the new processes of self-identification.[4] I would go further and distinguish a new literary genre that is based on the revaluation of suffering that these critics have identified. I call the new genre patience literature, which "features and praises, explicitly or implicitly, the 'ability to endure,' to keep on being the same person despite oppressive suffering, that Shaw notices as a developing aspect of self-definition in characters from various Hellenic, Jewish, and Latin works, starting about 200 years before Christ."[5]

Examples of patience literature occur in both secular and sacred cultural materials, for instance, romantic adventure stories such as Longus's *Daphnis and Chloe* and Achilles Tatius's *The Adventures of Leucippe and Clitophon*, and exemplary biographies as varied in their content as Tertullian's story of Leaena, Perpetua's highly evocative dreams and martyrdom, and Blandina's torture and execution.[6] The case of the last-named conveniently provides representative attributes of a typical example of patience literature. Her story is preserved only in Eusebius's *Historia Ecclesia* (written in Greek), in a letter traditionally called "The Martyrs of Lyon and Vienne." The events occur about 177 C.E. After acknowledging that readers might be predisposed to judge Blandina as "cheap" and "ugly," "The Martyrs of Lyon and Vienne" provokes questioning of this seemingly sexist attitude because Blandina, a slave, becomes a "symbol of social reversal": she defeats expectations and eclipses her mistress's fame.[7] This martyr's trials, in three successive episodes,

---

[2] Perkins, "Space, Place, Voice in the *Acts* of the Martyrs and the Greek Romance," in *Mimesis and Intertextuality in Antiquity and Christianity* (ed. Dennis R. MacDonald; SAC; Harrisburg, PA: Trinity Press International, 2001), 117.

[3] See Ignatius, *Epistle to the Trallians*, in P. Th. Camelot, ed., *Ignatius of Antioch, Lettres* (4th ed.; SC 10; Paris: Cerf, 1969), 4.1.

[4] Perkins, "Space, Place, Voice," 118; eadem, *The Suffering Self: Pain and Narrative Representation in the Early Christian Era* (London: Routledge, 1995), 109, 123. See Shaw, "Body," 311; see also 300.

[5] Robin Waugh, *The Genre of Medieval Patience Literature: Development, Duplication, and Gender* (New Middle Ages; New York: Palgrave Macmillan, 2012), 7. See also Shaw, "Body," 279; see also 278.

[6] Longus, *Daphnis and Chloe* (trans. George Thornley, rev. J. M. Edmonds; LCL; London: William Heinemann, 1935), 1.28.50-52, 2.20.95-97. Tertullian, *Apologeticum*, ed. E. Dekkers, in Tertullian, *Opera* (CCSL 1; Turnhout: Brepols, 1954) 50.8 (p. 170). For the lives of Perpetua and Blandina, see Herbert Musurillo, ed. and trans., *The Acts of the Christian Martyrs* (OECT; Oxford: Clarendon, 1972). Subsequent references to the martyrdoms will be to this edition, using parenthetical page references in the text. I also use Musurillo's facing-page translations.

[7] Virginia Burrus, *Saving Shame: Martyrs, Saints, and Other Abject Subjects* (Divinations; Philadelphia: University of Pennsylvania Press, 2008), 25. For female slaves, see Christine Trevett,

receive detailed descriptions, and Blandina's final appearance marks the climax of the narrative. She appears and dies last in her group of believers, outlasts the male adolescent who is tortured alongside her, supplants the male martyr who seemed to be the central figure of this *passio* at the outset, Vettius Epagathus, and receives much fulsome praise throughout the narrative (Musurillo, 65, 67). Blandina's martyrdom ends with the judgment that "the pagans themselves admitted that no woman had ever suffered so much in their experience" (81). This extreme language asserts that she supersedes all other martyrs as "the ultimate virtuoso of torture," a phrase by Elizabeth A. Castelli that rightly characterizes the typical protagonists of patience literature as exhibitors of a (sometimes rather jarring) mixture of heroic attributes and passive ones (see Musurillo, 63, 103, 131, 205, 217, 287).[8]

Obviously, Shaw's and Perkins's analyses fit the content of the earliest examples of patience literature as I have outlined it in a very convincing fashion.[9] But Shaw goes on to argue for the existence of a sharp polarization between traditional masculine values and feminine ones just before and after the *passios* start to appear in large numbers. He opposes "voice, activity, aggression, closure, penetration, and the ability to inflict pain and suffering" to "silence, passivity, submissiveness, openness, [and] suffering" ("Body," 279).[10] I am uncomfortable with this very schematic division, which is frequently taken for granted by specialists in many periods, including the early medieval one, and I am surprised at the paucity of criticism concerning Shaw's two proposed categories when such reevaluation of attitudes toward gender divisions allows so much scope for elaboration.[11]

In contrast to Shaw, some critics, for example, Castelli, argue that early saints' lives and accounts of martyrdoms "do not simply rearticulate the hegemonic

---

Christian Women and the Time of the Apostolic Fathers (AD c. 80–160): Corinth, Rome and Asia Minor (Cardiff: University of Wales Press, 2006), 201–3.

[8] Castelli, *Visions and Voyeurism: Holy Women and the Politics of Sight in Early Christianity* (Protocol of the Colloquy of the Center for Hermeneutical Studies n.s. 2; Berkeley: Center for Hermeneutical Studies, 1995), 19. I here draw on my *Genre of Medieval Patience Literature*, 13; see also 12.

[9] Daniel Boyarin produces an analysis of the origins of Western martyrdom, synthesizing material from many traditions. See his *Dying for God: Martyrdom and the Making of Christianity and Judaism* (Figurae; Stanford: Stanford University Press, 1999), 117. A recent historical account of early Christian martyrdoms occurs in Elizabeth A. Castelli, *Martyrdom and Memory: Early Christian Culture Making* (Gender, Theory, Religion; New York: Columbia University Press, 2004), 33–59. Of course all saints' lives are not examples of patience literature, and there are examples of patience literature that are not saints' lives.

[10] In setting up his categories, Shaw has certain attitudes toward the body in mind. The attitudes toward the body that figure in the revaluation of suffering are "startling" in their novelty, according to Perkins. See her "The Rhetoric of the Maternal Body in the *Passion of Perpetua*," in *Mapping Gender in Ancient Religious Discourses* (ed. Todd Penner and Caroline Vander Stichele; BibInt; Leiden: Brill, 2007), 317.

[11] See the discussions of gender issues by Castelli (*Martyrdom and Memory*, 59–68) and Boyarin (*Dying for God*, 67–92).

gendered order, nor do they simply deconstruct it; rather, they stretch its boundaries and, if only for a moment, call it into question." Such arguments seem to be gathering strength.[12] The evidence for such questioning of traditional gender roles exists in the remarkably egalitarian ideals of the early Christian apologists,[13] and in the startlingly expressive behaviors of many female characters in the early martyrologies: Agathonicē, Perpetua, Felicitas, Potamiaena, Irenē, Agapē, Chionē, and Crispina (see Musurillo, 25, 27, 29, 34–37, 67, 69, 75, 106–31, 280–93, 302–9).[14] One may conclude that, in "certain late antique and medieval compositions, women become famous for patience in the way that men are famous for the traditional heroic virtues, such as physical strength and courage, and that this new kind of fame leads to" gendered patience literature.[15] I do not mean to propose the existence of a utopia of feminine language that flourished in a kind of ideal world of early, egalitarian patience literature and sainthood before the usual male attitudes reasserted themselves. Patience literature, like almost all literary traditions, mainly and primarily supports the dominant, male-established attitudes. In order to analyze it thoroughly and effectively, one must do so "without *nostalgia*, that is outside of the myth of a purely maternal or paternal language, a lost native country of thought."[16] Nevertheless, one may observe engagements with the possibility of

---

[12] Elizabeth A. Castelli, "'I Will Make Mary Male': Pieties of the Body and Gender Transformation of Christian Women in Late Antiquity," in *Body Guards: The Cultural Politics of Gender Ambiguity* (ed. Julia Epstein and Kristina Straub; New York: Routledge, 1991), 33; see also 31, 42. I use Alcuin Blamires's term "profeminine" because it avoids the anachronisms and confusions that result when one tries to apply the term "feminist" to medieval texts. See Blamires, *The Case for Women in Medieval Culture* (Oxford: Clarendon, 1997), 171, 19–49. I do not mean to imply that any religion is more inherently sexist than any other.

[13] See Gal 3:28. I use *The Catholic Bible: Douay-Rheims Version* (Charlotte, NC: Saint Benedict Press, 2009), because it best represents the Bible in use in most western European locations during the Middle Ages. I am aware that the canon of scriptural texts was fluid and controversial during the late antique period. The egalitarian rhetoric in early Christian texts has been noted very frequently by many critics of many periods, but, almost certainly due to adamant sexism (see Evelyn Birge Vitz, "Gender and Martyrdom," *Medievalia et Humanistica* n.s. 26 [1999]: 92), it strangely still evades the attention that it deserves for its significance. See Clarissa W. Atkinson, *The Oldest Vocation: Christian Motherhood in the Middle Ages* (Ithaca, NY: Cornell University Press, 1991), 21; Bruce W. Winter, *Roman Wives, Roman Widows: The Appearance of New Women and the Pauline Communities* (Grand Rapids: Eerdmans, 2003), 8–9; Jo Ann McNamara, "Sexual Equality and the Cult of Virginity in Early Christian Thought," in *Women in Early Christianity* (ed. David M. Scholer; Studies in Early Christianity 14; New York: Garland, 1993), 220, 223; Barbara Newman, *From Virile Woman to WomanChrist: Studies in Medieval Religion and Literature* (Middle Ages Series; Philadelphia: University of Pennsylvania Press, 1995), 80; and Elisabeth Schüssler Fiorenza, *In Memory of Her: A Feminist Theological Reconstruction of Christian Origins* (New York: Crossroad, 1983), 175–84.

[14] See Waugh, *Genre of Medieval Patience Literature*, 15–24. For the great interest in female saints during this period, see Thomas J. Heffernan, *Sacred Biography: Saints and Their Biographers in the Middle Ages* (Oxford: Oxford University Press, 1988), 216–17.

[15] Waugh, *Genre of Medieval Patience Literature*, 1.

[16] Jacques Derrida, *Margins of Philosophy* (trans. Alan Bass; Chicago: University of Chicago

feminine political consciousness and even feminine language at several junctures of literary history, including the early medieval period.[17] Language is irretrievably male, so these engagements are extremely brief; but careful observation can expose them. They usually occur at "fortuitous conjuncture[s]" of crises in attitudes toward language and subjectivity, at moments when language itself is under strain because it proves inadequate for the expression of people's ideas.[18] New genres, of which patience literature is a representative example, also characteristically appear at such moments. The combination of relatively new religious beliefs with the emotional extremes that martyrs would experience during their interrogations, tortures, and other persecutions would seem to offer ideal conditions, then, for glimpses of attempts at newly conceived languages; hence, a few examples of patience literature allow extremely fleeting and usually paradoxical instances of women's speech and of speech-related actions to occur in highly individual spaces outside of the typical male-established structures. The events surrounding the inheritance of Job's three daughters at the end of the *Testament of Job*, taken together, probably represent the most explicit example of one of these engagements with feminine language. Not coincidentally, this text also directly fuses ideas of patience with feminine language,

---

Press, 1982), 27. Shaw is certainly correct in cautioning critics against wishful thinking and in noting that a few isolated examples of works composed by women, or a few works that would seem to put forward remarkably feminist attitudes, cannot make up a "great, but lost, tradition of female writers" (Shaw, "Passion of Perpetua," *Past and Present* 139 [1993]: 16 n. 41). Caroline Walker Bynum rightly issues similar warnings concerning any utopian views about the later Middle Ages (*Jesus as Mother: Studies in the Spirituality of the High Middle Ages* [Berkeley: University of California Press, 1982], 135–46).

[17] The late antique era is rich in the possibility of feminine political consciousness because the level of participation by women in patience narratives from both before and after the revaluation of endurance that Shaw proposes is relatively high when one considers how rarely female characters come to the fore in canonical works. See Shaw, "Passion of Perpetua," 13–15. To use terms of a more historical and less literary flavor, many critics have noted that the professed egalitarianism of Christianity must be inimical to the political beliefs associated with the Roman Empire. See Mary Ann Rossi, "The Passion of Perpetua, Everywoman of Late Antiquity," in *Pagan and Christian Anxiety: A Response to E. R. Dodds* (ed. R. C. Smith and J. Lounibos; Lanham, MD: University Press of America, 1984), 55; Giselle de Nie, "'Consciousness Fecund through God': From Male Fighter to Spiritual Bride-Mother in Late Antique Female Sanctity," in *Sanctity and Motherhood: Essays on Holy Mothers in the Middle Ages* (ed. Anneke B. Mulder-Bakker; New York: Garland, 1995), 104, 108; and Castelli, "'I Will Make Mary Male,'" 30. The "discourse of virginity" concerning, for example, Saint Thecla, "opposes the very notion of sexual hierarchy" and is "radically liberating," according to Maud Burnett McInerney, *Eloquent Virgins from Thecla to Joan of Arc* (New Middle Ages; New York: Palgrave Macmillan, 2003), 11.

[18] Shaw, "Passion of Perpetua," 20. An example of one of these crises is that the rhetoric of egalitarianism was often related to the late antique sensing of an imminent apocalypse, when all earthly social distinctions would be rendered irrelevant. See Tertullian, *Apol.* 1.42.8 (pp. 157–58). Both the apocalypse idea and the concentration of political upheaval and suffering come at least in part from Jewish tradition and Scripture. See Lee Patterson, *Temporal Circumstances: Form and History in the Canterbury Tales* (New Middle Ages; New York: Palgrave Macmillan, 2006), 140–45; and Boyarin, *Dying for God*, 1–41.

while Maria Haralambakis's recent proposal that the *Testament of Job* is closest to a saint's life in its generic characteristics bolsters even further the patience connection that I have made.[19]

To be fair, Shaw detects a melding of male and female virtues into one in the *Testament of Job*. This text is a Greek pseudepigraphic work that has been dated to both pre-Christian and post-Christian times: the range is ca. 200 B.C.E.–ca. 200 C.E. Early-twentieth-century critics tended to favor a pre-Christian date. H. F. D. Sparks notes that certain phrases in the text suggest that the author was "familiar with the New Testament as well as the Old," but he acknowledges that these passages are probably not "deliberate allusions," and that the *Testament of Job* contains no explicitly Christian content.[20] Since the few existing manuscripts of the text date from the eleventh and thirteenth centuries and the internal evidence is inconclusive, any proposed date for this work is a supposition. The first century C.E. seems a good compromise.[21] Shaw includes discussion of the *Testament of Job* in his article that proposes the early antique revaluation of suffering because this work would seem to fit his argument admirably.

Certainly this work is remarkable for promoting the virtue of patience explicitly, while the original OT book of Job does not: "Endurance is Job's cardinal virtue"; it is "better than anything" (Shaw, "Body," 282; *T. Job* 27).[22] In the book of Job, in contrast, the protagonist discourses over several chapters on the subject of his suffering (29; 30; 31), regrets his change in fortune, and even accuses God of cruelty and hatred (30:21). Instead, according to Shaw, one may note in the *Testament of*

---

[19] Haralambakis, *The Testament of Job: Text, Narrative, and Reception History* (Library of Second Temple Studies 80; London: Bloomsbury T&T Clark, 2012), 171–72. I would only adjust Haralambakis's genre identification by arguing for the *Testament of Job* as an example of patience literature versus hagiography. An advantage of the designation "patience literature" is that it allows for examples from both sacred and secular canons and traditions without privileging sacred over secular, or vice versa. Shaw's idea of the revaluation of suffering is inherent in cultural materials of both a sacred and secular nature, and evidence for this revaluation is apparent in both sacred and secular works as soon as one may detect it and continuously thereafter.

[20] See "The Testament of Job," in *AOT*, 617–19. The text occurs on pp. 622–48, and subsequent references will occur in my text parenthetically by chapter number. For the date of this work, see also B. Schaller, "Das Testament Hiobs und die Septuaginta-Übersetzung des Buches Hiob," *Bib* 61 (1980): 377–406; and Rudolph P. Spittler, "Testament of Job," in *OTP* 1:833–36, 864. For the possible origins of the *Testament of Job*, see H. C. Kee, "Satan, Magic, and Salvation in the Testament of Job," in *Society of Biblical Literature 1974 Seminar Papers* (ed. George MacRae; 2 vols.; Cambridge, MA: Society of Biblical Literature, 1974) 1:53–76.

[21] See Sparks, "Testament of Job," 617.

[22] For classical and medieval attempts at a positive definition of patience, see Ralph Hanna III, "Some Commonplaces of Late Medieval Patience Discussions: An Introduction," in *The Triumph of Patience: Medieval and Renaissance Studies* (ed. Gerald J. Schiffhorst; Orlando: University Presses of Florida, 1978), 68–77. Augustine says that patience is *aequo animo mala tolerare*, "to endure external evils with an even mind" (Augustine, *De patientia* [ed. Joseph Zycha; CSEL 41; Vienna: Tempsky, 1900]), ch. 2; see also chs. 17; 23; 29. I use Hanna's translations of the passages that he quotes. Augustine is influenced by Gal 5.22 and Eph 4.2.

Job "a usurpation of the former conception [*hypomonē*] by the now increasing[ly] dominant one of patience," which is associated with the pain of childbirth ("Body," 282 n. 36),[23] and these associations together with other factors cause Shaw to argue for a "not-too-covert" "'feminization' of the text as compared to its canonical OT predecessor" (281).[24] Yet, apparently for Shaw, feminization—a term that suggests the artificial and ephemeral application of rather insubstantial ideas—means the simple presence of more female characters than occur in the original work.[25] He largely ignores any *attitudes* to women that the *Testament of Job* might display, whereas the primary texts of patience literature nearly always betray bouts of confusion and contradiction that inevitably boil up when endurance (or any other virtue for that matter) is touted as desirable for both men and women. The virtue contest between the sexes that almost invariably ensues means that unexpected attitudes toward women arise in, for instance, the early accounts of martyrdoms, and these attitudes should contribute to Shaw's observations concerning the "feminized rhetoric" that he discovers, but they do not. Moreover, there is a decided movement toward what can only be described as feminine rhetoric in these works and in related works as well—and feminine rhetoric, as opposed to feminized rhetoric, allows readers to perceive glimpses of profeminine attitudes and to identify this work as an example of gendered patience literature.[26]

---

[23] Shaw sees Seneca's lengthy discussion of patience as evidence that the virtue's reputation is growing. Seneca admits no difference between female bravery and male, at least in substance: the only difference is in the way that the two corresponding virtues are shown. He distinguishes between mere endurance and "brave" endurance. See Seneca, *De ira*, in Seneca, *Moral Essays* (trans. John W. Basore; 3 vols.; LCL; London: William Heinemann, 1928), 1.2.12.6; Shaw, "Body," 292–94 and nn. 75–78, 82. The idea of having a well-controlled mind, according to Hanna, "represents the Christianization of the central Stoic virtue *apatheia*," and, in Seneca's works, "patience is elevated to a fully heroic self control" ("Some Commonplaces," 77; see also nn. 11 and 12).

[24] Shaw first uses the phrase "feminized rhetoric" to describe changes in the depictions of women that he observes in 4 Maccabees as opposed to 2 Maccabees (see "Body," 284; see also 283; and his "Passion of Perpetua," 13 and n. 36).

[25] Any incidence of female characters in Scriptures, apocryphal works, and the accounts of martyrs is noteworthy, due to its rarity. Shaw gives the most balanced account of the probable incidence of female as opposed to male martyrs in the early passionals (see "Passion of Perpetua," 3–15). He suggests that there may have been local variations in this comparison and notes the unusually high number of North African female martyrs (p. 14). Atkinson observes that, soon after the earliest period of Christianity, "powerful voices within the Christian movement were working to restore women to the patriarchal household" (*Oldest Vocation*, 18–19). In the later Middle Ages, female saints typically drop to about 20 percent of the corpus. See Catherine Sanok, *Her Life Historical: Exemplarity and Female Saints' Lives in Late Medieval England* (Middle Ages Series; Philadelphia: University of Pennsylvania Press, 2007), 39.

[26] The role of women in the *Testament of Job* remains controversial. On the one hand, see Susan R. Garrett, "The Weaker Sex in the *Testament of Job*," *JBL* 112 (1993): 69–70; John J. Collins, "Structure and Meaning of the *Testament of Job*," *Society of Biblical Literature 1974 Seminar Papers*, 1:44; and Spittler, "Testament of Job," 864. On the other, see Rebecca Lesses, "The Daughters of

The *Testament of Job*, like the original book of Job, comes across as (among other things) a study in certain contrasts between the sexes during which a man demonstrates endurance and a woman does not.[27] The most detailed depiction of a woman in the *Testament* is of Job's wife, to whom it gives a name, Sitidos (she is not named in the book of Job). Sitidos dies happily in the course of the narrative, but her valuing of material things—for example, her hair that she is obliged to sell—contrasts with Job's renunciation of them. More importantly, Job's suffering always leaves his personal status intact. Neighboring chieftains come to visit him even in the worst depths of his personal losses and even during the most humiliating and painful manifestations of his illnesses. But Job's new-found poverty leads to Sitidos becoming a slave, a loss of social status that she, unlike her husband, laments at length (22–25; 39). Readers would thus be justified in concluding that a man's status is inherent and unassailable, while a woman's is much more external to her, more unstable, and almost entirely dependent on her relationship to a man.

On the other hand, overtly "profeminine" ideas (as opposed to Shaw's idea of "feminization") emerge when, near its end, the story focuses on Job's daughters. They become the "main characters," according to Shaw ("Body," 283), and this role is certainly unusual for women during this period.[28] Yet the daughters' association with their father's patience makes them even more unusual and significant. Since Job's second family is, among other things, one of God's rewards for his loyalty, any children that outlive him would be in some ways the products of his patience. Moreover, he passes the wisdom of patience down to them in the form of his testament, his story, and in the form of more tangible inheritances, as becomes clear when he details the bequests in an oral version of his will (45). Notably, both the original OT account and the *Testament of Job* depict him in the unusual act of bestowing goods upon daughters as well as sons: "And there were not found in all the earth women so beautiful as the daughters of Job: and their father gave them inheritance among their brethren" (Job 42:15). This even-handedness confirms that his endurance has caused him to think in more egalitarian terms than previously concerning the sexes; it also may suggest that, by the time the *Testament of Job* was written, women and patience were often associated with one another—but not as Shaw defines this association, with his attribution of passivity to women.

Unlike the daughters in the *Testament of Job*, the sons receive land, a traditionally male preserve and the type of inheritance traditionally regarded as the most

---

Job," in *Searching the Scriptures*, vol. 2, *A Feminist Commentary* (ed. Elisabeth Schüssler Fiorenza; New York: Crossroad, 1994), 140–43, 147.

[27] See Robert A. Kugler and Richard L. Rohrbaugh, "On Women and Honor in the *Testament of Job*," *JSP* 14 (2004): 60–61.

[28] See Collins, "Structure and Meaning in the *Testament of Job*," 48, Pieter W. van der Horst, "Images of Women in the *Testament of Job*," in *Studies on the Testament of Job* (ed. Michael A. Knibb and Pieter W. van der Horst; SNTSMS 66; Cambridge: Cambridge University Press, 1989), 105–6; and Nancy Klancher, "The Male Soul in Drag: Women-as-Job in the *Testament of Job*," *JSP* 19 (2010): 231–36.

lasting. The unusually assertive girls also receive an inheritance, one *chordē* ("girdle") each, but only after they have asked, "Father, are we not also your children? Why have you not given us a share in your property?" When they complain further and ask how they are to make a living with such objects, statements that come close to demonstrating a highly unusual ambition by women in Scripture to be both independent and equal to men, Job claims that his daughters' inheritance is "better than that of your seven brothers" (*T. Job* 46).[29] The girls' gifts are

> of many colours, such as no man could possibly describe; for they were not of earth but of heaven, flashing with sparks of fire like the rays of the sun. And he gave one cord each to his daughters, saying, "Take them and gird them round you, that they may keep you safe all the days of your life and fill you with every good thing." (46)

I am surprised that these cords have not received more attention, because they certainly seem to propose a female inheritance distinct from any male one.[30] Anything girded around the waist symbolizes fertility, and these girdles also embody powers of healing and personal security—ideas traditionally associated with women.[31] Yet Job's gifts are also emblems of masculine power that he has gained through his personal relationship with (the male) God. The Lord demands that Job "gird up [his] loins like a man," presumably with one or more of these same belts, in order to endure his trials (47). Significantly, his seven sons receive no inheritance that suggests intimations of heaven, whereas his three daughters do. Correspondingly, the women are named in the *Testament of Job* just as they are in the original book of Job (42:13–14). Job's sons are not.

---

[29] For the original term for these girdles, see *The Testament of Job according to the SV Text* (ed. Robert A. Kraft et al.; SBLTT 5, Pseudepigrapha Series 4; Missoula, MT: Society of Biblical Literature and Scholars Press, 1974), 79 n. 46.8. Klancher notes that the cords connect Job with his legacy and his daughters, but she argues that the daughters are mere reflections of their father ("Male Soul in Drag," 234, 237–38). However, I find these women more complicated than Klancher's view would suggest.

[30] A detailed study of the daughters' cords and their ritual purpose has recently appeared: Jennifer Zilm, "Multi-Coloured like Woven Works: Gender, Ritual Clothing and Praying with the Angels in the Dead Sea Scrolls and the Testament of Job," in *Prayer and Poetry in the Dead Sea Scrolls and Related Literature: Essays in Honor of Eileen Schuller on the Occasion of her 65th Birthday* (ed. Jeremy Penner, Ken M. Penner, and Cecilia Wassen; STDJ 98; Leiden: Brill, 2012), 437–51. See also Jane Schaberg, *The Resurrection of Mary Magdalene: Legends, Apocrypha, and the Christian Testament* (New York: Continuum, 2002), 312–13.

[31] There are many established traditions concerning inheritance in ancient Jewish society. For the many rabbinic traditions behind this text, see Peter Machinist, "Job's Daughters and Their Inheritance in the *Testament of Job* and Its Biblical Congeners," in *The Echoes of Many Texts: Reflections on Jewish and Christian Traditions. Essays in Honor of Lou H. Silberman* (ed. William G. Dever and J. Edward Wright; BJS 313; Atlanta: Scholars Press, 1996), 67–80; Randall D. Chestnutt, "Revelatory Experiences Attributed to Biblical Women in Early Jewish Literature," in *"Women like This": New Perspectives on Jewish Women in the Greco-Roman World* (ed. Amy-Jill Levine; SBLEJL 1; Atlanta: Scholars Press, 1991), 107–25; and Schaberg, *Resurrection of Mary Magdalene*, 311.

Though one may certainly see land as the quintessential gift from God, emblematic of the covenant and of the future fertility and prosperity of the people of Israel, such a gift is earthly, whereas the girdles come from heaven. They are greater gifts than the sons' precisely because they are more symbolic and mystical than land. According to the text, they are so ideal as to defy description (46). Furthermore, the *Testament* has foreshadowed their appearance by including near the start of the narrative a promise by God of fame and other extremely desirable benefits that Job will attain by remaining faithful (4). Since Job healed himself with the cords after God announced his restoration, they are (among other things) highly charged representations not only of his triumph and story but also of his direct dialogue with the Lord, his reception of wisdom through suffering, and all of the other God-ordained benefits of his life. Since the belts are miraculous, "of heaven," and come to the daughters (at one remove) from God, they represent God's promise of heaven to believers. Moreover, their power is more than emblematic. The text demonstrates that they retain magical powers after Job hands them over. He says,

> And after [the girding] my body received strength through the Lord.... And the Lord spoke to me in power, showing me what has been and what will be. Consequently, my children, with these cords you will never now have the Enemy arrayed against you nor even his thoughts in your hearts, because it is the Father's amulet. Get up, then, and gird them round you before I die, so that you may be able to see those who are coming for my soul and marvel at God's creatures. (47)

His prediction of visionary and prophetic powers comes true. When the first daughter, Hemera, puts on her girdle, "she assumed another heart, no longer minding earthly things" (48). Her sisters, at their girdings, take on the same kind of "other heart."

The female-directed inheritance from God through Job to these women is significant also in that it amounts to a new language (cf. Acts 2:1–21). When Hemera puts her belt on, "she g[i]ve[s] utterance in the speech of angels, sending up a hymn to God after the pattern of the angels' hymnody; and the Spirit let the hymns she uttered be recorded on her robe" (*T. Job* 48). Angels are usually deemed to be either sexless or male when the issue of their sex comes up, so this miraculous language, arriving in both oral and written form, is relayed to Hemera from presumably masculine figures and comes ultimately from a masculine source: God. Yet there is at least the suggestion that this angelic language is essentially feminine once she utters it, because there is no account of Job's sons taking part in these instances of ecstatic speech, and the text omits to say if anyone besides Hemera can read the hymns that are recorded on her robe.[32] In fact, one could interpret the three instances of ecstatic speech from each daughter in turn as so exclusive that

---

[32] The exclusivity of the ecstatic statements to Job's daughters is not in every version of the *Testament of Job*. The Coptic version, unlike the Greek one, features Job's brother, Nereos, who writes down the hymns of the women. See Haralambakis, *Testament of Job*, 118.

they amount to speeches in three separate languages. Each vision and spoken manifestation thereof are described as quite distinct in content from the others when, in other respects, the women's visionary experiences are similar. Cassia's "mouth took up the speech of the heavenly powers, and she lauded the worship of the heavenly sanctuary" (49). Amaltheias-Keras "spoke in the language of the cherubim, extolling the Lord of Virtues, and proclaiming their glory" (50).

Moreover, their language(s) seem to be akin to music, and this connection is telling when music makes up so much a part of Julia Kristeva's theory of the existence of an exclusively feminine language.[33] In the same vein, Job, once he realizes his approaching death, gives two of the daughters musical instruments: a lyre and a tambourine. The third receives a censer, affirming a priestlike role for all three. Musical instruments, together with the dispensing of incense, intimate cultic activity, perhaps deliberately recalling that of Miriam and Judith (Exod 15:20-21; Jdt 16:12-19). Job's daughters, as they "g[i]ve praise and honour, each in her special tongue," then receive a vision of their father's soul being taken up into heaven, with only Job and the daughters participating in this vision, "but no one else" (52). Clearly, access to God, complete with unique languages and visions, is passed only into the female line in this instance, and Job's patience under extreme endurance would seem to be a crucial factor in the engendering and continuation of this familial relationship with God. In fact, I interpret the revaluation of endurance as personified in Job during this work as the beginning of his career as a hero of patience (he lacks patience in the OT version of the story), and I interpret the inheritance of his daughters as an explicit inheritance of their father's patience. Indeed, his subsequent and remarkable reputation as a patience figure during the Middle Ages and beyond suggests that the *Testament of Job*—or at least the traditions represented in this text—was more influential than critics have previously thought.

The inheritance moment also marks the beginning of the gendering of patience literature. If patience is the "essence" of Job, as has become proverbial, then it matters that his female descendants are much more thoroughly described than his male ones—not only in the *Testament of Job* but also in the OT version of his story, while the ecstatic experiences of the three daughters could not be more explicit in presenting feminine rhetoric as opposed to feminized rhetoric. Admittedly, the *Testament* is unlikely to act as a major source for later works or to become one of the more important texts in the history of patience literature, because in general it seems to lack influence.[34] It fails to gain acceptance as a canonical work

---

[33] See Julia Kristeva, *Desire in Language: A Semiotic Approach to Literature and Art* (ed. Leon S. Roudiez; trans. Thomas Gora, Alice Jardine, and Roudiez; European Perspectives; New York: Columbia University Press, 1980), 133-34. Significantly, Eulalia, a female martyr described by Prudentius boasts a name that means "she who speaks well" (Shaw, "Body," 306). See *Peristephanon*, in *Prudentius* (ed. H. J. Thomson; 2 vols.; LCL; Cambridge, MA: Harvard University Press, 1969]. vol. 2, lines 142-56).

[34] For the reception history of this work, see Haralambakis, *Testament of Job*, 141-72.

among the other books of the OT, while Job himself (a man) goes on to become the quintessential and eventually proverbial figure of patience in much of Western literature and in other kinds of cultural material through the widest possible dissemination of his story in canonical Scripture. The *Testament of Job* did not receive nearly as much interest as other apocryphal texts did, and do. Nevertheless, the twin ideas of women as the inheritors of heroic patience and as the ecstatic speakers of an exclusive language are more obvious in this text than in any other.

One may certainly then read any martyrologies that feature female protagonists (and there are quite a few of them) as potential participants in a tradition of female patience—certainly the fact that a suddenly emerging body of literature often describes women using pseudo-heroic language is a very remarkable development in literary history (see Musurillo, 79–81). For instance Perpetua demonstrates *constantia et animi sublimitate* (124), "perseverance and nobility of soul" (125), and stares down the mob as she enters the arena to be martyred (126–27). So why has the idea of heroic patience as a particularly female attribute not been discussed more thoroughly and positively by the requisite critics?

One reason is an unfortunate yet hugely popular misinterpretation of Michel Foucault's social criticism. Shaw's article, for instance, relies on an interpretation of Foucault's ideas concerning power and sexuality, and these ideas can be oversimplified and taken out of context if, for instance, one uses the descriptions of aspects of sexuality in *The Use of Pleasure* to set up a distinction between Foucault's earlier, more theoretical (and hence perhaps more difficult) ideas and his later, more descriptive ideas concerning dominant men and passive women. Famously, Foucault quotes Aristotle in order to distinguish between "agents" and "patients": "the female, as female, is passive, and the male, as male, is active,'" as if this division had a peculiar authority.[35] But, in the first volume of his *History of Sexuality*, Foucault is very specific about the actual efficacy of any kind of "top down" manifestation of power. Power instead is "multiple" and "mobile," so that any kind of power distinction, let alone an identifiable hierarchy between identifiable agents and patients, is always fluid, localized, and questionable.[36]

Haralambakis concentrates on the Eastern European tradition rather than that of Western Europe during her discussion.

[35] Foucault, *The History of Sexuality*, vol. 2, *The Use of Pleasure* (trans. Robert Hurley; New York: Vintage, 1990) 46; see also 47. Shaw uses Aristotle as one of his examples of writers who make distinctions between male and female virtues: "submission and lack of resistance comes from effeminacy or cowardice" ("Body," 285). Cf. Castelli, "'I Will Make Mary Male,'" 31: "Masculine and feminine, male and female, man and woman are not always self-evident and parallel categories in ancient discourses." See also n. 4. Moreover, Eve Kosofsky Sedgwick has largely disposed of any idea that one may draw general conclusions concerning identity politics based on general attitudes toward sex acts (*Epistemology of the Closet* [Berkeley: University of California Press, 1990], 25–26).

[36] Foucault, *The History of Sexuality*, vol. 1, *An Introduction* (trans. Robert Hurley; New York: Vintage, 1990), 98; Derrida, *Margins of Philosophy*, 17.

One need only examine the behaviors of the protagonists of examples of patience literature in order to question the proposed hierarchy of active men versus passive women. For instance, the silence of the martyrs during the dialogue portions of their *passio*s can often be interpreted, somewhat paradoxically, as active.[37] Papylus, a protagonist in *The Martyrdom of Saints Carpus, Papylus, and Agathonicē*, which exists in both a Greek and a Latin version, is silent only after he has said, "I am a Christian, and you cannot hear any more from me than this; for there is nothing greater or nobler that I can say." He then declines to "utter a sound" during the ensuing tortures (Musurillo, 27). His silence, therefore, is an act of nonverbal communication that helps to prove his last point, reidentifies him, furthers his debate with the authorities, and fulfills his stated promise (27).[38] The Latin recension of the same story presents the active-silence motif in a slightly different way. The martyr says *iam uero me amplius audire non poteris* ("you will hear nothing further from me") after the proconsul has said *quid dicis* ("what say you?"), a request that the persecutor repeats after the martyr's torture. Though this version presents Papylus as less aggressive than he appears in the Greek recension, his silence cannot be merely passive, because it works as an explicit reply to—and as a comprehensive rejection of—the proconsul's questions and desires (30–33). In general, the martyrs' acts of silence or speech are so overmastering that they result in "the power of judgment claimed by the torturer [being] wrested from him," in the words of Virginia Burrus.[39] And there are many examples of early female martyrs who are just as active and talkative as their male counterparts: Margaret of Antioch, Crispina, Eulalia, Perpetua, and Agnes, to name just five.[40]

A second reason why Shaw in particular seems to shore up a connection

[37] Materials in patience literature can usually be divided into dialogue portions and suffering portions. The dialogue portion usually precedes the suffering portion and typically offers a chance for protagonists to (re)state their beliefs, (re)define their breaks with authority, and (re)identify themselves. In most martyrdoms, the dialogue portions take the form of legal or quasi-legal proceedings. See Waugh, *Genre of Medieval Patience Literature*, 24–27.

[38] See Robert Mills, "Can the Virgin Martyr Speak?" in *Medieval Virginities* (ed. Anke Bernau, Ruth Evans, and Sarah Salih; Religion and Culture in the Middle Ages; Toronto: University of Toronto Press, 2003), 195. This suspension between active and passive suits many later figures in patience literature. See, for instance, the discussion of saints in Martha Easton, "Pain, Torture, and Death in the Huntington Library *Legenda aurea*," in *Gender and Holiness: Men, Women, and Saints in Late Medieval Europe* (ed. Samantha J. E. Riches and Sarah Salih; Routledge Studies in Medieval Religion and Culture 1; London: Routledge, 2002), 62, and the discussion of Geoffrey Chaucer's depiction of Constance in Elizabeth Robertson, "The 'Elvysh' Power of Constance: Christian Feminism in Geoffrey Chaucer's *The Man of Law's Tale*," *Studies in the Age of Chaucer* 23 (2001): 173–74. See also Larissa Tracy, *Women of the Gilte Legende: A Selection of Middle English Saints Lives* (Cambridge: Brewer, 2003), 121; and McInerney, *Eloquent Virgins*, 9.

[39] Burrus, *Saving Shame*, 25; see also 26–27.

[40] See Vitz, "Gender and Martyrdom," 86; see also Mills, "Can the Virgin Martyr Speak?" 187–88, 194. Women's speech becomes a motif in later hagiography. See Tracy, *Women of the Gilte Legende*, 5, 21.

between female protagonists of patience works and passivity is his selective treatment of his chosen texts. Instead of qualifying or decentering his very schematic view of power relations between men and women outlined at the start of his article, he shifts his attention from an arresting discussion of Achilles Tatius's second-century Greek romance *The Adventures of Leucippe and Clitophon* to a discussion of the late fourth-century polemic Jerome's *Epistola 1*.[41] The latter work depicts an anonymous woman falsely accused of adultery and then tortured. It is highly sexualized, very theatrical, and it arrives later than the most influential *passios*. Jerome's contemporaries, moreover, were already distinguishing such stories as representative of a new kind of more theologically informed martyrdom than had been the case previously ("Body," 272–74).[42] Nevertheless, Shaw tends to gloss over this chronological gap between his two chosen texts and tends to downplay the profound generic differences between a romance and a patristic treatise.[43] To be sure, his close critical focus on Leucippe, the heroine of *The Adventures of Leucippe and Clitophon*, and on the woman falsely accused of adultery in Jerome's *Epistola 1* allows him to link femininity and passivity in an almost formulaic fashion (Achilles Tatius 6.21.345). But this tight focus means that he delays discussion of the martyrologies during his major argument. It would be much harder for him to argue that the more typical texts of the patience genre follow his two categories of "active and aggressive values entailed in manliness" as opposed to "the passive value of merely being able to endure" ("Body," 279). How, for instance, would he deal with Blandina, who eclipses the role of her mistress, suffers the same tortures as her male counterparts, and overmatches all of them by being the only martyr in her story who is described as "filled with . . . power" (Musurillo, 67)?[44]

[41] Jerome, *Epistola 1*, in F. A. Wright, ed., *Select Letters of St. Jerome* (LCL; London: William Heinemann, 1933), 1.7–9. See also Musurillo, 27–29. Jerome was particularly antifeminist and misogynist. See Newman, *From Virile Woman to WomanChrist*, 81.

[42] See Ambrose, *De Virginibus* (ed. Egnatius Cazzaniga; Corpus scriptorum latinorum Paravianum; Turin: G. B. Paravia, 1948), 1.2.8.

[43] He also tends to downplay the roles of women in *The Acts of Martyrs*, where they appear in groups, and alongside men. This slighting seems odd considering the historical significance of the martyrs. Eusebius in his *History* "describes the ordeals of no fewer than 146, naming ninety-seven of them" (G. A. Williamson, "Introduction" in Eusebius, *The History of the Church from Christ to Constantine* [trans. Williamson; Harmondsworth: Penguin, 1965], 23). Eusebius frequently praises the martyrs greatly and would hardly have included them in his *History* if he did not see them as an integral part of the narrative of the Christian church that he was writing. The alarm of Pliny the Younger at the sheer numbers of Christian martyrs in the second century C.E. also supports their historical significance. See Pliny the Younger, *Epistularum Libri Decem* (ed. R. A. B. Mynors; Scriptorum classicorum bibliotheca Oxoniensis; Oxford: Clarendon, 1963), 10.96.8, p. 339. For a translation, see Henry Bettenson, ed. and trans., *Documents of the Christian Church* (World's Classics; London: Oxford University Press, 1943), 5.

[44] For the power that the martyrs gain through the spectacle of their tortures, see Peter Brown, *The Cult of the Saints: Its Rise and Function in Latin Christianity* (Haskell Lectures in History of Religions n.s. 2; Chicago: University of Chicago Press, 1981), 106–27. Shaw's treatment of Blandina's story is puzzling. In his argument concerning the revaluation of suffering, he

To an extent, Shaw's approach to his chosen texts is justifiable. By treating them primarily as discrete works, regardless of their status as textual, scriptural, or historical authorities, he can concentrate on the evidence for endurance as a virtue pure and simple and treat these sources with a relatively even hand, privileging no account. Instead he can identify certain motifs, attitudes, patterns, and developments of his chosen texts in an objective fashion. However, I think that this new historicist approach leads him astray.[45] It is possible instead to argue, as Daniel Boyarin does, that "in the fourth century, we have a much more complex structure of gender in which both the masculinized aggressivity of the female martyr as *virago* and an almost contradictory feminized passivity as *virgo* are produced simultaneously."[46] And surely one may posit an even "more complex structure of gender" than stereotypical terms such as *virago* and *virgo* imply. Boyarin's observation would mean that cultural materials of all kinds in the late antique era frequently cross the boundaries between the "masculine" and "feminine" attributes that Shaw sets up and, in contrast to Shaw's tendency to slight women in his study of patience, I find that the incidence of women in patience literature from both before and after the revaluation of endurance as a virtue, an incidence that is parallel to the *Testament of Job* because this text straddles the two periods set out by Shaw, is a significant development. It is also difficult to accept Shaw's suggested disposal of virtues between the two genders as dominant when the classical authors do not in the end support it.[47] Indeed, Shaw admits that, in the classical age, any debate concerning the precise roles of "feminine" and "masculine" attitudes was often complex, heated, difficult to understand, and full of contradictory ideas ("Body," 284, 291–95). Having said all of this, I agree with Shaw's arguments much more often than I disagree with them, and he is most responsible for articulating

---

mentions her only after he has put forward his major argument concerning *hypomonē* ("Body," 308–9), so that she comes across as merely an example of the new, "ennobling" effect of the patience virtue. The fact that her *passio* and other works mark the establishment of an unusually heroic role for female protagonists seems to elude him, while, in another article, he compares her unfavorably with the North African martyr Perpetua, in an uncharacteristically subjective manner (see Shaw, "Passion of Perpetua," 17–19). Cf. Burrus, *Saving Shame*, 24, 26–27; Castelli, *Visions and Voyeurism*, 19; and Francine Cardman, "Acts of the Women Martyrs," in Scholer, *Women in Early Christianity*, 99, 102–3.

[45] See Hunter Cadzow, "New Historicism," in *The Johns Hopkins Guide to Literary Theory and Criticism* (ed. Michael Groden and Martin Kreiswirth; Baltimore: Johns Hopkins University Press, 1994), 534–40.

[46] Boyarin, *Dying for God*, 75.

[47] For instance, Cicero, so important in developing the political ideas of his era and, particularly, principles that backed up the preeminence of Rome, simply assumes that patience is important to any citizen: *Patientia est honestatis aut utilitatis causa rerum arduarum ac difficilium voluntaria ac diuturna perpessio*, "Patience is the willed and continuous endurance of laborious and difficult things for the sake of virtue or benefit" (*De inventione*, ed. Eduard Stroebel, in *Scripta quae manserunt omnia*, fasc. 2, *Rhetorici libri duo qui vocantur de inventione* [Leipzig: Teubner, 1965], 2.54.163, p. 149). For the translation and the use of this definition by Thomas Aquinas, see Hanna, "Some Commonplaces," 67–68 and n. 5.

the major texts of early patience literature so that the genre can become viable as a critical principle.

Feminine rhetoric is discernible in the most important patience works of the late antique period, despite the scholarly neglect of this rhetoric, and despite the necessary warning to overly idealistic critics that only glimpses of such rhetoric can ever emerge from the gloomy abyss of patriarchal tradition. There is no feminist utopia in the ancient world, even with the precocious appearance of egalitarian pronouncements at the onset of Christianity. However, one must not bury the pro-feminine attitudes that undeniably exist in patience literature under an idea of *hypomonē* that is too literary or too simplistic.

More importantly, the *Testament of Job* demonstrates most clearly the idea that women inherit, inhabit, and can claim rights to the virtue of patience from Job, when patience is often interpreted as a powerful, even miraculous attribute. The application of this virtue to women very specifically generates an important tradition that extends into and remains a characteristic tradition throughout the Middle Ages in the West. Geoffrey Chaucer writes in his *Clerk's Tale* (ca. 1390, appearing in Fragment IV of *The Canterbury Tales*):

> Men speke of Job, and moost for his humblesse,
> As clerkes, whan hem list, konne wel endite,
> Namely of men, but as in soothfastnesse,
> Though clerkes preise wommen but a lite,
> Ther kan no man in humblesse hym acquite
> As womman kan, ne kan been half so trewe
> As wommen been, but it be falle of newe.[48]

This passage occurs in the course of Chaucer's version of the story of Griselda, the most popular secular patience figure of the Middle Ages. With its featuring of a female protagonist who undergoes the most appalling mental tortures merely in order to fulfill a vow that she took under duress, Chaucer's *Clerk's Tale* represents the genre of patience literature at its most extreme.[49] This story, the *Testament of Job*, and the early *passios* that feature female protagonists all demonstrate in their very different ways the generation of an important tradition in Western culture, where women become famous for patience and endurance just as men can gain honor through exhibiting the traditional manly virtues.

---

[48] Geoffrey Chaucer, *The Clerk's Tale*, lines 932–38. See *The Riverside Chaucer* (ed. Larry D. Benson; 3rd ed.; Boston: Houghton Mifflin, 1987). William Langland (ca. 1387) uses the Virgin Mary and Mary Magdalene as his specific examples of patience (*Piers Plowman: An Edition of the C-Text* [ed. Derek Pearsall; York Medieval Texts; Berkeley: University of California Press, 1978], Passus 12, lines 131–36; see also lines 170–76, and Passus 15, lines 181–84, 274–78). Klancher notes similarities between the *Testament of Job* and early medieval works but does not discuss patience ("Male Soul in Drag," 239–43).

[49] See J. Burke Severs, *The Literary Relationships of Chaucer's "Clerkes Tale"* (New Haven: Yale University Press, 1942), 3–37; and Charlotte C. Morse, "The Exemplary Griselda," *Studies in the Age of Chaucer* 7 (1985): 55.

A Flaw in McIver and Carroll's Experiments to Determine Written Sources in the Gospels

MARK GOODACRE
Goodacre@duke.edu
Duke University, Durham, NC 27708

Robert McIver and Marie Carroll published an article in *JBL* in 2002 in which they discussed experiments with Australian undergraduate students that might help with determining the existence of written sources in the Gospels. They suggested that sixteen words in exact conjoined sequence provided a clear indicator of the presence of copying. However, McIver and Carroll transferred the results of their experiments in English to the Greek Synoptics without making any adjustments for the differences in language. A noninflected language like contemporary English takes more words to say something than an inflected language like Koine Greek. The problem can be illustrated by taking McIver and Carroll's list of Synoptic parallels that feature sixteen-word sequential agreements and higher, and comparing these parallels with English translations. In practically every case, the English sequential agreements are substantially higher. The presence of this important flaw in the conceptualizing of the experiments places a major question mark over McIver and Carroll's case.

In an article published in 2002, Robert K. McIver and Marie Carroll discuss a series of experiments with Australian undergraduate students to determine what would count as evidence for the copying of written sources. They attempt to explain the implications of their results for the study of the Synoptic Problem.[1] In the relatively short period since the publication of their work, it has often been cited

[1] Robert K. McIver and Marie Carroll, "Experiments to Develop Criteria for Determining the Existence of Written Sources, and Their Potential Implications for the Synoptic Problem," *JBL* 121 (2002): 667–87; and "Distinguishing Characteristics of Orally Transmitted Material When Compared to Material Transmitted by Literary Means," *Applied Cognitive Psychology* 18 (2004): 1251–69. For an excellent discussion of the first of these articles, drawing attention to some key difficulties in the application of the results, see John Poirier, "Memory, Written Sources and the Synoptic Problem: A Response to Robert K. McIver and Marie Carroll," *JBL* 123 (2004): 315–22.

favorably in discussions of the transmission of early Christian tradition,[2] and its main contention, that the presence of sixteen or more words in conjoined sequence[3] indicates the presence of written sources, is now accepted by some scholars as having been established.[4] Some are already engaged in the work of applying the criterion to related areas.[5]

There is a flaw in the way that McIver and Carroll apply the results of their experimental data to the texts of the Synoptic Gospels. The mistake is simple but important: their experimental data are in English whereas the Synoptic Gospels are in Greek.[6] Thus, although they regard the "strong cultural differences between the students taking part in these experiments and the anonymous writers who produced the Synoptic Gospels" as "self-evident,"[7] they do not take into account the key differences in language between contemporary English and Koine Greek. Having established their sixteen-word criterion for determining the presence of

---

[2] Most recently in Dale C. Allison, *Constructing Jesus: Memory, Imagination, and History* (Grand Rapids: Baker Academic, 2010), 9 n. 48, 30 n. 124. See also Birger A. Pearson, "A Q Community in Galilee?" *NTS* 50 (2004): 476–94, esp. 483.

[3] The figure is given as eighteen words in "Distinguishing Characteristics," 1259, 1264–65, but without reference to or correction of the sixteen-word figure in "Experiments to Develop." The figures are given on the basis of the same diagrams in both articles ("Experiments to Develop," 679, 680; and "Distinguishing Characteristics," 1259), although in one article the relevant experiment is labeled "Experiment 5" ("Experiments to Develop," 668–73) and in the other it is labeled "Experiment 1" ("Distinguishing Characteristics," 1254–60). The descriptions of the experiments have a lot in common, but discrepancies include the number of students involved—either forty-three ("Experiments to Develop," 668) or forty-two ("Distinguishing Characteristics," 1254)—and the expression "this is vital," present three times in "the instructions" given to students in one article ("Experiments to Develop," 669) but absent in the other ("Distinguishing Characteristics," 1254–55).

[4] April D. DeConick ("Human Memory and the Sayings of Jesus: Contemporary Experimental Exercises in the Transmission of Jesus Traditions," in *Jesus, the Voice and the Text: Beyond the Oral and Written Gospel* [ed. Tom Thatcher; Waco: Baylor University Press, 2008], 135–80) attempts to build on McIver and Carroll's work by doing further experiments with undergraduate students and applying the results to the development of the early Christian tradition, in the process concluding that "exact reproduction of sequences of sixteen or more words in length is suggestive of copying from a written source, confirming what McIver and Carroll found in an earlier study" (p. 145; cf. 178).

[5] James R. Edwards (*The Hebrew Gospel and the Development of the Synoptic Tradition* [Grand Rapids: Eerdmans, 2009], 250–51) accepts the conclusion of the article and attempts to apply McIver and Carroll's statistics to support Matthean posteriority. The fullest application is in James T. Sparks, *The Chronicler's Genealogies: Towards an Understanding of 1 Chronicles 1–9* (AcBib 28; Atlanta: Society of Biblical Literature, 2008), ch. 4, esp. 291–98. Sparks applies McIver and Carroll's sixteen-word criterion in attempting to establish the Chronicler's use of Genesis.

[6] The same error is made by DeConick, "Human Memory." The results of the experiments in contemporary English are transferred directly to the Synoptic Gospels in Koine Greek, without any discussion of the differences between the two languages.

[7] McIver and Carroll, "Experiments to Develop," 677.

copying from a written source in English,[8] they transfer the criterion without analysis or comment to the Greek Gospels.

This issue is important because it takes many more words to say something in contemporary English than it takes to say something similar in Koine Greek. Therefore, sixteen words in English correlates to fewer words in Greek, and so the sixteen-word criterion is much too high for Greek.[9] The point does not need to remain a purely abstract one. It can be illustrated by looking at English translations of passages that satisfy McIver and Carroll's criterion of sixteen or more words in conjoined sequence. Their example of the highest number of words in sequential agreement is Matt 10:21–22//Mark 13:12–13.[10] They count thirty-one Greek words in exact sequence:

Matthew 10:21–22	Mark 13:12–13
²¹Παραδώσει δὲ ἀδελφὸς ἀδελφὸν εἰς θάνατον καὶ πατὴρ τέκνον, καὶ ἐπαναστήσονται τέκνα ἐπὶ γονεῖς καὶ θανατώσουσιν αὐτούς. ²²καὶ ἔσεσθε μισούμενοι ὑπὸ πάντων διὰ τὸ ὄνομά μου· ὁ δὲ ὑπομείνας εἰς τέλος οὗτος σωθήσεται.	¹²καὶ παραδώσει ἀδελφὸς ἀδελφὸν εἰς θάνατον καὶ πατὴρ τέκνον, καὶ ἐπαναστήσονται τέκνα ἐπὶ γονεῖς καὶ θανατώσουσιν αὐτούς· ¹³καὶ ἔσεσθε μισούμενοι ὑπὸ πάντων διὰ τὸ ὄνομά μου· ὁ δὲ ὑπομείνας εἰς τέλος οὗτος σωθήσεται.

This sequential agreement of thirty-one words takes forty-five words to render in English translation.

Matthew 10:21–22 (NRSV)	Mark 13:12–13 (NRSV)
²¹Brother will betray brother to death, and a father his child, and children will rise against parents and have them put to death; ²²and you will be hated by all because of my name. But the one who endures to the end will be saved.	¹²Brother will betray brother to death, and a father his child, and children will rise against parents and have them put to death; ¹³and you will be hated by all because of my name. But the one who endures to the end will be saved.

---

[8] See p. 794 n. 3 above. I will talk about it as the "sixteen-word" criterion here since I am responding to the *JBL* version of the research, but it is worth remembering each time that the figure rises to eighteen in the *Applied Cognitive Psychology* version of the research.

[9] The same issue is true in the case of Hebrew and English, which affects James T. Sparks's application of McIver and Carroll in *The Chronicler's Genealogies*. For example, Sparks's second parallel featuring sixteen or more words in conjoined sequence is Gen 10:15–18a//1 Chr 1:13b–16 (p. 298) which features twenty-one consecutive words in Hebrew. There is a conjoined sequence of thirty words in the NRSV, thirty-three if one extends further back into 1 Chr 1:12 and parallel.

[10] McIver and Carroll, "Experiments to Develop," 681.

The difference between the two languages is largely self-evident. It includes issues such as the lack of an indefinite article in Greek and the lack of possessive pronouns in certain phrases, so in the above example, πατὴρ τέκνον is translated in the NRSV as "a father his child," doubling the number of words. Similarly, verbs are expressed in Greek without the necessity of a personal pronoun or auxiliary words, so in the above example, ἔσεσθε μισούμενοι is expressed in English as "you will be hated," again doubling the number of words. The point is a basic one in elementary Greek and does not require extended illustration, but it is fundamental to the difficulty of transferring results from experiments in one language to another language without any critical reflection.

The difficulty is in large part that McIver and Carroll are comparing results from experiments using a noninflected language with an inflected language. This is an issue because their experiments focus especially on conjoined sequences of words. A noninflected language like English is far more likely to retain word order across two parallels because word order is often intrinsic to the meaning. In Greek, by contrast, word order is less important in the determination of meaning. This has the effect of diminishing the likely extent of parallel conjoined sequences in Greek.

The point can be illustrated in a parallel such as Matt 9:5–6//Mark 2:9–11//Luke 5:23–24, which features a twenty-one-word triple agreement in English translation, the kind of agreement that comfortably satisfies McIver and Carroll's threshold for evidence of copying. This synopsis shows the passage in the NRSV, with the triple sequential agreement of twenty-one words underlined:

Matthew 9:5–6 (NRSV)	Mark 2:9–11 (NRSV)	Luke 5:23–4 (NRSV)
"For which is easier, to say,	"Which is easier, to say to the paralytic,	"Which is easier, to say,
'Your sins are forgiven,' or to say, 'Stand up	'Your sins are forgiven,' or to say, 'Stand up and take your mat	'Your sins are forgiven you,' or to say, 'Stand up
and walk'? ⁶ But so that you may know that the Son of Man has authority on earth to forgive sins"— he then said to the paralytic— "Stand up, take your bed and go to your home."	and walk'? ¹⁰ But so that you may know that the Son of Man has authority on earth to forgive sins"— he said to the paralytic— ¹¹ "I say to you, stand up, take your mat and go to your home."	and walk'? ²⁴ But so that you may know that the Son of Man has authority on earth to forgive sins"— he said to the one who was paralyzed—"I say to you, stand up and take your bed and go to your home."

This twenty-one-word sequential triple agreement in English, which lengthens to twenty-six words in Matthew and Luke (adding "Or to say 'Stand up …'"), is substantially higher than McIver and Carroll's sixteen-word criterion, but in the Greek texts of the Gospels, the actual sequential triple agreement is only six words.

Matthew 9:5-7	Mark 2:9-11	Luke 5:23-24
τί γάρ ἐστιν εὐκοπώτερον, εἰπεῖν, Ἀφίενταί σου αἱ ἁμαρτίαι, ἢ εἰπεῖν· Ἔγειρε καὶ περιπάτει; ⁶ ἵνα δὲ εἰδῆτε ὅτι ἐξουσίαν ἔχει ὁ υἱὸς τοῦ ἀνθρώπου ἐπὶ τῆς γῆς ἀφιέναι ἁμαρτίας, τότε λέγει τῷ παραλυτικῷ, Ἐγερθεὶς ἆρόν σου τὴν κλίνην καὶ ὕπαγε εἰς τὸν οἶκόν σου.	τί ἐστιν εὐκοπώτερον, εἰπεῖν τῷ παραλυτικῷ, Ἀφέωνταί σου αἱ ἁμαρτίαι, ἢ εἰπεῖν· Ἔγειρε καὶ ἆρον τὸν κράβαττόν σου καὶ περιπάτει; ¹⁰ ἵνα δὲ εἰδῆτε ὅτι ἐξουσίαν ἔχει ὁ υἱὸς τοῦ ἀνθρώπου ἀφιέναι ἁμαρτίας ἐπὶ τῆς γῆς, λέγει τῷ παραλυτικῷ ¹¹ Σοὶ λέγω, ἔγειρε ἆρον τὸν κράβαττόν σου καὶ ὕπαγε εἰς τὸν οἶκόν σου.	τί ἐστιν εὐκοπώτερον, εἰπεῖν, Ἀφέωνταί σοι αἱ ἁμαρτίαι σου, ἢ εἰπεῖν· Ἔγειρε καὶ περιπάτει; ²⁴ ἵνα δὲ εἰδῆτε ὅτι ὁ υἱὸς τοῦ ἀνθρώπου ἐξουσίαν ἔχει ἐπὶ τῆς γῆς ἀφιέναι ἁμαρτίας, εἶπεν τῷ παραλελυμένῳ, Σοὶ λέγω, ἔγειρε καὶ ἄρας τὸ κλινίδιόν σου πορεύου εἰς τὸν οἶκόν σου.

What this illustrates is that the chances for conjoined sequence in parallel passages is greater in contemporary English than it is in first-century Koine. Where the NRSV has twenty-one words in conjoined sequence across all three Synoptics (rising to twenty-six in Matthew and Luke), the Greek has only six (καὶ περιπάτει; ἵνα δὲ εἰδῆτε ὅτι..., rising to twelve in Matthew//Mark, καὶ περιπάτει; ἵνα δὲ εἰδῆτε ὅτι ἐξουσίαν ἔχει ὁ υἱὸς τοῦ ἀνθρώπου).

The same kind of thing can be clearly illustrated elsewhere. Matthew 26:13// Mark 14:9, for example, features a conjoined sequence of nineteen words in the NRSV. This is the kind of sequential agreement that is well above McIver and Carroll's sixteen word threshold:

Matthew 26:13 (NRSV)	Mark 14:9 (NRSV)
Truly I tell you, wherever this good news is proclaimed in the whole world, what she has done will be told in remembrance of her.	Truly I tell you, wherever the good news is proclaimed in the whole world, what she has done will be told in remembrance of her.

The contrast with the Greek texts of Matthew and Luke again illustrates the point:

Matthew 26:13	Mark 14:9
ἀμὴν, λέγω ὑμῖν, ὅπου ἐὰν κηρυχθῇ τὸ εὐαγγέλιον τοῦτο ἐν ὅλῳ τῷ κόσμῳ, λαληθήσεται καὶ ὃ ἐποίησεν αὕτη εἰς μνημόσυνον αὐτῆς.	ἀμὴν δὲ, λέγω ὑμῖν, ὅπου ἐὰν κηρυχθῇ τὸ εὐαγγέλιον εἰς ὅλον τὸν κόσμον, καὶ ὃ ἐποίησεν αὕτη λαληθήσεται εἰς μνημόσυνον αὐτῆς.

The differing position of λαληθήσεται in Matthew and Mark generates a shorter conjoined sequence of words in Greek than one sees in English translation, only four words in comparison with the nineteen in the English of the NRSV. In English, the subject "what she has done" goes before the verb ("will be told"), whereas in Koine, the subject (καὶ ὃ ἐποίησεν αὕτη) can go either before the verb (λαληθήσεται), as in Matthew, or after it, as in Mark. Similarly, the difference in prepositions between Matthew (ἐν) and Mark (εἰς) means that identical words are in different cases (ὅλῳ τῷ κόσμῳ in Matthew; ὅλον τὸν κόσμον in Mark), which again reduces the number of words in exact sequence in Koine and increases it in English. Parallels like this, with only seven words in exact sequence in Greek, come nowhere near satisfying McIver and Carroll's criterion for determining the existence of written sources.

In other words, English is more likely to feature lengthy conjoined sequences of words, given that it is a noninflected language with fewer options in relation to the ordering of words. This should have been factored into McIver and Carroll's attempt to transfer their contemporary English experimental results to ancient texts written in Greek.

It is possible to get an indication of how far the differences in language affected McIver and Carroll's conclusions. They compiled a list of twenty-three passages[11] that feature exact sequential agreements of sixteen words or more.[12] For each of these, one can compare the sequential agreements in English translation as an indicator of the extent to which the length of sequential agreements differs in the two languages. Moreover, the advantage of comparing the Greek texts here with English translations is that this compares like with like, so that subject matter, at least, is the same. In order to avoid experimenter bias, I will use the NRSV rather than my own translations for the purposes of comparison. In this chart, the first column gives the location of McIver and Carroll's parallels in the order in which they present them;[13] the second column gives the number of Greek words in exact sequence (corrected where necessary);[14] the third column is my count of the number of English words in the same parallel in exact sequence in the NRSV:

---

[11] McIver and Carroll list only one sequential parallel in each of their twenty-three passages although some of those passages contain more than one. See Poirier, "Memory, Written Sources," 319.

[12] They further pare these down to "nine parallel passages ... where copying has almost certainly occurred" ("Experiments to Develop," 680) by taking out examples of aphorisms and poetry.

[13] Note, however, that McIver and Carroll only give the location of the entire pericope in which the parallel is found. For precise locations (even the word number), see Poirier, "Memory, Written Sources," 320.

[14] Here Poirier's more detailed and accurate table is very helpful, "Memory, Written Sources," 320.

Parallel	No. of Greek words in exact sequence	No. of English words in exact sequence (NRSV)
Matt 10:21–22//Mark 13:12–13	31	45
Mark 10:14–15//Luke 18:16–17	29	37
Matt 11:25–27//Luke 10:21–22	27[15]	51
Matt 24:50–51//Luke 12:46	26[16]	25[17]
Mark 1:24–25//Luke 4:34–35	26	38
Matt 6:24//Luke 16:13	26	32
Matt 3:9–10//Luke 3:8–9	24	55[18]
Matt 7:7–8//Luke 11:9–10	24	52
Matt 8:20//Luke 9:58	24	33[19]
Matt 12:41//Luke 11:32	24	32
Matt 16:24–25//Mark 8:34–35	23	39
Mark 12:38–39//Luke 20:46	14[20]	42
Matt 24:18–20//Mark 13:16–18	23	31
Matt 26:24//Mark 14:21	23	37
Matt 11:7–8//Luke 7:24–25	19[21]	42
Matt 8:9–10//Luke 7:8–9	25[22]	36
Matt 15:8–9//Mark 7:6–7	20	25
Matt 22:44//Mark 12.36	19	20

[15] McIver and Carroll's figure is 28. It is corrected by Poirier to 27.

[16] McIver and Carroll's figure is 28. It is corrected by Poirier to 25, but this does not include the article τῶν that appears with the synonyms ὑποκριτῶν (Matthew) and ἀπίστων (Luke).

[17] The NRSV translates the identical sentences differently across the Matthean and Lukan parallels. Thus, καὶ διχοτομήσει αὐτόν, identical in Matthew and Luke, is translated with "and" in Luke but without it in Matthew. Cf. the RSV, which has thirty-three words in sequential agreement here ("the master of that servant will come on a day when he does not expect him and at an hour he does not know, and will punish him, and put him with the …").

[18] The NRSV here translates Matthew and Luke identically, although the Greek differs. Matthew's ἤδη δὲ ἡ ἀξίνη is translated the same way as Luke's ἤδη δὲ καὶ ἡ ἀξίνη. Luke's additional καί disrupts the sequential agreement.

[19] The NRSV extends backwards into Matt 8:19//Luke 9:57, "I will follow you wherever you go".

[20] McIver and Carroll's figure is 23; Poirier corrects this to 14. McIver and Carroll here treat οἱ κατεσθίοντες (Mark) and οἳ κατεσθίουσιν (Luke 20:47) as identical, though their policy elsewhere is to count only complete identity in their exact sequences. Their list would have been far longer if they had treated other cases like this as exact parallels.

[21] McIver and Carroll's figure is 22; Poirier corrects this to 19.

[22] McIver and Carroll's figure is 21; Poirier corrects this to 25.

Parallel	No. of Greek words in exact sequence	No. of English words in exact sequence (NRSV)
Matt 8:2–3//Luke 5:12–13	18[23]	7[24]
Matt 20:28//Mark 10:45	17	21
Matt 15:32//Mark 8:2–3	16	21
Matt 16:25//Luke 9:24	16	24
Matt 24:33–34//Mark 13:29–30	16	44[25]

In practically every case,[26] the English translations feature substantially more words in exact sequential agreement, sometimes dramatically more. On occasion after occasion, English shows a greater tendency, in translations of the same material, to lengthier conjoined sequences of words. Given these substantive differences between the two languages, it is clear that the sixteen word threshold for Greek, chosen by McIver and Carroll on the basis of experiments in English, is much too low.

Attention to this important point about the difference between English and Greek would have resulted in a vastly greater number of passages that show evidence of copying in the Synoptic Gospels. McIver and Carroll have derived a criterion from work with one language and have applied it to texts in another language, in spite of the fact that it takes many more words to say a similar thing in English than it does in Greek. Their experiments are therefore problematic with respect to their goal of determining the existence of written sources in the Synoptic Gospels, and their sixteen-word criterion should be abandoned.

---

[23] McIver and Carroll's figure is 17; Poirier corrects this to 18.

[24] The NRSV here translates identical Greek differently, thus breaking up the sequential agreement. Contrast the RSV, which has twenty-six words in verbatim agreement in English.

[25] The agreement in the NRSV spans Matt 24:33–36//Mark 13:29–32, from "you know" to "that day."

[26] The exception is Matt 8:2–3//Luke 5:12–13, where the NRSV translates the same Greek differently in each case, thus disturbing the sequential agreement. See n. 24 above.

Paul's Letter to the Romans, the Ten Commandments, and Pagan "Justification by Faith"

For Alan Segal ז״ל

PAULA FREDRIKSEN
augfred@bu.edu
The Hebrew University, Jerusalem 91905, Israel

E. P. Sanders's *Paul and Palestinian Judaism* (1977) challenged the utility of the phrase "justification by faith" as a key to anything other than Lutheran scholarship. This note argues that the phrase does offer us insight into the historical Paul, provided we interpret it within its native context, an apocalyptic stream of first-century Hellenistic Judaism that took its message to pagans. Noting that *dikaiosynē* functioned commonly as a code for the Second Table of the Law, and that *pistis* in the first century meant not "belief" or "faith" but "conviction, steadfastness, loyalty," the argument concludes that the pagans' *dikaōthentes ek pisteōs* indicates these people's pneumatically granted ability to act toward one another in community according to the dictates of the Ten Commandments.

E. P. Sanders's *Paul and Palestinian Judaism* (1977) revolutionized NT studies. Credited with initiating the "new perspective on Paul,"[1] Sanders no less initiated a new perspective on Paul's native religious context. Unabashedly exposing the deep and defining anti-Judaism of so much Christian scholarship,[2] Sanders radically undermined the old, theologically generated caricature of Judaism as a "legalistic" system of works righteousness pitted against Paul's liberating message of "justification by faith."[3] That latter concept, he argued, might serve as a key to understanding Lutheran scholarship, but it had little application to the historical Paul.

---

[1] Sanders, *Paul and Palestinian Judaism* (Philadelphia: Fortress, 1977); see also his *Paul, the Law, and the Jewish People* (Philadelphia: Fortress, 1983). The phrase is James D. G. Dunn's, "The New Perspective on Paul," *BJRL* 65 (1983): 95–122; see also Dunn, *The New Perspective on Paul* (rev. ed.; Grand Rapids: Eerdmans, 2008).

[2] See especially Sanders's critical bibliographical review in *Paul and Palestinian Judaism*, 33–59, 434–42.

[3] In place of this model of Judaism and "works righteousness," Sanders proposed what he called "covenantal nomism," a pattern of religion resting on grace, faith, and obedience. God

As a slogan, "justification by faith" powerfully synopsizes many foundational Christian ideas: the priority of grace, the theology of the cross, the universality of sin (in its Catholic iterations, of original sin). Many of these ideas were definitively shaped in the course of much later arguments: Augustine's against Pelagius, Young Man Luther's against Renaissance Rome. "Justification by faith" has served conceptually and polemically as a lodestar of Lutheran tradition, and of NT scholarship more broadly. In these contexts, it presents a sharp contrast between (Christian) "faith" and (Jewish) "law."

Despite its doctrinal freightedness, however, some NT scholars have continued to insist on the phrase's historical utility as a key to understanding Paul.[4] These scholars may be right, but not for the reasons they think. To understand what Paul means by "justification by faith" and how it functions specifically within his εὐαγγέλιον ἐν τοῖς ἔθνεσιν, we need to place the phrase back into its originary social context: committed communities of apocalyptically minded late Second Temple Jews and pagans. Like the Purloined Letter, our clue word for guiding us in this effort has been hiding in plain sight. What is meant, in this Jewish context, by δικαιοσύνη?

I. Piety and Justice: The Ten Commandments

Let us begin where the historical core of Jesus of Nazareth's story begins, on the banks of the River Jordan. This is Josephus's description of John the Baptizer in *Antiquities* 18:

> John exhorted the Jews to practice ἀρετή ["virtue"], to practice δικαιοσύνη ["justice"] toward their fellows and εὐσέβεια ["piety"] toward God, and in so doing to join in immersion.... The immersion was for the purification of the flesh once the soul had been cleansed through δικαιοσύνη ["right conduct"]. (*A.J.* 18.116–19)

The "virtue" or "moral excellence" that Josephus's John urges on his Jewish hearers here is defined as "justice" and "piety." These two words are not moral abstractions: they signal a core tradition of the biblical covenant, the Ten Commandments. The first five commandments, the First Table of the Law, concern relations with God, coded here as εὐσέβεια ("piety"). The next five, or Second Table, regulate relations between people, δικαιοσύνη ("justice" or "righteousness"). Thus:

---

graciously chose Israel from among the nations, binding Israel to himself in a covenanted relationship. Israel's grateful response to God's gracious election was to live faithfully according to the covenant's commands. "Obedience maintains one's position in the covenant, but it does not earn God's grace as such" (Sanders, *Paul and Palestinian Judaism*, 420; see too 75, 81–85).

[4] Stephen Westerholm offers an up-to-date review of current discussion (*Justification Reconsidered: Rethinking a Pauline Theme* [Grand Rapids: Eerdmans 2013]).

εὐσέβεια: Piety toward God	δικαιοσύνη: Justice toward Others
1. No other gods	6. No murder
2. No graven images (idols)	7. No adultery
3. No abuse of God's name	8. No theft
4. Keep the Sabbath	9. No lying
5. Honor parents	10. No coveting[5]

According to Josephus, then, the Baptizer's call to repentance (תשובה [tĕšûbâ] in later rabbinic idiom, "turn") meant, precisely, *re*turning to God's commandments as revealed in the Torah. Similarly, Josephus's contemporaries, the Synoptic evangelists, portray a Jesus who, like John, summoned fellow Jews to repentance ("Μετανοεῖτε!" Mark 1:15; Matt 4:17). Asked what were the greatest commandments, Mark's Jesus replies by citing Deut 6:4. "Hear O Israel, the Lord our God, the Lord is one. And you shall love the Lord your God with all your heart, and with all your soul, and with all your might"—in other words, εὐσέβεια, the First Table of the Law. And "you shall love your neighbor as yourself"—that is, δικαιοσύνη, the Second Table of the Law (Lev 19:18; Mark 12:29–31; Matt 22:34–40; Luke 10:25–28). In brief, Mark's passage encodes the Ten Commandments. Elsewhere, his Jesus invokes them directly: "You know the commandments: 'You shall not murder; you shall not commit adultery; you shall not steal; you shall not bear false witness; you shall not defraud; honor your father and your mother'" (Mark 10:19). Matthew's Jesus repeats and reinforces this message in his Sermon on the Mount (Matt 5:21–22, against murder; vv. 27–30, against adultery; vv. 31–37 against lying/"swearing

---

[5] The Bible arranges these commandments variously: see Exod 20:1–17 and Deut 5:6–21. Sanders notes that "these two words [εὐσέβεια and δικαιοσύνη] were used very widely by Greek-speaking Jews to summarize their religion" (*The Historical Figure of Jesus* [London: Penguin 1993], 92). The words εὐσέβεια and δικαιοσύνη also appear in Philo's summary of the law's two chief principles or κεφάλαια (*kephalaia*; *Spec.* 2.63; cf. *Decal.* 19, on "honoring parents" within the law's First Table). David Flusser surveys the variety of twofold summaries of Torah (love of God and of neighbor; piety and justice) from *Jubilees* to Lactantius in "The Ten Commandments and the New Testament," in *The Ten Commandments in History and Tradition* (ed. Ben-Zion Segal; Publications of the Perry Foundation for Biblical Research, the Hebrew University of Jerusalem; Jerusalem: Magnes, 1990), 219–46. Similarly, *b. Mak.* 24a runs the numbers down from 613 commandments to two (Isa 56:1) to one (Hab 2:4, the righteous man will live by his אמונה, "strength" or "steadfastness"; cf. Paul's ἐκ πίστεως ζήσεται [Gal 3:11]). On אמונה not as "faith" but as "firmness, steadfastness, fidelity," see BDB, 53. I thank Avraham Isaacs and Jay Pomrenze for walking me through selected biblical and rabbinic Hebrew texts with this term. This same tendency to streamline moral teachings appears in the philosophical epitomes of contemporary Greco-Roman culture (Epicurus's *Kyriai Doxai*, Epictetus's *Encheiridion*); see Hans Dieter Betz, *The Sermon on the Mount: A Commentary on the Sermon on the Mount, Including the Sermon on the Plain (Matthew 5:3–7:27 and Luke 6:20–49)* (Hermeneia; Minneapolis: Fortress, 1995), 76–79, with notes to the key literature.

falsely").[6] The Jesus of Synoptic tradition, in other words, like Josephus's Baptizer, foregrounds the Ten Commandments.

II. Paul and His Pagans

What about Paul? Paul's circumstances differed pointedly from those of the Baptizer and of Jesus. His "mission field" was the cities of the eastern empire. His hearers were not Jews but pagans.[7] And these he called to repent not of "Jewish" sins (i.e., breaking the commandments) but of "pagan" sins (most especially idolatry and its perennial rhetorical companion, πορνεία, "fornication").[8] Nonetheless—and despite Paul's insistence that pagans-in-Christ not "convert" and assume Jewish practices, thus Jewish law[9]—these pagans' religious reformation went hand in hand

---

[6] See Sanders's comments on this Matthean passage (*Historical Figure*, 210–12); see also Flusser, "Ten Commandments," 234. Cf. Luke 11:42, another coded reference, where neglecting "judgment" (τὴν κρίσιν) indicates neglecting justice. Emphasis on the Ten Commandments in mid-first-century Palestinian Judaism is perhaps reflected as well in *tefillin* from Qumran. The later tractate *y. Ber.* 9b comments that, while the Ten Commandments used to be recited every day in the temple, they no longer are "on account of the מינים ['sectarians']," who hold that no other commandments were given on Sinai. See Ephraim Urbach, *The Sages, Their Concepts and Beliefs* (2 vols.; Jerusalem: Magnes, 1975), 2:844 n. 75.

[7] Modern English uses two words, "pagan" and "gentile," where the Greek has only one, ἔθνη. "Pagan" refers to religion: the person referred to is neither a Jew nor a Christian. "Gentile" refers to ethnicity: the person referred to is not a Jew. In Paul's day, however, with few exceptions, pagans were Gentiles and Gentiles were pagans: relations between humanity and divinity were commonly configured along ethnic lines. Despite the anachronism of the term, then—"pagan" is a fourth-century Christian coinage—I have kept "pagan" as my translation of ἔθνη to signal to the reader that these non-Jews were intrinsically in relationship with their gods. See, too, in defense of this term, C. P. Jones, "The Fuzziness of 'Paganism,'" *Common Knowledge* 18 (2012): 249–54. On the existence of all gods in antiquity, even in the view of "monotheists" like Jews and Christians, see P. Fredriksen, "Judaizing the Nations: The Ritual Demands of Paul's Gospel," *NTS* 56 (2010): 232–52, esp. 235–36. All of my own articles cited here are available in PDF on my Boston University web page: www.bu.edu/religion/faculty/fredriksen.

[8] On the ways that their respective audiences define the views of Jesus and of Paul on "sin," see Paula Fredriksen, *Sin: The Early History of an Idea* (Princeton: Princeton University Press, 2012), 6–49.

[9] In so doing, Paul assumed a normative Jewish stance: Jews did not hold non-Jews responsible for and to Jewish ancestral custom. Accordingly, we can infer nothing about Paul's own personal level of Jewish observance from the fact that he tells pagans that they do not have to be observant. See my articles "Judaizing the Nations," 241–44; "How Later Contexts Affect Pauline Content, or, Retrospect Is the Mother of Anachronism," in *Jews and Christians in the First and Second Centuries: How to Write Their History* (ed. Peter J. Tomson and Joshua Schwartz; CRINT 13; Leiden: Brill, 2014), 17–51; "Paul, Practical Pluralism, and the Invention of Religious Persecution in Roman Antiquity," in *Understanding Religious Pluralism: Perspectives from Religious Studies and Theology* (ed. Peter C. Phan and Jonathan Ray; Eugene, OR: Wipf & Stock, 2014),

with their social/ethical reformation, and their living according to Jewish law precisely indexed this reformation. Keeping which Jewish law? Keeping what Jewish laws? Sabbath excepted (for good reason: see just below), their keeping nine of the Ten Commandments.

The word εὐσέβεια, which signaled the First Table of the Law, appears nowhere in Paul. We can only speculate why not. Perhaps Paul avoided referring directly to the Law's First Table because Sabbath observance featured in that list, and Paul had argued heatedly against his missionary competition that pagans-in-Christ were not obligated to Jewish ancestral practices. Or perhaps Paul conceived of these pagans' new piety in a special way, since it had been brought about not through their own efforts (ἐξ ἔργων, "by works"), but rather by eschatological fiat of God through Christ (χάριτι, "by grace"). Their new orientation toward God, however, conformed precisely to the mandates of Jewish worship, in accordance with the Law's First Table: No other gods, and no idols.[10]

Why did Paul make this Judaizing demand of his pagans? Unlike the Baptizer,

---

87–113; and "The Question of Worship: Gods, Pagans, and the Redemption of Israel," in *Paul within Judaism* (ed. Mark Nanos and Magnus Zetterholm; Minneapolis: Fortress, 2015), 175–201.

For further discussion of the inclusion of the nations in Israel's redemption, with primary references, see Joachim Jeremias, *Jesus' Promise to the Nations* (London: SCM, 1952), 46–75; E. P. Sanders, *Jesus and Judaism* (Philadelphia: Fortress, 1985), 212–21; James M. Scott, *Paul and the Nations: The Old Testament and Jewish Background of Paul's Mission to the Nations, with Special Reference to the Destination of Galatians* (WUNT 84; Tübingen: Mohr Siebeck, 1995), especially for the (traditional) Jewish phrasing of "the nations and all Israel"; and more broadly, Terence L. Donaldson, *Judaism and the Gentiles: Jewish Patterns of Universalism (to 135 CE)* (Waco: Baylor University Press, 2007).

[10] What does Paul mean by "law"? The secondary literature, enormous and factious, cannot be reviewed here. Paul's orientation toward the temple, though, is positive (Rom 9:4; 15 passim), and he seems to envisage the integration of his pagans in its cult, on which see esp. F. W. Horn, "Paulus und die Herodianische Tempel," *NTS* 53 (2007): 184–203; Fredriksen, "Judaizing the Nations," 244–49. Where Paul does speak negatively about law/Torah, however, he speaks *to pagans* and refers to Jewish ancestral custom configured as circumcision, Sabbath, and food laws (though this last is complicated too) as "works of the law" (Gal 2:16; Rom 3:20). For this reason, I would take him to speak against performance of these "works of the law" *by non-Jews*.

Do Jews, then, also need to be "justified by faith in Christ"? Much Pauline scholarship, "new perspective" and otherwise, says yes; the *Sonderweg* scholars say no: see, e.g., John G. Gager, *Reinventing Paul* (Oxford: Oxford University Press, 2004); before him, Lloyd Gaston, *Paul and the Torah* (Vancouver: University of British Columbia Press, 1987); Stanley K. Stowers, *A Rereading of Romans: Justice, Jews, and Gentiles* (New Haven: Yale University Press, 1994). Both sides make good points, and we have no statement from Paul about the Jewish observance of Jewish ancestral practices one way or the other. It does seem to me, however, that *de minimis* Paul expects some sort of vindicating final acknowledgment on the part of his "kinsmen according to the flesh" (currently non–Christ-following Israel) that his views on messiah and on the impending end were correct: Rom 10:3–4 (Christ as law's τέλος); Rom 11:25–27 (directed to πᾶς Ἰσραήλ, "all Israel"). Such acknowledgment, however, implies no derogation of Torah.

and unlike Jesus of Nazareth, Paul had seen the risen Christ (1 Cor 9:1; 15:8; Gal 1:16). This eschatological event convinced him of the rightness of Jesus' urgent prophecy: the kingdom truly was at hand; indeed, within the ἐκκλησία, on the evidence of Christ's resurrection, it had in some sense already begun. Transformed by this vision from opponent to apostle (sometime around 34 C.E.), Paul undertook his mission, convinced by that same vision that he knew what time it was on God's clock. Some twenty-odd years later, he reaffirmed this conviction. "Salvation is now nearer to us," he told Christ-following pagans in Rome,[11] "than when we ἐπιστεύ-σαμεν" (Rom 13:11; I will translate the verb below).

In the ever-shortening meanwhile, Paul called his pagans from the worship of their own gods to an exclusive commitment to the one true god, Paul's god, the god of Israel. These people were not *re*turning to their native god and their native ancestral laws (the Jewish meaning of μετάνοια), but *turning to* him for the first time (ἐπιστρέφω in various forms, e.g., 1 Thess 1:9).[12] "Indeed there are many gods and many lords," Paul writes to his community in Corinth, "yet *for us* there is one god, the Father ... and one lord, Jesus Christ" (1 Cor 8:5–6). Of course Paul, and Paul's pagan assemblies, had then to cope with the anger of these lower gods, who lashed back.[13] But they were fortified by holy πνεῦμα communicated to them through immersion into Christ's death and resurrection (Rom 8:9–17); enabled by that spirit to utter prophecies, to speak in tongues, to heal, and to discern between spirits (1 Cor 12:1–11); validated in their apocalyptic convictions by these very charismata. In πίστις, they awaited Christ's imminent return, his defeat of these hostile powers, the transformation of the quick and the dead, and the redemption of

---

[11] I assume that Paul's letter addresses Christ-following pagans in Rome (Rom 1:6; cf. 11:13), not a mixed assembly of Jews and pagans both.

[12] On ἐπιστρέφω as "turning" *as opposed to* "converting," see Fredriksen, "Judaizing the Nations," 242–44.

[13] The θεὸς τοῦ αἰῶνος τούτου ("the god of this age") had blinded the minds of unbelievers (2 Cor 4:4; pagans? Jews?). The ἀρχόντων τοῦ αἰῶνος τούτου ("the rulers of this age"), if by this phrase Paul intends astral powers, have crucified the son of Paul's god (1 Cor 2:8). The divinities formerly worshiped by his congregations in Galatia, he says, are not "gods by nature" but mere cosmic lightweights, στοιχεῖα ("elements") unworthy of fear or worship (Gal 4:8–9: note that Paul demeans their status but does not deny their existence). Such gods, in fact, are mere δαιμονία, subordinate deities, "demons" (1 Cor 10:20–21). "Indeed, there are many gods and many lords," he tells his pagans in Corinth (1 Cor 8:5–6); but soon these lower powers, currently worshiped through images, will themselves acknowledge the God of Israel when Christ defeats them and establishes the kingdom of his father (in 1 Cor 15:24–27, these powers are "destroyed"; in Rom 8:38, they are liberated). In the end, these beings, wherever they are—above the earth or upon the earth or below the earth—will also bend their knees to Jesus (Phil 2:10).

For the definition of ἄρχων as a subordinate and evil divine entity, see BAGD (1979), definition 3; δύναμις, definition 6; ἐξουσία, definition 4.β; στοιχεῖα, definitions 3 and 4. For Paul's many references to other gods, see James D. G. Dunn, *The Theology of Paul the Apostle* (Grand Rapids: Eerdmans, 1998), 33–38, 104–10.

creation (including, perhaps, of these lower gods).¹⁴ Scripture had foreseen that God would δικαιοῖ τὰ ἔθνη ἐκ πίστεως (Gal 3:8, "justify the Gentiles by faith" [NRSV]), and now, through Christ, he had. In the brief time remaining, infused with holy spirit, these pagans ἐν Χριστῷ were enabled by and through their πίστις in Christ, and through God's (or Christ's) πνεῦμα, to fulfill the law and to conduct community life in accordance with it (e.g., Gal 5:13–25). They were δικαιωθέντες ἐκ πίστεως (Rom 5:1). What does Paul mean by this phrase?

III. *Pneuma*, Steadfastness, and Doing Justice

Here the connotations of our modern English words impede translation of our ancient Greek texts, which depend on nuanced construals of πίστις, εὐσέβεια, and δικαιοσύνη. Our word "faith," for example, refracted through the prism of a long Christian cultural history that runs at least from Tertullian (*credo quia absurdum*) to Søren Kierkegaard, has come to imply all sorts of psychological inner states concerning authenticity or sincerity of "belief." In antiquity, πίστις and its Latin equivalent, *fides*, connoted, rather, "steadfastness," "conviction," "loyalty."¹⁵ For this reason, I would translate Rom 13:11, cited above, as "Salvation is nearer to us now than it was when we first became convinced" (cf. RSV: "than when we first believed"). So too with "piety." Less about religious sentiment than about showing respect (a synonym for εὐσέβεια was φόβος, "fear"),¹⁶ εὐσέβεια and its Latin equivalent, *pietas*, indexed a respectful attentiveness in the execution of inherited protocols of worship—what we call "religion" but what ancient authors, Paul included, thought of as a kind of family patrimony, "ancestral custom."¹⁷ And Paul's use of δικαιοσύνη and its related verbal forms presents daunting challenges to English, which lacks much-needed precision.¹⁸

Alert to these problems, how can we translate Paul without anachronism?

---

¹⁴ For redemption of creation, including these beings, see Rom 8:18–39; perhaps of lower gods, Phil 2:10 (all those superhuman knees, cf. Ps 97.7), though cf. 1 Cor 15:24 (these beings are "destroyed").

¹⁵ Hence Paul's use of "obedience" with "commitment" or "conviction" or "steadfastness" (cf. "faith"—not "*the*" faith, as RSV Rom 1:5).

¹⁶ See εὐσέβεια in T. Muraoka, *A Greek-English Lexicon of the Septuagint* (rev. ed.; Louvain: Peeters, 2009), 305.

¹⁷ Cf. the concepts of *mos maiorem*, *fides patrum*, παράδοσεις τῶν πατρικῶν (Gal 1:14), τὰ πατριὰ ἤθη, οἱ πάτριοι νόμοι. According to Benjamin Isaac, "In the Roman world, religion and ethnic loyalties were inseparable" (*The Invention of Racism in Classical Antiquity* [Princeton: Princeton University Press, 2005], 500).

¹⁸ Sanders offers a lengthy consideration of the defects of English for translating Paul's δικαιοσύνη and similar words in *Paul, A Very Short Introduction* (Oxford: Oxford University Press, 1991), 52–90; see esp. 54–55. I will adopt his awkward neologism "righteoused" above, since it is preferable to "justified."

I suggest that we navigate by the Ten Commandments. As our passage from *Antiquities* 18 indicates, δικαιοσύνη signals the Second Table of the Law, just as εὐσέβεια does the First. And while Paul never uses εὐσέβεια, δικαιοσύνη, by comparison, appears frequently: thirty-six times in Romans alone.

When Paul's pagans, then, adhered steadfastly to the good news brought by his message ("believed in the gospel"), they ceased worshiping their own gods and committed themselves to the god of Israel through his son (the cluster of ideas around πιστεύω). Made right by God toward God, they were likewise pneumatically enabled to make right toward each other by acting rightly toward each other, "not like the ἔθνη who do not know God" (1 Thess 4:5; cf. Rom 1:18–32). Their πίστις in Christ (confidence that he had died, had been raised, and was soon coming back) righteoused them (through the giving of πνεῦμα, which also effected adoption[19]) so that they could "fulfill the law," specifically, the Law's Second Table, δικαιοσύνη.[20] Thus, in the same place where Paul reviews the sins of the flesh that Christ-following pagans have left behind (Rom 13:13–14), and where he speaks urgently of the impending end (13:11–12), he also lists the commandments of the Second Table (13:9–10). "Righteoused" pagans, spirit-filled, enabled by their commitment to Christ and, through him, to God, act "righteously" toward others in community.

This is what Paul meant by "justification by faith."

---

[19] Paul's use of adoption here conforms to quotidian culture: Roman adoption customarily entailed assuming responsibility for gods not inherently one's own. It also conforms to antiquity's view that gods and humans form family groups. If pagans now worship Israel's god, then they are adopted into that god's family. (God, not Abraham, is whom they call "Abba"; Rom 8:15; Gal 4:6.) The pagans' adoption is *not* κατὰ σάρκα but κατὰ πνεῦμα: the ethnic distinction between Israel and adopted pagans continues, albeit in an attenuated way, in the kingdom (Rom 15:9–12) (Fredriksen, "Judaizing the Nations," 243–44). On the fixity and fluidity of Paul's ethnic reasoning on this point, see further Caroline Johnson Hodge, "The Question of Social Interaction: Gentiles in Pauline Communities as Gentiles—but Also Not," in Nanos and Zetterholm, *Paul within Judaism*.

[20] Does "being righteoused"/justification *enable* and lead to "righteousness," or does "being righteoused"/justification *constitute* righteousness? I wonder whether this is a distinction that Paul would draw, or even see: it is, however, a hallmark issue for Protestant theology. Translating δικαιοσύνη (back) into Hebrew, would we distinguish (in meaning in addition to part of speech) between צדק (righteousness), צדוק (the state of being right or righteous), and צדיק (the one who is righteous)? How much weight would and could such distinctions bear? I thank Larry Hurtado for thinking over these questions with me.

JBL 133, no. 4 (2014): 809–835

Paul's Understanding of the Resurrection in 1 Corinthians 15:36–54

JAMES WARE
jw44@evansville.edu
University of Evansville, Evansville, IN 47722

The present essay contributes to the current discussion regarding the nature of the resurrection in 1 Corinthians 15. The article begins with a capsule summary of the chapter's history of interpretation, which is generally unfamiliar to NT scholars but provides crucial perspective on the current discussion. The article then offers a new proposal regarding the literary and syntactic structure of Paul's exposition of the resurrection body in 1 Cor 15:36–54. Building on prior structural analysis of the text, the essay points to key but previously neglected features of the passage's composition, arguing that the specific way in which Paul shapes his exposition has crucial implications for his understanding of the nature of the resurrection event. In concert with this structural analysis, the article also seeks to advance scholarly discussion of two much-debated elements of Paul's thought in the passage, providing a fresh discussion of the nature of the "change" that Paul envisions in 15:51–52, and an analysis of Paul's description of the risen body as a *sōma pneumatikon* in 15:44. The structure of Paul's argument in 1 Cor 15:36–54 proposed here has, I argue, significant ramifications for the long-standing debate regarding the nature of the resurrection in Paul.

This article attempts to illumine the current debate regarding the nature of the resurrection that Paul envisions in 1 Corinthians 15. Did the apostle envision the revival and glorious transformation of the body of flesh and bones laid in the tomb? Or did he conceive of the resurrection as involving the bestowal of a new, nonmaterial body discontinuous with the earthly, physical body? Or did he perhaps envision an ethereally material body composed not of flesh but of a heavenly pneumatic substance? Each of these positions finds proponents in current Pauline scholarship. I seek to contribute to this discussion in the following four ways. First, I will place this contemporary debate in a wider context by providing a brief history of interpretation of this chapter (focused narrowly on understandings of the nature of the resurrection event envisioned in the passage) from antiquity until the present. Second, I will offer a new proposal regarding the literary structure of the chapter, which I believe will shed new and significant light on the current discussion.

809

Third, in the course of this structural analysis I will offer a fresh discussion and proposal concerning the nature of the "change" that Paul envisions for the risen body in 1 Cor 15:51–52. Fourth, I will also seek to provide a more precise analysis than has yet been offered regarding a critical term in Paul's argument—Paul's reference to the risen body as a *sōma pneumatikon* in 1 Cor 15:44. I will argue that the exegetical key to Paul's conception of the nature of the resurrection in this chapter is the (hitherto neglected) structure of Paul's own argument in 1 Cor 15:36–54.

I. A Brief (Focalized) History of Interpretation of 1 Corinthians 15

The history of interpretation of this chapter, although largely unknown to most NT specialists, provides a larger theological and historical perspective that is (as we will see) of crucial relevance for the current debate. Due to limitations of space, I will not attempt a history of interpretation in the full sense of the term. Rather, the thumbnail sketch here will focus, quite narrowly and specifically, on interpretation of the nature of the resurrection envisioned by the apostle within the chapter.

In the line of interpretation extending from Irenaeus in the second century to Augustine in the fifth, 1 Corinthians 15 was interpreted in terms of a resurrection of the flesh, identifying the resurrected body of this passage with the earthly, fleshly body raised to life and transformed to be imperishable.[1] By contrast, so-called Gnostic interpreters such as the Valentinians and Ophites, although exhibiting a diversity of approaches that defy easy systematization, characteristically read this chapter in ways that excluded a literal resurrection of the body.[2] In the third century the brilliant Alexandrian exegete Origen (although the precise nature of his views remains controversial) apparently introduced something like a mediating position, interpreting 1 Corinthians 15 as involving a bodily resurrection, but the resurrection of a heavenly or spiritual body composed of ethereal matter, distinct from the earthly body of flesh.[3] Origen's reading of the passage exerted considerable

---

[1] See François Altermath, *Du corps psychique au corps spirituel: Interprétation de 1 Cor. 15,35–49 par les auteurs chrétiens des quatre premiers siècles* (BGBE 18; Tübingen: Mohr Siebeck, 1977). Cf. Irenaeus, *Haer.* 5.7–14; Tertullian, *Res.* 48–57; Methodius, *Res.* 1.13–14; 3.5–6; Rufinus, *Symb.* 41–47; Jerome, *Epist.* 108.23–24; Augustine, *Civ.* 20.20; 22.21–24.

[2] See Elaine Pagels, "'The Mystery of the Resurrection': A Gnostic Reading of 1 Corinthians 15," *JBL* 93 (1974): 276–88; and Outi Lehtipuu, "'Flesh and Blood Cannot Inherit the Kingdom of God': The Transformation of the Flesh in the Early Christian Debates concerning Resurrection," in *Metamorphoses: Resurrection, Body and Transformative Practices in Early Christianity* (ed. Turid Karlsen Seim and Jorunn Økland; Ekstasis 1; Berlin: de Gruyter, 2009), 147–68. Cf. *Gos. Phil.* 56.26–57.22; Irenaeus, *Haer.* 1.30.13.

[3] See Henry Chadwick, "Origen, Celsus, and the Resurrection of the Body," *HTR* 41 (1948): 83–102; and Henri Crouzel, "La doctrine origènienne du corps réssuscité," *BLE* 31 (1980):

influence; it is evident, for example, in the interpretation of this chapter in the writings of Didymus the Blind, Origen's highly respected successor in the catechetical school at Alexandria.[4] However, Origen's interpretation of the passage also met with strong opposition, and his views on the resurrection were eventually condemned by the fifth ecumenical council (Constantinople II).[5] The understanding of 1 Corinthians 15 in terms of a resurrection of the flesh, expounded by such figures as Irenaeus, Tertullian, Jerome, and Augustine, became constitutive for the reading of this passage in subsequent centuries. This reading in turn served to reinforce and develop a generally received Christian theological understanding of resurrection as the reconstitution and glorious transformation of the present mortal body, a transformation involving "enhancement of what is, not metamorphosis into what is not."[6] M. E. Dahl described this orthodox conception as involving the claim that "the resurrection body is *this* body restored and improved in a miraculous manner."[7] The confession of the resurrection of the fleshly body found an important place in the baptismal and conciliar creeds of the ancient church, in papal and conciliar decrees of the medieval church, and in the confessional formulas of the magisterial Reformation.[8] Exegesis of 1 Corinthians 15 was carried out

---

175–200, 241–66. Crouzel's article is widely considered the authoritative study of the subject. Key primary texts include *Sel. Ps.* 11.384 (on Ps 1:5); *Comm. Matt.* 17.29–30; *Princ.* 2.10–11; and *Cels.* 5.18–23.

[4] Didymus, *Ps. T.* 328–30; cf. 259.4–16. For discussion, see Richard A. Layton, *Didymus the Blind and His Circle in Late-Antique Alexandria: Virtue and Narrative in Biblical Scholarship* (Urbana: University of Illinois Press, 2004) 45–47, 151–57.

[5] Leading opponents of Origen's exegesis of 1 Corinthians 15 were Methodius (*Res.* 2–3) and Jerome (*Jo. Hier.* 25–36), but also among Origen's chief supporters, such as Gregory of Nyssa and Rufinus, his interpretation of that chapter as excluding the earthly flesh from salvation was rejected (cf. Gregory of Nyssa, *De anima* 1898–1923; *In sanctum pascha* 251–70; Rufinus, *Symb.* 42–45). Origen's views on the nature of the resurrection body were declared heretical at Constantinople II (553) in anathemas X and XI of the so-called Fifteen Anathemas against Origen.

[6] Caroline Walker Bynum, *The Resurrection of the Body in Western Christianity, 200–1336* (Lectures on the History of Religions n.s. 15; New York: Columbia University Press, 1999), 8.

[7] M. E. Dahl, *The Resurrection of the Body: A Study of 1 Corinthians 15* (SBT 36; London: SCM, 1962), 7.

[8] Cf. the Old Roman Creed (ca. 175 C.E.): πιστεύω εἰς ... σαρκὸς ἀνάστασιν ("I believe in ... the resurrection of the flesh"); Creed of Jerusalem (ca. 350 C.E.): πιστεύομεν ... εἰς σαρκὸς ἀνάστασιν ("we believe ... in the resurrection of the flesh"); *Apostolic Constitutions* 7.41 (fourth century C.E.): βαπτίζομαι καὶ ... εἰς σαρκὸς ἀνάστασιν ("I am baptized also ... into the resurrection of the flesh"); Creed of the First Council of Toledo (400 C.E.): *resurrectionem vero humanae credimus carnis* ("we believe indeed in the resurrection of our human flesh"); Apostles' Creed (sixth century C.E.): *credo in ... carnis resurrectionem* ("I believe in ... the resurrection of the flesh"); Symbol of Faith of Leo IX (1053 C.E.): *credo etiam veram resurrectionem eiusdem carnis, quam nunc gesto* ("I believe also in the true resurrection of the same flesh which I now have"); Symbol of the IV Lateran Council (thirteenth century): *omnes homines in fine saeculi cum suis propriis resurgent corporibus quae nunc gestant* ("at the end of the age all human beings will rise again with their very same bodies

in the context of this conviction, shared alike by Catholic, Orthodox, and Protestant interpreters, that the resurrection that Paul expounds in this chapter was a resurrection of the flesh.

However, an important shift took place in the modern period. In an influential monograph published in 1896, Ernst Teichmann argued for a spiritualized notion of resurrection in 1 Corinthians 15, as a key step in a claimed development of Paul's eschatology from the Jewish concept of the resurrection of the flesh to a Hellenistic concept of disembodied immortality.[9] Teichmann argued, in a reading with clear affinities to Origen's earlier mediating view, that in this chapter Paul envisions a "spiritual" resurrection body, that is, a body no longer made up of flesh but composed of spirit, or πνεῦμα, a fine pneumatic "stuff" of which the heavenly bodies are composed.[10] In striking contrast to the traditional interpretation, Paul explicitly *opposes*, according to Teichmann's view, a resurrection of the flesh in 1 Corinthians 15.[11] However, Teichmann's interpretation of 1 Corinthians 15 was subject to two influential critiques, first by Albert Schweitzer and again, much later, by Joachim Jeremias.[12] These led to an increasing abandonment of Teichmann's and similar views, and a rallying to the patristic interpretation of resurrection in Paul as involving the miraculous reconstitution and transformation of the flesh. As a result, in 1986 Ben F. Meyer, in an outline of the history of research on the resurrection in Paul during the previous one hundred years, could report that Teichmann's interpretation of Paul's thought as involving the annihilation rather than the transformation of the fleshly body was "a dead letter for the vast majority today."[13] That estimate was certainly overstated but was indicative of a general trend. Meyer's own essay contributed to this trend, offering a classic case for the thesis that Paul's concept of the resurrection involved the revivification (and transformation to

---

which they now have"); Westminster Confession (seventeenth century): "all the dead shall be raised up, with the selfsame bodies, and none other (although with different qualities)."

[9] Teichmann, *Die paulinischen Vorstellungen von Auferstehung und Gericht und ihre Beziehung zur jüdischen Apokalyptik* (Freiburg: Mohr, 1896), 33–62.

[10] Ibid., 42–53.

[11] Ibid., 5. An important precursor to Teichmann's study was the work of Otto Pfleiderer (*Paulinism: A Contribution to the History of Primitive Christian Theology*, vol. 1, *Exposition of Paul's Doctrine* [trans. Edward Peters; London: Williams & Norgate, 1877]). Similarly to Teichmann, Pfleiderer argued that Paul's conception of the resurrection in 1 Corinthians 15 involved not "the old fleshly body" but instead the clothing of the pure spiritual part with a corresponding "spiritual corporeity, which not being fleshly is no more subject to decay, and is analogous to the heavenly body of the risen Christ, which consists … of heavenly light-substance (δόξα)" (p. 260; cf. 128, 131–32).

[12] See Schweitzer, *Paul and His Interpreters: A Critical History* (London: A. & C. Black, 1912), 76; and Jeremias, "Flesh and Blood Cannot Inherit the Kingdom of God (1 Cor. XV.50)," *NTS* 2 (1956): 151–59.

[13] Meyer, "Did Paul's View of the Resurrection of the Dead Undergo Development?" *TS* 47 (1986): 374.

imperishability) of the present body. A number of recent treatments have similarly argued that, in 1 Corinthians 15, Paul envisions the resurrection of the flesh.[14] However, an interpretation of the chapter largely along the lines suggested by Teichmann has in recent years gained an increasing amount of scholarly support. Today a number of interpreters argue that, in 1 Corinthians 15, Paul envisions a heavenly or "spiritual" body, which excludes participation of the earthly, mortal body in final salvation.[15]

Perhaps the most influential case in recent times for this understanding of resurrection in Paul is Dale Martin's exposition of 1 Corinthians 15 in ch. 5 of his monograph *The Corinthian Body*.[16] Martin's work has served to clarify the discussion in important ways, two of which call for particular mention. First, in contrast to hazy hypotheses about a "realized eschatology" mind-set among the Corinthians, Martin argues persuasively that "everything we know about the position of the strong [i.e., those at Corinth who denied the resurrection] can be accounted for by recourse to popular philosophy," in particular, a pervasive body/soul dualism that

---

[14] See Anthony Thiselton, *The First Epistle to the Corinthians: A Commentary on the Greek Text* (NIGTC; Grand Rapids: Eerdmans, 2000), 1257–1306; N. T. Wright, *Christian Origins and the Question of God*, vol. 3, *The Resurrection of the Son of God* (Minneapolis: Fortress, 2003), 340–61; Richard B. Hays, *First Corinthians* (IBC; Louisville: John Knox, 1997), 270–75; E. Earle Ellis, "Sōma in 1 Corinthians," *Int* 44 (1990): 132–44; Martin Hengel, "Das Begräbnis Jesu bei Paulus und die leibliche Auferstehung aus dem Grabe," in *Auferstehung - Resurrection: The Fourth Durham-Tübingen Research Symposium. Resurrection, Transfiguration, and Exaltation in Old Testament, Ancient Judaism and Early Christianity* (ed. Friedrich Avemarie and Hermann Lichtenberger; WUNT 135; Tübingen: Mohr Siebeck, 2001), 119–83; and Andrew Johnson, "Turning the World Upside Down in 1 Corinthians 15: Epistemology, the Resurrected Body and the New Creation," *EvQ* 75 (2003): 291–309. See also the earlier studies of Ronald Sider, "St. Paul's Conception of the Resurrection Body in 1 Corinthians XV.35–54," *NTS* 21 (1975): 428–39; and Bernhard Spörlein, *Die Leugnung der Auferstehung: Eine historisch-kritische Untersuchung zu I Kor 15* (Biblische Untersuchungen 7; Regensburg: Pustet, 1971), 109–21.

[15] See, e.g., Paula Fredriksen, "Vile Bodies: Paul and Augustine on the Resurrection of the Flesh," in *Biblical Hermeneutics in Historical Perspective: Studies in Honor of Karlfried Froehlich on His Sixtieth Birthday* (ed. Mark S. Burrows and Paul Rorem; Grand Rapids: Eerdmans, 1991), 75–87; Nikolaus Walter, "Leibliche Auferstehung? Zur Frage der Hellenisierung der Auferweckungshoffnung bei Paulus," in *Paulus, Apostel Jesu Christi: Festschrift für Günter Klein zum 70. Geburtstag* (ed. Michael Trowitzsch; Tübingen: Mohr Siebeck, 1998), 59; Andreas Lindemann, *Der Erste Korintherbrief* (HNT 9.1; Tübingen: Mohr Siebeck, 2000), 324–73 (the "more likely" interpretation); James D. G. Dunn, "How Are the Dead Raised? With What Body Do They Come? Reflections on 1 Corinthians 15," *SwJT* 45 (2002): 4–18; Peter Lampe, "Paul's Concept of a Spiritual Body," in *Resurrection: Theological and Scientific Assessments* (ed. Ted Peters, Robert John Russell, and Michael Welker; Grand Rapids: Eerdmans, 2002), 103–14; Jerry Sumney, "Post-Mortem Existence and Resurrection of the Body in Paul," *HBT* 31 (2009): 12–26; and Daniel A. Smith, *Revisiting the Empty Tomb: The Early History of Easter* (Minneapolis: Fortress, 2010), 27–45. For an influential version of this thesis from the previous generation, see Hans Grass, *Ostergeschehen und Osterberichte* (Göttingen: Vandenhoeck & Ruprecht, 1962), 146–73.

[16] Martin, *The Corinthian Body* (New Haven: Yale University Press, 1995).

exalted the spiritual and disparaged the body.¹⁷ Second, Martin reminds us that the sort of dualism that underlay the rejection of the resurrection at Corinth was not necessarily commensurate with our modern Cartesian contrast between matter and nonmaterial spirit. On some ancient views, spirit as well as body was conceived of as material or substantial, albeit the body of a lower, grosser form of matter, and spirit or *pneuma* of a higher, finer sort.¹⁸

How, according to Martin, does Paul respond to those at Corinth who challenged the resurrection? Martin argues that, on one level, Paul overturns these dualistic assumptions of the strong at Corinth by insisting on the future resurrection of the *body*. However, on another level, he compromises with these assumptions by *redefining* the body that is raised—not the body of flesh and bones but "a heavenly body composed of pneuma."¹⁹ Martin thus rejects an interpretation of resurrection in Paul such as that of Paul W. Gooch, who argues that Paul envisions a resurrection that is entirely nonbodily.²⁰ Rather, Martin claims, Paul thinks of what is raised as a "body" because he conceives of *pneuma* or spirit as a corporeal substance—the substance of which the heavenly bodies are composed and of which the resurrection body, too, will be composed, fitting it for heavenly habitation.²¹ But such an understanding of the resurrected body involves, according to Martin, Paul's "conscious rejection" of "the resurrection of the flesh."²² "Paul, for his part, rejects the notion of a resurrection of corpses or of flesh and blood."²³ Martin suggests that Paul reenvisions the risen body in this way, that is, as a body composed of heavenly "stuff" or matter, "so as to make it an acceptable category for immortality according to philosophical physiology."²⁴

Among those scholars who have built on the foundation of Martin's seminal work, especially significant contributions have been made by Jeffrey R. Asher and Troels Engberg-Pedersen.²⁵ Engberg-Pedersen's contribution is of particular importance. Although building on Martin's thesis that Paul's conception of the

---

¹⁷ Ibid., 108–17, 129.

¹⁸ Ibid., 108–23.

¹⁹ Ibid., 120.

²⁰ Gooch, "On Disembodied Resurrected Persons: A Study in the Logic of Christian Eschatology," *RelS* 17 (1981): 199–213.

²¹ Martin, *Corinthian Body* 126, 128–29, 276 n. 82.

²² Ibid., 123.

²³ Ibid., 130.

²⁴ Ibid.

²⁵ See Asher, *Polarity and Change in 1 Corinthians 15: A Study of Metaphysics, Rhetoric, and Resurrection* (HUT 42; Tübingen: Mohr Siebeck, 2000); cf. idem, "ΣΠΕΙΡΕΤΑΙ: Paul's Anthropogenic Metaphor in 1 Corinthians 15:42–44," *JBL* 120 (2001): 101–22. See also Engberg-Pedersen, "Complete and Incomplete Transformation in Paul: A Philosophical Reading of Paul on Body and Spirit," in Seim and Økland, *Metamorphoses*, 123–46; idem, "The Material Spirit: Cosmology and Ethics in Paul," *NTS* 55 (2009): 179–97; and, most recently, idem, *Cosmology and Self in the Apostle Paul: The Material Spirit* (Oxford: Oxford University Press, 2010), 8–38.

resurrection involved a body composed not of flesh but of the corporeal substance of *pneuma*, Engberg-Pedersen seeks to go beyond it by situating this putative Pauline conception of a body of material pneumatic substance more precisely within Greco-Roman philosophical thought. Engberg-Pedersen argues that Paul's "notion of the pneumatic resurrection body presupposes Stoic cosmology."[26] According to Engberg-Pedersen, Paul's treatment of the resurrection body in 1 Corinthians 15 reveals that the *pneuma* is in Paul's thought conceived, in Stoic and panentheistic fashion, as a material entity made up of the same ethereal substance as the sun, moon, and stars.[27] In the Stoic view of the afterlife, the ethereally material soul "leaves the body of flesh and blood behind and rises ... to take its place in heaven alongside other heavenly bodies made up of pneuma."[28] Paul's fundamentally Stoic conception likewise envisions salvation as a heavenly ascent to astral immortality, but an ascent not of the soul but of the *body*, which is *transformed* into ethereally material *pneuma*.[29] The result is a Pauline variation on the Stoic conception, which nonetheless "does not differ very much" from the Stoic understanding: "In Paul, the body of flesh and blood is transformed as a *whole—but into the very same* state as in Stoicism."[30] On Engberg-Pedersen's reading, Paul's conception of resurrection, involving a unique fusion of Jewish apocalyptic elements and Stoic cosmology, envisions an ethereally corporeal resurrection body that excludes the reconstitution of the body of flesh and bones.[31]

The thumbnail history of interpretation above illumines a point of critical relevance for the current debate regarding the conception of the resurrection body in 1 Corinthians 15. This debate is often framed in terms of "materialist" versus "nonmaterialist" readings of resurrection in Paul. But such categories actually obscure the key points at issue, whether in ancient, premodern, or current discussion of the passage. Not two, but three distinct views may be delineated. (1) A number of scholars argue, in concurrence with ancient interpreters such as Irenaeus, Jerome, and Augustine, that Paul's conception of the resurrection in 1 Corinthians 15 involves the resurrection (and glorious transformation to imperishability) of the once-dead *body of flesh and bones* from the tomb. (2) Other interpreters, however, congruent with Valentinian readings of this chapter extant as

---

[26] Engberg-Pedersen, *Cosmology and Self,* 37; see the entire section 26–38. See also idem, "Material Spirit," 180–87; idem, "Transformation," 124–29.

[27] See Engberg-Pedersen, *Cosmology and Self,* 8–38, 39–40, 43–44, 55, 62, 72, 103–5, 173–81. Engberg-Pedersen's thesis regarding Paul's conception of the resurrection body in 1 Corinthians 15 plays a crucial role in his reconstruction of Pauline theology, for it serves as the primary exegetical basis for his larger thesis, that Paul's theology reflects a Stoic philosophical framework and is essentially Stoic in its central features; see esp. Engberg-Pedersen, *Paul and the Stoics* (Edinburgh: T&T Clark, 2000).

[28] Engberg-Pedersen, *Cosmology and Self,* 32.

[29] Ibid., 26–34.

[30] Ibid., 32 (italics Engberg-Pedersen's).

[31] Ibid., 26–34.

early as the second century, argue that Paul in this chapter envisions a *nonmaterial body*, which excludes participation of the earthly, fleshly body in final salvation. (3) In a view with striking affinities to the reading of Teichmann in the nineteenth century and Origen in the third, Engberg-Pedersen, Martin, and Asher have recently argued that Paul's concept of the resurrection envisions an *ethereally material body* composed not of flesh but of the corporeal substance of *pneuma*. Moreover, each of these major positions represents a competing claim regarding the setting of Paul's concept of the resurrection in its ancient context. The first view maintains that Paul's conception of the resurrection in 1 Corinthians 15 assumes the mainstream ancient Jewish belief in the revivification of the entombed body and its transformation to imperishability. The second view, by contrast, argues that Paul's understanding represents a modification of the common Jewish viewpoint, in a Hellenistic or Platonizing direction. The third view, as advocated by Engberg-Pedersen, argues that the conception of resurrection in 1 Corinthians 15 involves a novel blend of Jewish apocalyptic expectations and Stoic cosmological speculation.

As this capsule history of interpretation has thus shown, the question is not, as it is often posed, whether Paul envisioned the resurrection as "material" or "nonmaterial," as "bodily" or "nonbodily," but whether Paul conceived of the resurrection as the bestowal of a new, incorporeal body, transformation into an ethereally corporeal body distinct from the present one, or the revivification of the body of flesh and bones laid in the tomb and its transformation to imperishability. Put in other terms, does Paul's treatment in the chapter reflect the dominant Jewish expectation of the resurrection of the present body to imperishability, or a modification of that conception in either a Platonic or Stoic direction? James D. G. Dunn defines the question, in light of recent study, with precision: "The real debate is whether Paul conceived of the resurrection body in terms of a reconstitution of the *flesh*."[32]

This debate has extraordinarily important implications for Paul's thought. If, on the one hand, Paul envisioned resurrection to either a disembodied or ethereally embodied state, Paul conceived of human redemption as a liberation from the present body and earthly existence, in order to share in the life of the heavenly realms. If, on the other hand, Paul envisioned a resurrection of the flesh, Paul conceived of human redemption as the restoration of the present body and its liberation from death, in order to share in the life of a renewed created order. The latter is a hope for the redemption of this world and this body; the former is a hope that this body and this world will be transcended in a world above. These contrasting claims regarding the apostle's vision of humanity's ultimate future entail radically different construals of Pauline soteriology, Christology, anthropology, and ethics. There is thus no area of Pauline theology that the debate concerning the nature of resurrection in Paul does not touch.

---

[32] Dunn, "1 Corinthians 15," 16 (italics Dunn's).

In this essay, I seek to make a contribution to this debate. In addressing this question, I will focus my efforts by interacting principally with the recent important studies of Martin, Asher, and Engberg-Pedersen. I will concentrate on the crux of Paul's exposition of the resurrection body, 1 Cor 15:36-54. Of course, a full exegesis of this lengthy and complex passage is well beyond the limits of this essay. Rather, I will examine key exegetical issues relating to the debate on the resurrection in Paul. Moreover, space will preclude full discussion of the setting of 1 Cor 15:36-54 within the larger context of views of the afterlife in the ancient world. I will instead focus, quite narrowly, on close analysis of hitherto neglected features of the rhetorical structure, syntax, and vocabulary of the passage. Yet, in so doing, I will seek to advance the debate regarding the proper contextualization of this passage in its ancient philosophical and conceptual milieu. For the question whether this passage reflects the mainstream Jewish concept of the revivification of the entombed body, a Platonizing concept of disembodied immortality, or a Stoicizing concept of ethereally material but nonfleshly existence *can be determined only by a close analysis of Paul's own language and the underlying structure of his thought.* The exegetical key to the nature of the resurrection in Paul is thus the structure of Paul's own argument in 1 Corinthians 15. This article will offer a new analysis and proposal regarding the literary and rhetorical structure of Paul's argument. In light of this analysis I will argue, against the grain of much contemporary interpretation of 1 Corinthians 15, that the resurrection Paul envisions in this chapter involves the eschatological restoration to life of the mortal body of flesh and bones, and its transformation to be imperishable.

II. THE STRUCTURE OF 1 CORINTHIANS 15:36-54 AND ITS IMPLICATIONS

It is widely recognized that 1 Cor 15:36-54 forms an integral unit within the wider chapter, focused on an exploration of the nature of the resurrection body.[33] General agreement also exists regarding the following core structural features of

---

[33] For discussion of the structure of the wider chapter, see Margaret M. Mitchell, *Paul and the Rhetoric of Reconciliation: An Exegetical Investigation of the Language and Composition of 1 Corinthians* (Louisville: Westminster John Knox, 1993), 283-91; Duane F. Watson, "Paul's Rhetorical Strategy in 1 Corinthians 15," in *Rhetoric and the New Testament: Essays from the 1992 Heidelberg Conference* (ed. Stanley E. Porter and Thomas H. Olbricht; JSNTSup 90; Sheffield: JSOT Press, 1993), 231-49; Michael Bünker, *Briefformular und rhetorische Disposition im 1 Korintherbrief* (GTA 28; Göttingen: Vandenhoeck & Ruprecht, 1983), 59-72; David E. Garland, *1 Corinthians* (BECNT; Grand Rapids: Baker Academic, 2003), 679-80; Wolfgang Schrage, *Der erste Brief an die Korinther* (4 vols.; EKKNT; Neukirchen-Vluyn: Neukirchener Verlag, 2001), 4:9; and Hans Conzelmann, *Der erste Brief an die Korinther* (2nd ed.; KEK; Göttingen: Vandenhoeck & Ruprecht, 1981), 343.

the unit: (1) The passage functions as a unified response to the twofold objection of the interlocutor in v. 35: "How are the dead raised? And with what kind of body do they come?"[34] (2) Verses 36–49 and 50–54 nonetheless form distinct units within the larger passage.[35] At the same time, Joachim Jeremias's well-known suggestion that Paul's response is arranged in a chiastic pattern, vv. 36–49 addressing the interlocutor's second question ("And with what kind of body do they come?"), and vv. 50–57 taking up the first ("How are the dead raised?") appears forced and has generally not been followed.[36] (3) Verse 42 marks a new section within the larger passage, as Paul begins the application (οὕτως καὶ ἡ ἀνάστασις τῶν νεκρῶν, 15:42) of the series of analogies in vv. 36–41. (4) The unit vv. 42–49 further subdivides into vv. 42–44a, an artful series of four antitheses, and vv. 44b–49, an explanation of the concept of the *sōma pneumatikon* introduced in v. 44a.[37] (5) A concentric or envelope structure within vv. 50–54a (or 50–53) further demarcates these verses as a unit distinct from both the section preceding (vv. 42–49) and the section following (vv. 54b–57).[38] (6) A striking feature of the passage as a whole, which sets it apart from the rest of the chapter, is that the entire unit 15:36–54 is strongly marked by a series of antitheses, as Paul sets the present body and the coming resurrection body in stark contrast.[39]

I regard each of these structural observations as persuasive; however, they are of only limited value in addressing the exegetical issues relating to the debate regarding the resurrection in 1 Corinthians 15. In this essay I offer a new proposal regarding a key feature of the conceptual and syntactic structure of 1 Cor 15:36–54. I am convinced that the structure of Paul's argument can be set forth with greater precision than has been done previously, and that a fuller grasp of Paul's literary shaping of the passage can make important contributions to the current debate.

I propose that Paul's argument in 1 Cor 15:36–54 is structured by *twelve* antithetically paired verbs (that is, six pairs of verbs) denoting death (or the mortal state) and resurrection (or the risen state) in vv. 36–49, followed by *seven* verbs denoting resurrection or transformation in vv. 50–54. These two segments of Paul's argument may be delineated as follows. The section of twelve paired verbs in vv. 36–49 develops a series of contrasts or oppositions between the present body and the risen body. In 15:36–37 the antemortem body, represented by the seed, "dies" (ἀποθάνῃ) but is "made alive" (ζῳοποιεῖται) by God. In 15:42–44, in a skillful

---

[34] Correctly emphasized by Asher, *Polarity*, 147–57.
[35] The evidence is marshaled most fully by Werner Stenger, "Beobachtungen zur Argumentationsstruktur von 1 Kor 15," *LB* 45 (1979): 100–101.
[36] Jeremias, "Flesh and Blood," 156–57; for cogent criticisms of Jeremias's proposal, see John Gillman, "Transformation in 1 Cor 15,50–53," *ETL* 58 (1982): 309–22.
[37] Stenger, "Argumentationsstruktur," 116–20.
[38] See Gillman, "Transformation," 315–22; Stenger, "Argumentationsstruktur," 121–25; Asher, *Polarity*, 164–65 n. 42.
[39] This is a major emphasis of Asher's study; see *Polarity*, 8–12, 93–117, 134–37, 141–45.

series of eight antithetically paired verbs, the body is "sown" (σπείρεται) in decay, dishonor, and weakness, as a *sōma psychikon*, but is "raised" (ἐγείρεται) in incorruption, glory, and power, as a *sōma pneumatikon*. In 15:49, we "were clothed" (ἐφορέσαμεν) with the image of Adam, but we "will be clothed" (φορέσομεν) with the image of Christ. Throughout the section 15:36-49, Paul effectively highlights the connections between the paired verbs by a series of rhetorical devices, including parallelism, asyndeton, assonance, and repetition.

The second section in 15:50-54 marks a shift from the structure of paired antithetical verbs in 15:36-49. The hinge point appears to be Paul's declaration in v. 50 that "flesh and blood cannot inherit the kingdom of God, nor does what is perishable inherit that which is imperishable." This is immediately followed by the revelation of the mystery in v. 51: "we shall not all sleep, but we shall all be changed." Paul employs the contrasting pairs of verbs denoting death and resurrection (vv. 36, 42–44, 49) prior to v. 50, but from that point forward he uses only verbs denoting resurrection or transformation (vv. 51, 52, 53–54). In this latter section (15:50–54) Paul employs seven verbs to describe this coming resurrection and tranformation: ἀλάσσω (twice), ἐγείρω (once), and ἐνδύω (four times).

Paul's use in 15:53–54 of eight antithetically paired substantives complements the eight antithetically paired verbs in 15:42–44, thus constituting a skillful *inclusio* bracketing the entire section 15:42–54. The inclusion is strengthened by the first pair of contrasted substantives in vv. 53–54 (τὸ φθαρτὸν τοῦτο/ἀφθαρσία), which mirrors the first verbal pair in v. 42 (σπείρεται ἐν φθορᾷ/ἐγείρεται ἐν ἀφθαρσίᾳ). The second pair of contrasted substantives in vv. 53–54 (τὸ θνητὸν τοῦτο/ἀθανασία) recalls the first verbal pair in the passage (ζῳοποιεῖται/ἀποθάνῃ, 15:36), thus forming a further inclusion which frames the passage as a whole. The final substantive in this second pair (ἀθανασία, 15:54a) in turn skillfully prepares the way for the announcement of the destruction of death (θάνατος) in the passage that follows, 15:54b-57. The structure of the entire passage (15:36–54) may be set out as on the following page.

A grasp of the structure of Paul's exposition, I am convinced, is essential in order to understand the function of the series of oppositions between the mortal body and the risen body in Paul's argument. These contrasts play a crucial role in Martin's analysis of the passage.[40] For Martin, this sequence of contrasts establishes an ontological distinction between this present body and the risen body, which rules out their somatic identity:

> Paul reaffirms the resurrection of their *bodies*; but to convince Christians influenced by philosophy, he admits that he himself does not believe in a resurrection of *this* body.[41]

---

[40] Martin, *Corinthian Body*, 126–30.
[41] Ibid., 130 (italics Martin's).

	Subject	Verb	Predicate Complements
36	ὃ σπείρεις (that which you sow)	ἀποθάνῃ (dies)	—
		ζωοποιεῖται (is made alive)	—
42	(τὸ σῶμα [the body]) (cf. 36–41, 44)	σπείρεται (is sown)	ἐν φθορᾷ (in decay)
		ἐγείρεται (is raised)	ἐν ἀφθαρσίᾳ (in incorruption)
43		σπείρεται (is sown)	ἐν ἀτιμίᾳ (in dishonor)
		ἐγείρεται (is raised)	ἐν δόξῃ (in glory)
		σπείρεται (is sown)	ἐν ἀσθενείᾳ (in weakness)
		ἐγείρεται (is raised)	ἐν δυνάμει (in power)
44		σπείρεται (is sown)	σῶμα ψυχικόν (a body given life by the soul)
		ἐγείρεται (is raised)	σῶμα πνευματικόν (a body given life by the Spirit)
49	(ἡμεῖς [we])	ἐφορέσαμεν (we were clothed)	τὴν εἰκόνα τοῦ χοϊκοῦ (with the image of the man of dust)
		φορέσομεν (we will be clothed)	καὶ τὴν εἰκόνα τοῦ ἐπουρανίου (also with the image of the man from heaven)
51	πάντες (all)	ἀλλαγησόμεθα (we will be changed)	—
52	οἱ νεκροί (the dead)	ἐγερθήσονται (will be raised)	ἄφθαρτοι (imperishable)
	ἡμεῖς (we)	ἀλλαγησόμεθα (will be changed)	—
53	τὸ φθαρτὸν τοῦτο (this perishable body)	δεῖ ἐνδύσασθαι (must be clothed with)	ἀφθαρσίαν (imperishability)
	τὸ θνητὸν τοῦτο (this mortal body)	δεῖ ἐνδύσασθαι (must be clothed with)	ἀθανασίαν (immortality)
54	τὸ φθαρτὸν τοῦτο (this perishable body)	ἐνδύσηται (is clothed with)	ἀφθαρσίαν (imperishability)
	τὸ θνητὸν τοῦτο (this mortal body)	ἐνδύσηται (is clothed with)	ἀθανασίαν (immortality)

The transformation expected at the eschaton will cause the Christian body to shed the lower parts of its current nature and be left with the purer, transformed part of the pneuma. Christians will have bodies without flesh, blood, or soul—composed solely of pneumatic substance—light, airy, luminous bodies.[42]

Martin's reading of the function of the oppositions between the mortal and risen state in Paul's argument has been widely followed. Asher, for example, maintains that Paul's contrasts express a cosmic polarity that prohibits a "terrestrial human form or substance" from partaking of immortality.[43] Dunn similarly argues that Paul's series of contrasting pairs (e.g., corruption/incorruption, dishonor/glory) serves to underline the impossibility that "the physical body, weak and subject to corruption and death" should share in resurrection life.[44] For many interpreters, it seems, Paul's series of oppositions between the present and risen body, with their reference to what is sown being x and what is raised being y (15:42–44; cf. 15:52–54), points to a radical discontinuity between the mortal body and the risen body in Paul's thought, which precludes the possibility that Paul believed in a resurrection of *this* body.

However, close examination of the structure proposed here, I would argue, reveals that this assumption fails to grasp the actual function of the contrasts in Paul's argument. Four observations will be crucial as we unpack the implications of Paul's structure. These observations relate to (1) the subject of Paul's antithetical verb pairs in 15:36–49; (2) the subject of Paul's verbs of resurrection and change in 15:50–54; (3) the nature of the verbs Paul employs in the passage for the resurrection event; and (4) the predicate complements of Paul's verbs and verbal pairs in 15:36–54.

The Subject of Paul's Paired Verbs in 15:36–49

My first observation: the *subject* of the antithetical verbal pairs in 15:36–49 is *one and the same* both for verbs denoting death and for those denoting resurrection. This pattern is evident throughout the entire section 15:36–49. In v. 36 the seed, representative of the present mortal body, "dies" but "is made alive" again by God. In vv. 42–44 the subject remains the perishable body, which is "sown" in mortality and death but "raised" to imperishable life. In v. 49 a single subject is clothed first with the image of Adam and thereafter with the image of Christ. In the structure of 15:36–49, the contrasts occur not in the *subject* of these periods but in their *predicates* (verbs and verbal complements).

This simple observation, which is nonetheless commonly ignored by commentators, has profound exegetical implications. But before exploring these, an

---

[42] Ibid., 132.
[43] Asher, *Polarity*, 153.
[44] Dunn, "1 Corinthians 15," 16; cf. also Teichmann, *Die paulinischen Vorstellungen*, 48.

important question must be addressed. Within 15:36–49, the subject of the eight paired verbs in vv. 42–44 is not expressed. The structural analysis above assumes, with the great majority of interpreters, that the implied subject of these passive verbs is τὸ σῶμα. Is this assumption warranted?

A few scholars have argued that these verbs, as "impersonal passives," have no implicit subject but refer merely to the activity of sowing and raising (i.e., "there is a sowing"/"there is a raising").[45] However, this view has its source in a misunderstanding of Greek syntax. Unlike English, German, and other modern languages, there are no true impersonal verbs—that is, finite verbs that lack a subject—in ancient Greek. Those ancient Greek verbs regularly translated into the modern languages as impersonal verbs invariably have an implied subject in their original settings, which is indicated by lexical or contextual factors.[46] So-called impersonal passives do not merely express the verbal idea but always have a subject implied within their context.[47]

What, then, is the implied subject of the paired verbs in 1 Cor 15:42–44? It is evident from the following contextual factors that the subject of those verbs is the present, perishable body:

1. In the preceding analogy Paul has identified the seed that is *sown* (ὃ σπείρεις, v. 36; ὃ σπείρεις, v. 37; cf. τῶν σπερμάτων, v. 38) with the present mortal *body* (vv. 36–38). The obvious implication is that, when he uses this same verb (σπείρεται, vv. 42–44 [four times]) in the application of the analogy, the subject is the present body.

2. The contrasts in 15:42–44 apply the series of analogies in 15:36–41 (οὕτως καὶ ἡ ἀνάστασις τῶν νεκρῶν, v. 42). These analogies contrast various kinds of *flesh*

---

[45] So C. K. Barrett, *A Commentary on the First Epistle to the Corinthians* (BNTC; New York: Harper & Row, 1968), 372; Gillman, "Transformation," 327–28; Stenger, "Argumentationsstruktur," 117.

[46] See Raphael Kühner and Bernhard Gerth, *Ausführliche Grammatik der griechischen Sprache* (Hannover: Hahnsche, 1904), 2.1:36 ("Unpersönliche Verben … kennt die griechische Sprache nicht"); A. T. Robertson, *A Grammar of the Greek New Testament in the Light of Historical Research* (4th ed.; Nashville: Broadman, 1934), 391–93 ("The conclusion of the whole matter is that the subject is either expressed or implied by various linguistic devices" [p. 393]). Using a somewhat different nomenclature, Herbert Weir Smyth designates a class of "impersonal" and "quasi-impersonal" verbs in ancient Greek, but points out that in both cases a subject is invariably implied, in the former class by lexical features and in the latter class "derived from the context" (*A Greek Grammar for Colleges* [Cambridge, MA: Harvard University Press, 1920], 260). The discussion in Friedrich Blass, Albert Debrunner, and Freidrich Rehkopf (*Grammatik des neutestamentlichen Griechisch* [18th ed.; Göttingen: Vandenhoeck & Ruprecht, 2001], 107–8) is inadequate.

[47] So Robertson, *Grammar*, 392: in so-called impersonal passives "the subject is involved in the action of the verb." See also Smyth, *Greek Grammar*, 260: in impersonal passives "the subject is merely indicated in the verbal ending" (cf. p. 396). Thus (to cite one representative example), in 1 Pet 4:6 the implied subject of εὐηγγελίσθη is τὸ εὐαγγέλιον.

(v. 39) and various kinds of *bodies* (vv. 37–38, 40–41). In 15:36–41 the word σῶμα occurs five times. This context indicates that the subject of the contrasts in 15:42–44, in which the analogy is applied, is the human *body*.

3. In the first antithesis in 15:42, the subject of σπείρεται is said to be sown "in corruption" (ἐν φθορᾷ). In my view, the verb σπείρεται in vv. 42–44, in light of the preceding analogy (ὃ σπείρεις, vv. 36, 37), most likely refers to the act of *burial*. If so, the implied subject is the body, which is buried and decays in the earth. Other interpreters, however, take σπείρεται as a reference not to burial but to *present mortal existence*.[48] On this view, the implied subject is the living but mortal body that is subject to decay. In either case, the implied subject is the mortal body, and the modifier ἐν φθορᾷ accents its perishable and corruptible nature.

4. In the fourth antithesis in 15:44, the subject of σπείρεται is said to be sown as a σῶμα ψυχικόν. This predicate complement identifies the subject as a body, and the following context (vv. 44b–49) further identifies the σῶμα ψυχικόν as the present mortal body.

All of these factors indicate that the subject of the paired verbs σπείρεται and ἐγείρεται in 15:42–44 is the present, perishable body. But here a further objection must be considered. It is sometimes assumed that Paul's ellipsis of the subject in vv. 42–44 permits the conclusion that the paired verbs have *distinct* subjects, the subject of the first verb indeed being the present body, but the subject of the second verb referring to a new resurrection body distinct from the mortal body.[49] Such a construal of the text, however, is simply not consistent with ancient Greek usage. Within the conventions of ancient Greek syntax, consecutive verbs, apart from the introduction of a new subject, are understood to have the same subject as the verb preceding (e.g., Matt 6:26; 16:21; Mark 4:32; 1 Cor 13:5–7; 15:3–4).[50] If a change of subject between consecutive verbs occurs, this must normally (for obvious reasons of clarity) be expressed (e.g., Matt 11:5; 13:4–8; 24:40–41; Mark 12:32; Luke 1:11–13; 12:24; Rom 14:4–6). Distinct subjects for the verbs in 15:42–44 would thus require a construction such as ὃ μὲν σπείρεται … ἄλλο ἐγείρεται ("one [body] is sown … another [body] is raised").[51] An exception to this rule occurs when the object of a previous verb, or a noun or pronoun within its clause, is taken up as the subject of the verb that follows (e.g., Mark 9:27; Luke 8:29; John 19:31).[52] However, this syntactic feature is not present in the passage under consideration. Other

---

[48] So Asher, "Anthropogenic Metaphor"; Garland, *1 Corinthians*, 732–33; Conzelmann, *Der erste Brief an die Korinther*, 346 n. 25.

[49] Such an understanding appears to underlie the exegesis of Martin (*Corinthian Body*, 126–30) and Dunn ("1 Corinthians 15," 10–17).

[50] For further discussion of the points that follow, see esp. Kühner-Gerth, *Grammatik*, 2.1:32–36; 2.2:560–71; and Smyth, *Greek Grammar*, 259–61. For ease of reference, I will confine the examples given here to the NT.

[51] Cf. Mark 4:4–8; Luke 23:33; Rom 14:5; 1 Cor 11:21; 12:8–10.

[52] Cf. Kühner-Gerth, *Grammatik*, 2.1:35; 2.2:561.

exceptions are rare and are signaled by unmistakable contextual factors (e.g., Matt 14:20; 22:30; Mark 4:27; Heb 4:8; 1 John 5:16). Such factors are lacking in 1 Cor 15:42–44. Moreover, the view that the subject changes between σπείρεται and ἐγείρεται involves the further improbable claim that the subject changes *repeatedly*, without grammatical indication, a total of seven times in the space of vv. 42–44. There is simply no precedent for such a phenomenon anywhere in ancient Greek literature.

The conventions of Greek syntax would thus appear to demand that the consecutive verbs in 1 Cor 15:42–44 have a single subject. Indeed, the identity of subject between these two verbs receives emphatic stress through the pointed assonance of the paired verbs (σπείρεται/ἐγείρεται).[53] The effect of the assonance is heightened by Paul's use of asyndeton (there are no connectors between the paired verbs) and repetition or anaphora (the two verbs are each repeated four times in 15:42–44). The overall rhetorical effect is to strongly emphasize that the paired verbs have a single subject—the present, earthly body of flesh and bone.

The evidence presented above is, in my view, sufficient to establish the point: the subject of the verbal pairs throughout 15:36–49 is *one and the same* both for verbs denoting death (or the mortal state) and for those denoting resurrection (or the risen state). The subject throughout is the present, perishable body, which "dies" but "is made alive" again by God (v. 36), which is "sown" (σπείρεται) in mortality and death but "raised" (ἐγείρεται) to imperishable life (vv. 42–44). The importance of this for Paul's understanding of the resurrection event can hardly be overstated. Paul does not describe resurrection as an event in which *x* (the present body) is sown but *y* (a body distinct from the present body) is raised, but in which a single *x* (the present body) is sown as a perishable *x* but raised as an imperishable *x*. The subject of the verbs in 15:36–49 denoting resurrection thus does not refer, as Martin claims, to some "immortal and incorruptible part" of the body that does not die, but rather refers to the mortal, corruptible body, which *dies* but in resurrection is *restored to life* and made incorruptible. The same perishable body that is "sown" in mortality and decay (σπείρεται) is thereafter "raised" to imperishable life (ἐγείρεται).[54] Martin, Asher, and Engberg-Pedersen argue that Paul's conception of resurrection excludes the mortal and perishable flesh from eschatological salvation. But Paul's sequence of paired verbs in 1 Cor 15:36–49 indicates that, in Paul's thought, it is precisely that which perishes—the mortal body—that in the resurrection is given new, imperishable life.

---

[53] Paul's skillful use of assonance in the pairing of σπείρεται and ἐγείρεται combines both *homoioarcton* (similarity of word beginnings) and *homoioptoton* (similarity of inflectional endings). See Blass-Debrunner-Rehkopf, *Grammatik*, 422.

[54] Cf. Sider, "Resurrection Body," 435; Johnson, "Turning the World Upside Down," 298; Spörlein, *Der Leugnung der Auferstehung*, 117.

The Subject of Paul's Verbs of Resurrection and Change in 15:50-54

This brings us to the second observation. When Paul shifts in 15:50-54 from paired verbs denoting death and resurrection to verbs denoting solely resurrection or transformation, here too it is the *present perishable body* that is the subject of this resurrection and transformation (vv. 51, 52, 53-54). The subjects of these verbs are respectively "we" (vv. 51, 52), "the dead" (v. 52), "this perishable body" (vv. 53-54), and "this mortal body" (vv. 53-54). The "we" in v. 52, who are contrasted with "the dead" (the "we" of v. 51 embraces both groups), are without controversy the living, *embodied* persons who remain until the coming of the Lord. "The dead" is the usual translation for οἱ νεκροί in v. 52. However, νεκρός differs from the English term in regularly denoting the dead in their *bodily* aspect, being most nearly equivalent to our "corpse."[55] In vv. 53-54, the subject that clothes itself with imperishability is explicitly "this perishable body" (τὸ φθαρτὸν τοῦτο) and "this mortal body" (τὸ θνητὸν τοῦτο).[56] As John Gillman observes, "The demonstrative adjective τοῦτο signals that it is precisely this earthly body, understood in a wholistic sense, which puts on immortality and incorruption."[57]

The force of the syntax can hardly be contested, but its far-reaching significance for Paul's understanding of the resurrection in 1 Corinthians 15 has not been sufficiently recognized. Throughout 15:50-54, the subject of the verbs Paul uses to describe the resurrection event is the corruptible body of flesh, whether laid in the tomb or still living at the parousia. It is this present body that is raised and transformed. The section 15:53-54 in particular forms a striking counterpoint to Martin's assertion that Paul "does not believe in a resurrection of *this* body," for in vv. 53-54 the subject that undergoes transformation is precisely the corruptible (φθαρτός) and mortal (θνητός) body of flesh and bones. Indeed, the fourfold repetition of "this" (τοῦτο) emphasizes that it is *this* mortal, perishable body that is the subject of the transformation. "The subject persists throughout the radical change."[58] Mortal flesh, far from being excluded from this divine, saving event, is the subject of that event.

---

[55] See J. H. Heinrich Schmidt, *Synonymik der griechischen Sprache* (4 vols.; Leipzig: Teubner, 1876-78), 4:54; and cf. Matt 11:5; 23:27; Luke 7:14-15; 24:5; Heb 11:35. This is recognized by both Martin (*Corinthian Body*, 122-23) and Engberg-Pedersen (*Cosmology and Self*, 26). However, its implications are not fully appreciated.

[56] As almost all interpreters are agreed, the implicit substantive, evident from the neuter adjectives, is σῶμα. A few interpreters suggest that τὸ φθαρτὸν τοῦτο and τὸ θνητὸν τοῦτο may be taken as abstract substantives ("this corruptibility of ours"/"this mortality of ours"); Barrett considers this a "possible" rendering (*First Epistle to the Corinthians*, 382). Paul's use of the demonstrative adjective τοῦτο makes this interpretation highly unlikely. In either case, however, the referent is clearly the present body in its corruptibility and mortality.

[57] Gillman, "Transformation," 331-32.

[58] Sider, "Resurrection Body," 438; cf. Spörlein, *Der Leugnung der Auferstehung*, 44.

The Nature of the Verbs Paul Employs for the Resurrection Event in 15:36–54

My third observation is closely related to the first two. We have seen that the subject of Paul's verbs throughout the passage is the present earthly body. What is the nature of the resurrection event of which this present body is the subject? In Martin's exegesis, the resurrection event in Paul is frequently described with verbs denoting divestment and annihilation of the mortal flesh.[59] In striking contrast, the five verbs that Paul employs in 1 Cor 15:36–54 for the resurrection event are ζῳοποιέω ("make alive"; vv. 36, 45; cf. 15:22), ἐγείρω ("raise to life"; vv. 42–44, 52; cf. 15:3, 12–17, 20, 29, 32, 35), φορέω ("be clothed"; v. 49), ἀλλάσσω ("change"; vv. 51, 52), and ἐνδύω ("clothe"; vv. 53, 54). Each of these verbs expresses, in different ways, not the annihilation or replacement of the fleshly body but its revival (ζῳοποιέω, ἐγείρω), investiture (φορέω, ἐνδύω), and transformation (ἀλλάσσω).

Asher and Engberg-Pedersen have each offered cogent criticisms of this aspect of Martin's reading of the passage.[60] As Asher notes, "Martin's understanding of the nature of the transformation that will take place does not take into account Paul's description of the resurrection as an investiture in vv. 53–54."[61] But Asher and Engberg-Pedersen's exegesis of these verbs is equally unsatisfying. In Paul's resurrection expectation as portrayed by Asher and Engberg-Pedersen, the result of the resurrection event is the replacement of the earthly body with a body composed of heavenly matter. The terrestrial body perishes and is replaced by another. By contrast, the verbs Paul employs for the resurrection describe the *revival* and *enhancement* of the mortal body. What was dead is "made alive" (v. 36). The once mortal body is transformed from a state of corruption (τὸ φθαρτὸν τοῦτο, vv. 53–54; cf. ἐν φθορᾷ, v. 42) to a state of freedom from corruption (ἀφθαρσίαν, vv. 53–54; cf. ἐν ἀφθαρσίᾳ, v. 42; ἄφθαρτοι, v. 52). The substance of flesh is not annihilated, but "raised" (v. 52), "transformed" (vv. 51–52), and "clothed" with imperishability and immortality (vv. 53–54).

Unfortunately, space precludes a full discussion here of these five verbs, each of which in different ways excludes the conception of a replacement of the earthly body with an ethereal one. I wish to focus briefly here on only one of these, the verb ἀλλάσσω ("change"; 15:51, 52). That discussion will lead in turn to my fourth and final observation regarding the structure of 15:36–54.

---

[59] In Paul's view of resurrection, according to Martin, "the raised body is *stripped* of flesh, blood, and soul" (*Corinthian Body*, 129); the mortal body must "*shed* the lower parts of its current nature" (p. 132), with both flesh and soul "*sloughed off* along the way" (p. 126) (all italics mine).

[60] See Engberg-Pedersen, *Cosmology and Self*, 32, 221 n. 85; Asher, *Polarity*, 156 n. 20.

[61] Asher, *Polarity*, 156 n. 20.

III. Paul's Language of "Change" within the Structure of 15:36–54

The implications of Paul's language of *change*, expressed by the verb ἀλλάσσω (15:51, 52), have not, I would argue, been fully appreciated in the current discussion. Paul's choice of this verb is highly significant, for, like the other verbs Paul employs for the resurrection event throughout 15:36–54, it does not imply the destruction, but rather the continued existence and enhancement, of its subject. Put most simply, change implies continuity as well as discontinuity; for *x* to *change*, *x* must *continue to exist* in order to be changed. Neither Martin's portrayal of resurrection in Paul as abandonment of the mortal body, nor the claim of Asher and Engberg-Pedersen that, in the resurrection, the body of flesh and bones ceases to exist, is consistent, it would seem, with the *continued existence* of the present body implied by Paul's language of "change."

Perhaps not surprisingly, among the proponents of an ethereal resurrection body in Paul, it is the philosophically trained Engberg-Pedersen who has grasped most perceptively the challenge that the structure of Paul's actual language presents to this interpretation—although the solution he adopts is, I will argue, not satisfactory. Unlike many interpreters, Engberg-Pedersen fully appreciates the significance of the fact that the subject of Paul's verbs of transformation is the present earthly body and what this means for the continuity of the present and risen body in Paul's thought:

> First on continuity. Definitely yes. That, I suggest, is in fact the very point of the τοῦτο that Paul repeats four times in 15:53–54: that "*this* corruptible (something)" and "*this* mortal (something)" (meaning this individual body) will put on incorruption and immortality. If "this mortal and corruptible something," which must consist of flesh and blood, is going to put on immortality and incorruption, then it must, as it were, *be* there for that operation to be successful.[62]

But how, then, is it possible for this Pauline conception of *continuity accompanied by change* to be accounted for in a conception of resurrection in Paul's thought involving (as in Engberg-Pedersen's view) the *replacement* of the body of flesh and bones by a body of ethereal *pneuma*? Engberg-Pedersen suggests the following solution:

> ... there will be a change, which will touch both the dead and the living. And this change (15:53–4) will mean that "*this* corruptible (something)" and "*this* mortal (something)" (meaning this *individual* body) puts on "incorruption" and "immortality." Here the process that Paul has in mind is the one that in the Aristotelian tradition was called "substantive change": that the whole substance

---

[62] Engberg-Pedersen, "Transformation," 128 (italics Engberg-Pedersen's).

changes into an altogether different, new substance.... It is not that the flesh and blood will in some sense be "shed" in such a way that it is only what *remains* that will be resurrected. No, the individual body of flesh and blood will be *transformed as a whole* so as to become through and through a pneumatic one.[63]

Engberg-Pedersen's proposed solution deserves closer examination. Aristotle's notion of "substantive change," to which Engberg-Pedersen calls attention, involves the substance or essence of a thing. In substantive change, a previously nonexistent entity comes into existence (Aristotle calls this γένεσις, "coming into being"), an existing entity is destroyed (the term Aristotle uses is φθορά, "corruption"), or a simultaneous process of destruction (φθορά) and generation (γένεσις) produces an entirely new entity (see Aristotle, *Cat.* 14; *Phys.* 5.1; *Gen. corr.* 1.3–4). This technical Aristotelian conception of substantive or essential change, differing from more common understandings of change in antiquity, involves a unique kind of "change" whereby a subject or substance passes into or out of existence, comes into being or ceases to be. An example Aristole gives of substantive change involving simultaneous corruption and origination is the process whereby water changes into air, or air into water (*Gen. corr.* 1.4). Engberg-Pedersen proposes that Paul uses "change" in this specialized sense of substantive change, to denote the "passing-away" of the body composed of flesh and the "coming-to-be" of the body composed of *pneuma*.[64]

This conception of "substantive change" contrasts with Aristotle's notion of "qualitative change" or "alteration" (ἀλλοίωσις). In qualitative change, the substance or essence of an entity remains intact, but the entity changes in its qualities, properties, or mode of existence (see Aristotle, *Phys.* 7.2; *Cael.* 1.3; *Cat.* 14; *Metaph.* 8.1.7–8). Qualitative change, or *alloiosis* (expressed by the noun ἀλλοίωσις or its verbal cognate ἀλλοιόω), involves the qualities, states, or dispositions that inhere in a subject—the subject becomes healthy or sick, warm or cold, white or black, but the underlying substance perdures.[65] This philosophical conception of qualitative or modal change coincides with the general nonphilosophical use of the vocabulary of "change" in antiquity, as both the philosophical concept of *alloiosis* and the popular usage involve the concept of transformation or alteration of an existing and perduring entity or subject.

Echoes of an Ancient Exegetical Debate

Does Paul's notion of "change" in 1 Cor 15:51–52 involve a qualitative change, in which the present body is enhanced and transformed, or a substantive change,

---

[63] Engberg-Pedersen, *Cosmology and Self,* 32 (italics Engberg-Pedersen's); cf. 220–21 n. 84.
[64] Engberg-Pedersen, "Transformation," 128.
[65] Chryssipus (*SVF* 2:494) defines *alloiosis* as "either change in regard to quality, or alteration of a previously existing quality" (ἀλλοίωσιν δὲ ἢ μεταβολὴν κατὰ τὸ ποιὸν ἢ ἀλλαγὴν τῆς προϋπαρχούσης ποιότητος). Cf. Galen, *De meth. med.* 10.88: ἀλλαγὴν εἶναι τοῦ προϋπάρχοντος τὴν ἀλλοίωσιν ("*alloiosis* is alteration of a preexisting quality"); and Didymus, *Ps.T.* 184.32: καὶ γὰρ ἡ ἀλλοίωσις μεταβολὴν ποιότητος σημαίνει ("for *alloiosis* signifies change in quality").

in which the present body is destroyed and replaced by another? Engberg-Pedersen's insightful raising of this issue mirrors a little-known ancient exegetical debate regarding this very question, which took place within the wider ancient debate over the interpretation of 1 Corinthians 15 discussed in section I of this study.[66] Within a widespread stream of interpretation of 1 Corinthians 15, the verb ἀλλάσσω ("change") in vv. 51–52 was understood in terms of qualitative change, and thus as closely synonymous with ἀλλοιόω. This is illustrated by the phenomenon that a number of ancient exegetes read the words ὑπὲρ τῶν ἀλλοιωθησομένων ("for those who will be changed"), found in a number of superscriptions in the Psalter, in explicit connection with the words πάντες δὲ ἀλλαγησόμεθα ("but we shall all be changed") in 1 Cor 15:51, as a reference to the coming bodily transformation at the resurrection.[67] On this interpretation, in the resurrection the substance of flesh is not destroyed but enlivened and enhanced with new glorious qualities. Among interpreters of Origen's school such as Didymus, by contrast, this equation of ἀλλάσσω in 1 Cor 15:51–52 with ἀλλοιόω, and thus with *alloiosis* or qualitative change, was explicitly rejected. Instead, ἀλλάσσω in these verses was understood in terms of substantive change—in the resurrection the flesh perishes, giving way to a new body of pneumatic substance.[68] Didymus in his lectures on the Psalms engages in a lengthy defense of this understanding of the "change" in 1 Cor 15:51–52 as a substantive one involving the replacement of the body of flesh with a body of ethereal matter.[69] This ancient debate is also reflected in the fragments of

---

[66] Unlike the wider debate, which has been treated extensively by modern scholars (see section I above), the only treatment in contemporary scholarship of the ancient debate regarding the verb ἀλλάσσω in 1 Cor 15:51–52 of which I am aware is the brief discussion in Layton, *Didymus the Blind*, 45–47. I am indebted to Layton's excellent discussion, but I also seek to enlarge upon it by means of additional evidence.

[67] See, e.g., Basil, *Hom. in Ps.* 44. According to Basil, the superscription "mystically signifies to us the promise of the resurrection, in which this change of quality shall be given to us" (τὸν τῆς ἀναστάσεως ἡμῖν παραινίσσεται λόγον, ἐν ᾗ ἡ ἀλλοίωσις ἡμῖν δοθήσεται). Didymus in his Psalms lectures reports that this interpretation was common (*Ps.T.* 328.23–25).

[68] Didymus, *Ps.T.* 328–30. Cf. Layton, *Didymus the Blind*, 45–47. For the conception, see Origen, *Princ.* 2.3.7: tunc ipsa quoque substantia corporalis optimis ac purissimis spiritibus sociata pro assumptionem vel qualitate vel meritis in aetherium statum permutata, secundum quod apostolos dicit, Et nos immutabimur, refulgebit ("Then also the bodily substance itself, united with the best and purest spiritual beings, will be changed into an ethereal state, refulgent with light, in conformity with either the character or virtues of those who receive it, just as the apostle says: 'And we will be changed'"). Cf. *Princ.* 2.10.3.

[69] Didymus, *Ps.T.* 329–30. See in particular *Ps.T.* 329.7–9, 18: ἐὰν οὖν κατὰ ἀλλοίωσιν ἀνάστασις γένηται, ἡ σὰρξ πάλιν σάρξ ἐστιν, τὸ φθαρτὸν πάλιν φθαρτόν ἐστιν· οὐ γὰρ ποιότητα λέγω τὸ φθαρτὸν ἢ τὴν σάρκα.... ταύτην οὖν ἀλλαγὴν λέγω, οὐκ ἐξ ὑποκειμένου εἰς ἄλλο ὑποκείμενον, ἀλλὰ εἰς γενάμενον ἐκ φθαρέντος γεγονέναι ("If therefore resurrection takes place as a qualitative change [ἀλλοίωσις], the flesh [ἡ σάρξ] is again flesh, the perishable body [τὸ φθαρτόν] is again perishable. For I deny that either the perishable body or the flesh is a quality [ποιότης].... This, then, I call change [ἀλλαγή], not when one being becomes another being, but when a new

Didymus's Psalms commentary found outside the Tura manuscript (which are universally recognized as reworked by an editor to remove the Origenist elements). In the edited version of Didymus's commentary on Psalm 68, contrary to Didymus's own views, the text explicitly approves the application of the words ὑπὲρ τῶν ἀλλοιωθησομένων in the Psalm's superscription to 1 Cor 15:51–52, reflecting an understanding of these verses in terms of *alloiosis* or qualitative change (*Comm. Ps.* 706a9–14).

The importance of this issue within the wider ancient debate over the nature of the resurrection body in 1 Corinthians 15 suggests that Engberg-Pedersen, in raising the question of the nature of the "change" that Paul envisions in 1 Cor 15:51–52, has astutely identified an issue of critical significance for the conception of resurrection in the chapter. I am also convinced that the structural features of the chapter discussed above are able to shed light on this question. This brings us to a fourth observation regarding Paul's shaping of his argument.

The Predicate Complements of Paul's Verbs in 15:36–54

Does the change of the present body that Paul envisions in 1 Cor 15:51–52 involve, as Engberg-Pedersen argues, the specialized notion of substantive change? This claim is crucial to Engberg-Pedersen's thesis of an ethereal resurrection body in Paul. For since "change" in its common signification implies the continued existence of that which is changed, the concept of a new, ethereal body is coherent with 1 Cor 15:51–52 if and only if one interprets this "change" specifically in terms of the Aristotelian concept of substantive change. But does such an interpretation of this "change" offer a plausible construal of Paul's thought in the passage? Several factors suggest that it does not.

First of all, one would expect Paul to use this language in its generally accessible nonphilosophical sense of alteration or transformation, rather than in a specialized philosophical sense involving destruction and origination. Moreover, even assuming a philosophical setting for Paul's language (which I think unlikely), the word Paul employs to describe the "change" that takes place at the resurrection (ἀλλάσσω) is unrelated to Aristotle's language for substantive or essential change (γένεσις "origination" or φθορά "corruption"), but instead closely corresponds to the philosophical language for qualitative change (ἀλλοιόω). But most decisive is a fourth and final observation regarding the structure of 1 Cor 15:36–54. This observation concerns the predicate complements (see the right-hand column of the diagram provided earlier in the article) of the verbs and verbal pairs in the passage. These complements are critical, for within the structure of Paul's exposition, in which the subject remains constant, the contrasts between the present and risen

---

substance comes into being from that which perishes [εἰς γενάμενον ἐκ φθαρέντος]." See also *Ps. T.* 259.4–16.

body are located entirely within Paul's verbs and verbal complements. Strikingly, these complements uniformly refer not to the substance of the body but to *qualities*, *states*, or *conditions* of the body: corruption, incorruption, dishonor, glory, weakness, power, mortality, and immortality. The complements that describe the new state of the risen body refer not to a change or annihilation of the body's *substance* but to a new *quality* or *mode* of existence, in which what was once perishable, dishonored, weak, and mortal is endowed with imperishability, glory, power, and immortality (vv. 42–43, 52–54).[70] Paul's series of oppositions does not describe two different bodies, distinct in substance, but two contrasting modes of existence of the same body, one prior to and the other subsequent to the resurrection.

Among these altered qualities, the artful inclusion bracketing the passage that I identified above (15:42/15:53–54) puts primary emphasis on the transformation from corruptibility (ἐν φθορᾷ, v. 42; τὸ φθαρτὸν τοῦτο [twice], vv. 53–54) to incorruptibility (ἐν ἀφθαρσίᾳ, v. 42; ἀφθαρσίαν [twice], vv. 53–54). Paul's predicate complements, I would argue, clearly describe the results of *qualitative* change (the common notion of change in antiquity)—the very body that is now corruptible and mortal is not replaced or destroyed, but *changed*, entering into a new mode of incorruptible, immortal existence (vv. 42–43, 53–54). The four "poles" of Paul's shaping of the passage we have examined—the unchanging subject of Paul's antithetical verb pairs in vv. 36–49, the present perishable body as the consistent subject of Paul's verbs of resurrection and transformation in vv. 50–54, verbs of revivification and investiture, and predicate complements describing a change of quality rather than of substance—all point in the same direction. The change Paul has in view involves, to use Caroline Walker Bynum's words, "enhancement of what is, not metamorphosis into what is not."[71]

IV. The ΣΩΜΑ ΠΝΕΥΜΑΤΙΚΟΝ in 1 Corinthians 15:44

Central to Engberg-Pedersen's proposal, and commonplace in modern scholarly reading of Paul, is the assumption that the σῶμα πνευματικόν in 1 Cor 15:44–46 refers to a body composed of spirit, or *pneuma*, distinct from the body of flesh laid in the tomb.[72] The purpose of the present section of this article is to examine this

---

[70] See Thiselton, *First Epistle to the Corinthians*, 1276.

[71] Bynum, *Resurrection of the Body*, 8. Space precludes discussion here of Paul's declaration in 1 Cor 15:50 that "flesh and blood cannot inherit the kingdom of God, nor does what is perishable inherit the imperishable." But I believe the evidence provided here is sufficient to demonstrate that the common scholarly reflex to use this verse as a "proof-text" for a Pauline denial of the resurrection of the flesh relies on a reading of this verse in isolation from Paul's larger argument in the chapter.

[72] See Engberg-Pedersen, *Cosmology and Self*, 26–34; cf. Martin, *Corinthian Body*, 117, 120, 126; Asher, *Polarity*, 153–68, esp. 153–54 n. 17; Sumney, "Post-Mortem Existence," 17–18; Dunn,

assumption critically, focusing on the meaning of this specific phrase in Paul's argument. In so doing I hope to provide a more precise analysis than those previously offered elsewhere. The following considerations are, in my view, decisive that by *sōma pneumatikon* Paul refers not to a body composed of material spirit but to the risen body of flesh and bones given life by the Spirit of God.

1. The notion that v. 44 introduces the concept of a new body, distinct in substance from the body sown in death, misunderstands the structure of Paul's syntax in this verse. The *sōma psychikon* and *sōma pneumatikon* do not function, as sometimes assumed, as the subject of the verbs in 15:44.[73] Once again a grasp of the structure of Paul's argument as outlined above is crucial. As shown above, the implied grammatical subject of the verbs in v. 44 is the mortal, fleshly body, which is sown in decay (σπείρεται) but thereafter is raised to immortal life (ἐγείρεται). The terms σῶμα ψυχικόν and σῶμα πνευματικόν function *predicatively* ("it is sown as a *sōma psychikon*; it is raised as a *sōma pneumatikon*") and thus describe two contrasting *modes of existence* of this same body, one prior to the resurrection, the other following the resurrection.

2. The understanding of the *sōma pneumatikon* as involving a "body composed of *pneuma*," distinct in substance from the earthly body, also ignores the actual lexical meaning and usage, in Paul and in the wider ancient world, of the key terms in question. This view is thus routinely bedeviled by the gratuitous assumption that the contrast Paul draws in 15:44 is that of *flesh* and *spirit*. Paula Fredriksen, for example, understands Paul to assert that "the Christian's fleshly body, whether living or dead, will be transformed, like Christ's, into a spiritual body."[74] However, the adjective that Paul here contrasts with πνευματικός is not σάρκινος (cognate with σάρξ), referring to the *flesh*, but ψυχικός (cognate with ψυχή), referring to the *soul*. This adjective is used in texts outside the NT, without exception, with reference to the properties or activities of the soul.[75] Modifying σῶμα as here, with reference to the present body, the adjective describes this body as *given life or activity by the soul*. The adjective has nothing to do with the body's composition but denotes the source of the mortal body's life and activity.

The meaning of the paired adjective ψυχικός in 15:44 is extremely significant, for it reveals that the exegesis of Engberg-Pedersen, Martin, and Asher involves a fundamental misunderstanding of the passage. For if (as these interpreters suggest) σῶμα πνευματικόν in this context describes the composition of the future body, as

---

"1 Corinthians 15," 11–18; so earlier Teichmann, *Die paulinischen Vorstellungen*, 48–53; Pfleiderer, *Paulinism*, 128, 131–32, 250.

[73] For this misconception, see, e.g., Gillman, "Transformation," 327–28; Stenger, "Argumentationsstruktur," 117.

[74] Fredriksen, "Vile Bodies," 81.

[75] E.g., 4 Macc 1:32; Aristotle, *Eth. nic.* 3.10.2; Epictetus, *Diatr.* 3.7.5–7; Plutarch, *Plac. philos.* 1.8. The three NT instances outside 15:44–46, which cohere with this wider usage, will be discussed immediately below.

a body composed only of spirit, its correlate σῶμα ψυχικόν would perforce describe the composition of the present body, as a body *composed only of soul*. Paul would assert the absence of flesh and bones not only from the risen body but from the present mortal body as well! The impossibility that ψυχικός here refers to the body's composition rules out the notion that its correlated adjective πνευματικός refers to the body's composition. Contrasted with ψυχικός, the adjective πνευματικός must similarly refer to the source of the body's life and activity, describing the risen body as *given life by the Spirit*.

3. The mode of existence described by the adjective πνευματικός is further clarified by the larger context of the letter, for the contrasted pair of adjectives ψυχικός/πνευματικός is crucially foreshadowed earlier in the epistle. In 1 Cor 2:14–15 ὁ ψυχικὸς ἄνθρωπος is constrasted with ὁ πνευματικὸς [ἄνθρωπος]. In this passage the contrast is clearly not between a person composed of flesh and blood and a person composed of celestial spirit or *pneuma*. Rather, ὁ ψυχικὸς ἄνθρωπος is the person who possesses only the natural life of the soul (ψυχή) and is bereft of the Holy Spirit, in contrast with ὁ πνευματικὸς [ἄνθρωπος], the person possessing and transformed by the Spirit of God (τὸ πνεῦμα τοῦ θεοῦ, 2:11–12).[76] Similarly elsewhere in 1 Corinthians, the adjective πνευματικός is uniformly used with reference to persons or things enlivened, empowered, or transformed by the Spirit of God, including flesh-and-blood human beings (2:15; 3:1; 14:37), edible manna and water (10:3–4), and a very palpable rock (10:4). Paul's use of this adjective in 10:3–4 with reference to the manna and water miraculously provided in the exodus is especially illuminating, for in these verses the adjective is used with reference to earthly, palpable substances of gross (not fine or ethereal) matter, clearly indicating not their composition but that they are given by the power of the Spirit. The adjective πνευματικός in Paul simply never means "composed of celestial *pneuma*," and such a concept is entirely foreign to his thought (see point 4 immediately below). Rather, this adjective in Paul always has in view the power and activity of the *Spirit of God*. Used with σῶμα in 15:44, the adjective πνευματικός indicates that the risen body will be given life and empowered by God's Spirit.

4. The understanding of the σῶμα πνευματικόν as the risen body given life by the Spirit, which I have argued is demanded by the context of the passage, also coheres with the larger context of Paul's thought. For although the expression σῶμα πνευματικόν is unique here in Paul, the concept of *the Spirit as the agent of resurrection life* is a major theme in Paul's theology (Rom 8:9–11; 8:23; 2 Cor 5:4–5; Gal 5:25; 6:7–8). According to this theology, the work of the Spirit in those who belong to Christ will culminate in the resurrection, when "the one who raised Christ from the dead will also *give life to your mortal bodies through his Spirit* who indwells you" (Rom 8:11). By contrast, the notion of a risen body composed of corporeal *pneuma*

---

[76] Cf. Jude 19, where ψυχικοί persons are defined as πνεῦμα μὴ ἔχοντες ("not having the Spirit"). Similarly in Jas 3:15, the adjective is used to describe human wisdom apart from the Spirit (3:13–18).

perforce entails (as Engberg-Pedersen has in my view convincingly demonstrated) a specifically Stoic and pantheistic understanding of the relation of the divine to the cosmos, with the corollary that Paul conceived of the Spirit of God as a corporeal entity, composed of the same substance as the sun, moon, and stars.[77] Space precludes discussion here, but I regard such a reconstruction of Paul's thought to be without historical plausibility (cf. Rom 1:20–25; 4:17; 11:33–36; 1 Cor 8:4–6; 10:7; 10:14; 1 Thess 1:9–10).[78] But the thesis of an ethereal resurrection body in Paul depends on such a pantheistic and Stoic reading of Paul and collapses without it.

In conclusion regarding the *sōma pneumatikon* of 15:44: the syntax of the passage, the lexical evidence of Paul's key terms in their wider ancient context, Paul's usage elsewhere in the letter, and the larger context of Paul's own thought each preclude the notion that the adjectives ψυχικός and πνευματικός in this passage refer to the body's composition. Rather, the term σῶμα ψυχικόν describes the present body as *given life by the soul*, the life given by the very breath of God (1 Cor 15:45a, ἐγένετο ὁ πρῶτος ἄνθρωπος Ἀδὰμ εἰς ψυχὴν ζῶσαν, "the first man, Adam, became *a soul that is living*" [echoing Gen 2:7]), but in Adam subject to mortality and decay (1 Cor 15:21–22). In the same way, the term σῶμα πνευματικόν describes the resurrected body as *given life by the Spirit* of God, the life given by Christ, the new Adam (1 Cor 15:45b, ὁ ἔσχατος Ἀδὰμ εἰς πνεῦμα ζωοποιοῦν, "the last Adam became *a Spirit that is life-giving*"), and thus bestowing on the body a mode of existence that is immortal and imperishable (1 Cor 15:20–26, 42–43, 46–49, 52–54). The σῶμα πνευματικόν in Paul's thought is not a body composed of ethereal *pneuma* but the body of flesh and bones endowed with imperishable life by the power of the Spirit.

V. Conclusion

Current debate regarding 1 Corinthians 15 involves competing claims concerning both Paul's conception of the resurrection in that chapter and the proper contextualization of Paul's understanding within its ancient milieu. Does Paul's treatment in the chapter reflect the mainstream Jewish expectation of the resurrection and transformation to imperishability of the once-dead body of flesh and bones; a Platonizing modification of the common Jewish conception involving the bestowal of a new, incorporeal body; or a unique fusion of Jewish apocalyptic hopes and Stoic cosmology, envisioning an ethereally material body composed not of

---

[77] See Engberg-Pedersen, *Cosmology and Self*, 8–38; idem, "Material Spirit," 184–87.

[78] On the profound differences between the conception of God in Paul's thought and in Stoicism, see James Ware, "Moral Progress and Divine Power in Seneca and Paul," in *Passions and Moral Progress in Greco-Roman Thought* (ed. John T. Fitzgerald; London/New York: Routledge, 2008), 267–83.

flesh but of the corporeal substance of *pneuma*? This debate regarding Paul's understanding of the resurrection, which has massive implications for Paul's larger theology, can be resolved, I have argued, only on the basis of close investigation of Paul's own language and the underlying structure of his thought in the chapter. The foregoing analysis of the (hitherto neglected) structure of Paul's defense of the resurrection in 1 Cor 15:36–54 thus has significant implications for the current discussion concerning the nature of the resurrection in Paul. Key to this analysis is a new proposal regarding the literary structure of 1 Cor 15:36–54. The specific way in which Paul shapes his argument, and the structure of the syntax in which his thought is given expression, preclude the notion that Paul in this chapter envisions a nonfleshly resurrection body composed either of nonmaterial "spirit" or of materially ethereal "spirit" or *pneuma*. Rather, I have argued, in 1 Cor 15:36–54 the resurrection is understood as the revivification and glorious transformation to immortality of the mortal body of flesh. Throughout 1 Cor 15:36–54 the subject of the verbs Paul uses to describe the resurrection event is the body of flesh and bones. Moreover, the verbs Paul employs for this event describe not the annihilation or replacement of the present body but its revival and transformation. It is *this* body that will be given life (15:36), raised (15:42, 43, 44, 52), and transformed (15:51, 52, 53, 54). Paul's predicate complements reveal that the "change" Paul envisions for the risen body in vv. 51–52 involves a change in its qualities rather than a destruction of its substance. Finally, in v. 44 both contextual and lexical considerations indicate that the phrase σῶμα πνευματικόν refers not to a body composed of *pneuma* but to the fleshly body given imperishable life by the power of the Spirit.

Following Martin's influential study, scholars routinely point to Paul's range of contrasts between the mode of existence of the antemortem body and the resurrection body to argue that Paul excludes the present, perishable body from participation in final salvation. But, as the foregoing analysis of 1 Cor 15:36–54 has shown, such an exegesis in fact misses the central point of Paul's argument, which is to show how the body that is now perishable will be endowed, through eschatological resurrection, with imperishable life. The structure of Paul's argument is not consistent with a Platonizing conception of disembodied immortality, nor, as Engberg-Pedersen suggests, with a fusion of Jewish and Stoic thought involving the replacement of this present body with an ethereal one, but reflects the mainstream Jewish concept of the resurrection of the body of flesh and bones from the tomb, familiar to us from Second Temple Jewish texts (see Isa 25:6–9; 26:11–19; Dan 12:2–3; Job 19:25–27 LXX; 2 Maccabees 7; *Sib. Or.* 4:179–92). In 1 Cor 15:36–54, resurrection is understood as the miraculous reconstitution of the mortal body of flesh and bones and its transformation so as to be imperishable.

New Titles from Liturgical Press

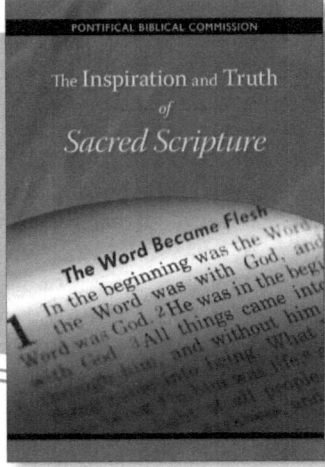

How Human Is God?
Seven Questions about God and Humanity in the Bible

Mark S. Smith

"Mark Smith has done it again! . . . Readers will regularly come away challenged to think more deeply and differently about issues and passages and the Bible as a whole than they have done before."
Peter Machinist
Harvard University

"All kinds of readers will find themselves enriched by Smith's clarity and his sensible, yet learned, reflections."
Jacqueline E. Lapsley
Princeton Theological Seminary

978-0-8146-3759-3
Paperback, 212 pp., $19.95
978-0-8146-3784-5 eBook, $17.99
B3759 Paperback & eBook Bundle, $24.49

The Inspiration and Truth of Sacred Scripture
The Word That Comes from God and Speaks of God for the Salvation of the World

Pontifical Biblical Commission

Translated by Thomas Esposito, OCist, and Stephen Gregg, OCist, and reviewed by Fearghus O'Fearghail

Foreword by Cardinal Gerhard Ludwig Müller

This book is the contribution of the Pontifical Biblical Commission toward a more adequate understanding of the concepts of inspiration and truth that respects both the nature of the Bible and its significance for the life of the Church.

978-0-8146-4903-9
Paperback, 216 pp., $19.95
978-0-8146-4904-6 eBook, $17.99
B4903 Paperback & eBook Bundle, $24.49

LITURGICAL PRESS www.litpress.org • 1-800-858-5450

The *JBL* Forum, an Occasional Exchange

This issue's *JBL* Forum focuses on the question of emotion. Françoise Mirguet examines the ways in which two texts, Josephus's *Jewish Antiquities* (books 1–11) and the *Testament of Zebulun,* insert or embed emotion in their rewriting or expansion of the Hebrew Bible. Although these works treat emotion in different ways, both take the perspective of the one who looks upon the pain of another and thereby permit a consideration of how compassion and pity function in the construction of the self. The responses are written by scholars who have each dealt with the topic of emotion in ancient texts: Sarah Judith Pearce from within the field of Second Temple Judaism, and David Konstan and Donald Lateiner from the field of Classics. Taken together, the contributions to this Forum illustrate (yet again) the importance of situating texts within the intellectual world of their authors—in this case, a world very much influenced by Aristotle—and remind us that questions that seem so germane to our twenty-first-century lives—identity and the construction of the self—were asked by others long before our own time.

As always, we invite your comments and responses via the Society of Biblical Literature website (log in with your SBL member number, http://www.sbl-site.org/publications/Journals_JBL_Login.aspx).

Adele Reinhartz
General Editor, *Journal of Biblical Literature*

Emotional Responses to the Pain of Others in Josephus's Rewritten Scriptures and the *Testament of Zebulun*: Between Power and Vulnerability

FRANÇOISE MIRGUET
Francoise.Mirguet@asu.edu
Arizona State University, Tempe, AZ 85287

The first eleven books of Josephus's *Jewish Antiquities* and the *Testament of Zebulun*, part of the *Testaments of the Twelve Patriarchs*, present a common insistence on emotional responses to the pain of others. This article studies how both texts construct the emotions that one is supposed to have when facing the suffering of others. For Josephus, the basic response to others' pain is pity, rooted in the rhetorical tradition but reinterpreted. Emotionally responding to others' pain depends on a cognitive appraisal and is characteristic of high moral character, which may contribute to creating a sense of superiority. In the *Testament of Zebulun*, the response to others' pain is primarily an embodied experience. The self may be unable to help the one in pain, and intense emotions then compensate for lack of action. Compassion is rooted in the realization of one's own vulnerability. Both discourses, in fact, illustrate a particular aspect of compassion, emphasizing either empowerment or vulnerability. In the conclusion, the article looks at emotional responses to others' pain as occasions for the self to position itself toward others while they are vulnerable, thus less threatening. By displaying appropriate emotions, the self redefines its position vis-à-vis its peers and manifests its belonging to the social group.

> Sympathizers have it better. They are in the position of being owed..., and by giving sympathy they increase their social and moral standing.
> —Candace Clark

> In pity and fear, we acknowledge our vulnerability before the circumstances of life.
> —Martha Nussbaum

It is a pleasure to thank Joel Gereboff, David Konstan, Ari Mermelstein, and André Wénin, who have read previous versions of this article and offered invaluable feedback. Special thanks to

Jewish texts written in Greek during the Hellenistic period often emphasize the emotions provoked in the self by the suffering of others. While this emotional response is expressed by different terms, which can, by convention, be rendered as pity (οἶκτος and ἔλεος), grief (ἀλγέω), sympathy (συμπάθεια), or a gut-felt compassion (root σπλαγχν-), it is also diversely constructed. The two texts studied here, Josephus's rewritten scriptures[1] in the first eleven books of the *Jewish Antiquities*, and the *Testament of Zebulun*, part of the *Testaments of the Twelve Patriarchs*, have been chosen for their different constructions of the pain felt for the others' suffering at each end of a spectrum that goes from an expression of privilege to a recognition of vulnerability.

For Josephus, the basic response to others' pain is pity; it is rooted in the rhetorical tradition but with expanded conditions. Emotionally responding to others' pain is a decision sometimes accompanied by assistance. It is characteristic of high moral character, which may contribute to creating a sense of superiority. In the *Testament of Zebulun*, the response to others' pain, expressed as pity and compassion, is primarily an embodied experience. The self may be unable to help the one in pain; the self's intense emotions then compensate for the lack of action. Compassion is rooted in the realization of one's own vulnerability. Both discourses, in fact, illustrate a particular aspect of compassion, whose definitions navigate between two poles—as do the two epigraphs to this article. Compassion, on one hand, is the privilege of those who do not suffer and who, by their very compassion, showcase their well-being and moral character. On the other hand, compassion is also the vulnerable feeling of those who recognize themselves in suffering others and realize that they are not immune to pain.

Besides their contrasted constructions of the emotions to others' pain, *Antiquities* 1–11 and the *Testament of Zebulun* have been chosen for their similar context and relation to scriptures. Both were written in Greek around the turn of the era, by Jewish authors (for at least the core of the text in the case of the *Testament of Zebulun*) influenced by the Hellenistic cultural environment. Both present a narrative frame, which is itself rooted in the grand narrative of the Jewish scriptures. Josephus rewrites the scriptural account (books 1–11 cover from creation to Esther, with an appendix on the rule of Alexander the Great),[2] while the *Testament of*

---

my friend and colleague Naomi Jackson for our lively conversations on this topic. This research started in spring 2013 at the Center for Hellenic Studies in Washington, D.C. I am grateful for this wonderful opportunity and for the daily conversations with the other fellows. Thank you also to John Woodford for editing the text.

My opening epigraphs are from Candace Clark, *Misery and Company: Sympathy in Everyday Life* (Chicago: University of Chicago Press, 1997), 228; and Martha C. Nussbaum, *The Therapy of Desire: Theory and Practice in Hellenistic Ethics* (Princeton: Princeton University Press, 1994), 91.

[1] I do not capitalize "scriptures" because the corpus used may not be entirely fixed and may entail texts with heterogeneous levels of authority.

[2] On rewritten scriptures and the debates about the notion, see, e.g., Molly Zahn, "Genre and Rewritten Scripture: A Reassessment," *JBL* 131 (2012): 271–88.

Zebulun expands the scriptural story of Joseph by adding new scenes involving scriptural characters. Both texts insert the motif of emotional responses to others' pain where it is absent in scriptures.

This article compares how these two texts construct the emotions that one is supposed to have when facing the suffering of others.[3] These observations allow me, in conclusion, to reflect on the common function of the emotion, despite its different constructions: emotional responses to others' pain are occasions for the self to position itself toward others while they are vulnerable, thus less threatening. By displaying appropriate emotions to the one in pain, the self redefines its position vis-à-vis its peers and manifests its belonging to the social group.

My research presupposes a historical and social constructivist perspective: emotions and the conventions linked to them are not universal but change over time (see, e.g., works by William Reddy or David Konstan), from culture to culture (Catherine Lutz), and even within a society (Barbara Rosenwein); emotions are part of broader social discourses that structure societies (Peter Stearns); emotions are also constructed by religions (John Corrigan).[4] Compassion, as a discourse, has a history that may still have to be written, as Karl F. Morrison observed in 1988.[5] Portions of that history actually have already been investigated: David Konstan has studied pity in ancient Greece;[6] Sarah McNamer has explored the construction of compassion in the Middle Ages;[7] different aspects of compassion in the present have been explored by Candace Clark, Susan Sontag, as well as Lauren Berlant and

---

[3] I will not focus here on the meaning of the words per se. For the roots συμπαθ- and σπλαγχ-, see my article "Compassion in the Making: Lexicographic Explorations in Judeo-Hellenistic Literature," *CHS Research Bulletin* 1/2 (2013), online, http://nrs.harvard.edu/urn-3:hlnc.essay:MirguetF.Compassion_in_the_Making_Lexicographic_Explorations.2013.

[4] The bibliography given here is only indicative. For an introduction to the historical study of emotions, see Barbara H. Rosenwein, "Worrying about Emotions in History," *AHR* 107 (2002): 821–45. For particular studies on emotions in history, see Carol Z. Stearns and Peter N. Stearns, eds., *Emotion and Social Change: Toward a New Psychohistory* (New York: Holmes & Meier, 1988); William M. Reddy, *The Navigation of Feeling: A Framework for the History of Emotions* (Cambridge: Cambridge University Press, 2001); David Konstan, *The Emotions of the Ancient Greeks: Studies in Aristotle and Classical Literature* (Robson Classical Lectures; Toronto: University of Toronto Press, 2006); Barbara H. Rosenwein, *Emotional Communities in the Early Middle Ages* (Ithaca, NY: Cornell University Press, 2006). On the cultural component of emotions, see in particular Catherine A. Lutz, *Unnatural Emotions: Everyday Sentiments on a Micronesian Atoll and Their Challenge to Western Theory* (Chicago: University of Chicago Press, 1988). On emotions and religion, see John Corrigan, ed., *Religion and Emotion: Approaches and Interpretations* (New York: Oxford University Press, 2004), esp. 3–31.

[5] Morrison, *I Am You: The Hermeneutics of Empathy in Western Literature, Theology, and Art* (Princeton: Princeton University Press, 1988), xix.

[6] Konstan, *Pity Transformed* (Classical Inter/faces; London: Duckworth, 2001). See also further bibliography later in this essay.

[7] McNamer, *Affective Meditation and the Invention of Medieval Compassion* (Middle Ages Series; Philadelphia: University of Pennsylvania Press, 2010).

other scholars;[8] Martha Nussbaum and Morrison have examined key moments in the Western history of compassion.[9] However, compassion has been largely overlooked in biblical and Judeo-Hellenistic studies.[10]

I. Josephus: Pity and Sympathy as Privilege

In his retelling of the Jewish scriptures in the first eleven books of the *Antiquities*, Josephus often enriches the emotional life of his characters, adding emotions or expanding the descriptions given in scriptures. Characters' actions are explained by their emotions (e.g., 1.259; 6.59), and characters are portrayed according to the way they handle emotions (4.328–29; 6.63). At times, Josephus interrupts the narrative to reflect on human emotions (6.153, 262–67); even legal passages may take emotions into account (4.219, 236, 244). Josephus also sometimes indicates which emotions an event should elicit (4.53). This omnipresence of emotions has been explained in different ways.

Hellenistic historians are, in general, prone to telling about their characters' emotions, which makes Josephus's emphasis on emotions typical among his contemporaries.[11] Angelos Chaniotis describes Hellenistic historiographical works in terms of theatricality and performativity, reading them in the light of the

---

[8] Clark, *Misery and Company*; Sontag, *Regarding the Pain of Others* (New York: Farrar, Straus & Giroux, 2003); Berlant, ed., *Compassion: The Culture and Politics of an Emotion* (Essays from the English Institute; New York: Routledge, 2004).

[9] Nussbaum, *Upheavals of Thought: The Intelligence of Emotions* (Cambridge: Cambridge University Press, 2001); Morrison, *I Am You*.

[10] See, however, Roman Heiligenthal, "Werke der Barmherzigkeit oder Almosen? Zur Bedeutung von ἐλεημοσύνη," *NovT* 25 (1983): 289–301; Ronald L. Giese Jr., "Compassion for the Lowly in Septuagint Proverbs," *JSP* 11 (1993): 109–17; Jan Joosten, "חסד 'bienveillance' et ἔλεος 'pitié': Réflexions sur une équivalence lexicale dans la Septante," in *"Car c'est l'amour qui me plaît, non le sacrifice...": Recherches sur Osée 6:6 et son interprétation juive et chrétienne* (ed. Eberhard Bons; JSJSup 88; Leiden: Brill, 2004), 25–42; Walter T. Wilson, "The Constitution of Compassion: Political Reflections on Philo's *De Humanitate*," in *Scripture and Traditions: Essays on Early Judaism and Christianity in Honor of Carl R. Holladay* (ed. Patrick Gray and Gail R. O'Day; NovTSup 129; Leiden: Brill, 2008), 33–46. On pity in early Christianity, see Paul M. Blowers, "Pity, Empathy, and the Tragic Spectacle of Human Suffering: Exploring the Emotional Culture of Compassion in Late Ancient Christianity," *JECS* 18 (2010): 1–27.

[11] Josephus recognizes that he sometimes voices his own emotions, in particular when reporting the fall of Jerusalem (*War* 1.9–11). We can surmise that Josephus expected such an emotional involvement to be acceptable to his sponsors and audience. The passage is discussed by Steve Mason, *Flavius Josephus on the Pharisees: A Composition-Critical Study* (StPB 39; Leiden: Brill, 1991), 65–69; John Marincola, *Authority and Tradition in Ancient Historiography* (Cambridge: Cambridge University Press, 1997), 168; Tamar Landau, *Out-Heroding Herod: Josephus, Rhetoric, and the Herod Narratives* (Ancient Judaism and Early Christianity 63; Leiden: Brill, 2006), 10–12.

Hellenistic cultural and political context. Emotional display, Chaniotis shows, served as a mode of communication, which explains why Hellenistic historians were so given to portraying their characters' emotions, to arousing their readers' emotions, and to elucidating the techniques by which the ancient leaders would control their audience's emotions.[12] In a similar way, John Marincola interprets the use of emotions as part of the rhetorical techniques used by historians. Emotions serve, first, to persuade readers and lead them to appropriate interpretations of the narrated events, and, second, to give readers "the vicarious experience of what it was like to be there"—a sense of the reality of the past.[13] Josephus's works are to be understood in this literary and historical context.

To my knowledge, there is no study in Josephan scholarship devoted to emotions per se. Scholars, however, have noted the literary role of emotions in the narrative, especially in the expansion or introduction of romantic motifs.[14] Studies dealing with Josephus's portraits of scriptural characters have examined particular emotions.[15] In general, Josephus's attribution of positive emotions to Jewish ancestors is explained as a way of making them moral models, according to the norms of the time, in particular, Stoic norms.[16] At times, the portrayal of emotions can also be viewed as a political tactic to respond to anti-Jewish polemics and to construct a more likable image of the Jews.[17] These observations are a good starting

---

[12] Chaniotis, "Empathy, Emotional Display, Theatricality, and Illusion in Hellenistic Historiography," in *Unveiling Emotions II: Emotions in Greece and Rome. Texts, Images, Material Culture* (ed. Angelos Chaniotis and Pierre Ducrey; Stuttgart: Steiner, 2013), 53–84. See also, by the same author, "Emotional Language in Hellenistic Decrees and Hellenistic Histories," in *Parole in movimento: Linguaggio politico e lessico storiografico nel mondo ellenistico. Atti del convegno internazionale, Roma, 21–23 febbraio 2011* (ed. Manuela Mari and John Thornton; Studi ellenistici 27; Pisa: F. Serra, 2013), 339–52.

[13] Marincola, "Beyond Pity and Fear: The Emotions of History," *Ancient Society* 33 (2003): 315. See also, by the same author, "Aristotle's *Poetics* and 'Tragic History,'" in *Parachoregema: Studies on Ancient Theatre in Honour of Professor Gregory M. Sifakis* (ed. D. Iakov and S. Tsitsiridis; Heraklion: Crete University Press, 2010), 445–59; and "Polybius, Phylarchus, and 'Tragic History': A Reconsideration," in *Polybius and His World: Essays in Memory of F. W. Walbank* (ed. Bruce Gilson and Thomas Harrison; Oxford: Oxford University Press, 2013), 73–90.

[14] See, e.g., Louis H. Feldman, *Josephus's Interpretation of the Bible* (Hellenistic Culture and Society 27; Berkeley: University of California Press, 1998), 185–86; idem, *Studies in Josephus' Rewritten Bible* (JSJSup 58; Leiden: Brill, 1998), 565.

[15] To give only a few examples, Louis H. Feldman discusses control of the passions ("Josephus' Portrait of Moses: Part Two," *JQR* 83 [1992]: 7–50, esp. 28–32). Feldman's "Josephus' Portrait of Joab," *EstBíb* 51 (1993): 323–51, has a section on envy. The section "Balaam" (Feldman, *Studies in Josephus' Rewritten Bible*, 110–36) examines hate, and Michael Avioz discusses homosexual love in "Josephus' Retelling of the Jonathan Narratives," *JSP* 22 (2012): 68–86.

[16] For example, Feldman notes that Moses "emerges as the Stoic-like sage," while Pharaoh, because of his intemperance, appears as "the opposite of the Stoic sage" ("Josephus' Portrait of Moses: Part Two," 28–29). See also, about different scriptural heroes, Feldman, *Studies in Josephus' Rewritten Bible*, 546–51.

[17] See Louis H. Feldman, *Flavius Josephus: Translation and Commentary*, vol. 3, *Judean*

point; they do not, however, address the broader emotional discourses that underlie Josephus's work.

Confrontation of the suffering of others is one of the narrative occasions where Josephus tends to expand scriptures by adding emotional reactions. Pity is the most frequent emotion in this situation, expressed either by οἶκτος or ἔλεος, as well as by cognate terms from both roots. Though contemporary English speakers may have some difficulty counting pity as an emotion, ἔλεος figures prominently in ancient lists of emotions.[18] Pity in the ancient Greek world has recently received much scholarly attention.[19] In particular, Konstan has elucidated the components of ancient pity on the basis of Aristotle's definition of ἔλεος in his *Rhetoric*, illustrated by a large collection of texts from different literary genres. Aristotle writes:

> Let pity [ἔλεος] be a pain [λύπη] about an apparent, destructive or painful, harm, happening to someone not deserving it [ἀναξίου], which one, or one of one's own, might expect to suffer oneself, and when it seems near. (*Rhet.* 2.8, 1385b.13–16)

Two elements are at the core of Aristotle's definition. For us to experience pity for someone in pain, the pain has to be undeserved (even if Aristotle himself concedes that some pity can be felt even in the case of a deserved fate),[20] and some possibility must exist, either for us or for those close to us, to suffer a similar fate in a not too distant future ("when it seems near").[21] Pity, as typical of ancient Greek emotions, has a strong cognitive component, since it is conditioned by judgments: whether the suffering is deserved, and whether it might happen to the self. Aristotle's definition thus combines the two elements of power and vulnerability mentioned above. On the one hand, the definition first supposes that the person who

---

Antiquities 1–4 (Leiden: Brill, 2000), 75 (on Abraham's pity for the Sodomites), and, more generally, Feldman, *Studies in Josephus' Rewritten Bible*, 557–60.

[18] See Aristotle, *Rhet.* 2.1, 1387a; *Eth. nic.* 1105b; *De an.* 403a; Dionysius of Halicarnassus, *Dem.* 22, 1.322.

[19] See esp. Nussbaum, *Therapy of Desire*, 86–96; David S. Levene, "Pity, Fear and the Historical Audience: Tacitus on the Fall of Vitellius," in *The Passions in Roman Thought and Literature* (ed. Susanna Morton Braund and Christopher Gill; Cambridge: Cambridge University Press, 1997), 128–49; Konstan, *Pity Transformed*; Stephen Halliwell, *The Aesthetics of Mimesis: Ancient Texts and Modern Problems* (Princeton: Princeton University Press, 2002), 207–33; Konstan, *Emotions of the Ancient Greeks*, 201–18; Rachel Hall Sternberg, *Tragedy Offstage: Suffering and Sympathy in Ancient Athens* (Austin: University of Texas Press, 2006); Norman B. Sandridge, "Feeling Vulnerable, but Not Too Vulnerable: Pity in Sophocles' *Oedipus Coloneus*, *Ajax* and *Philoctetes*," *CJ* 103 (2008): 433–48; Lucia Prauscello, "The Language of Pity: *Eleos* and *oiktos* in Sophocles' *Philoctetes*," *Cambridge Classical Journal* 56 (2010): 199–212; Dana LaCourse Munteanu, *Tragic Pathos: Pity and Fear in Greek Philosophy and Tragedy* (Cambridge: Cambridge University Press, 2012).

[20] See Konstan, *Pity Transformed*, 43–48; idem, *Emotions of the Ancient Greeks*, 205.

[21] Nussbaum adds a third cognitive component: the assessment that the suffering is serious (*Upheavals of Thought*, 306–11).

has pity is not suffering at the moment. As Konstan puts it, "it follows that we do not pity those who are suffering the same thing as we are"—"the pitier, then, must be in a superior position to the pitied."[22] Aristotle's definition also posits some distance between the one who pities and the one who is pitied: we do not pity our intimate relatives or beloved; we rather feel grief.[23] Finally, even the judgment of desert may entail a dominant position: when granting pity, I am the master of my own emotions, and I assume the role of judge over the other's suffering.[24] On the other hand, by recognizing that the other's suffering could also happen to me (or to someone close to me), I put myself in a position of vulnerability. I realize that I am not immune to pain, and I imagine myself in the situation experienced by the other. As Nussbaum writes, "the person who pities must believe that he or she is vulnerable in similar ways."[25]

Historiography has been particularly influenced by the rhetorical tradition in its understanding of emotions. As Marincola has written, "History, as a genre with a close association to oratory, plants its feet firmly in the ground of rhetoric, and rhetoric throughout antiquity employed the arousal of emotions as an important element in persuasion."[26] It will be no surprise to find the rhetorical understanding of pity, especially in its Aristotelian definition, in the background of Josephus's treatment of the emotion; however, we will also observe that Josephus expands the Aristotelian conditions for pity.

The first component of Aristotle's definition of pity is illustrated in Josephus's retelling of Judah's appeal to Joseph to spare their brother Benjamin. In the scriptural version, Judah tries to induce Joseph to adopt the brothers' point of view, and especially to feel the guilt that he would experience should their father die because of the loss of Benjamin (Gen 44:18–34). In Josephus's retelling, appeal to pity dominates, as Judah attempts to convince Joseph to adopt their father's perspective and thus feel his pain. Judah begins by making clear that he does not entreat Joseph's pity toward the brothers, who "deserve punishment" [τιμωρίας ἄξια] (*Ant.* 2.140): "we do not feel pity on ourselves [οὐ γὰρ αὐτοὺς ἐλεοῦντες]" (2.148). However, he implores Joseph to "have pity [οἰκτείροντες] for [our father's] old age" (2.148),[27] "a

---

[22] Konstan, *Pity Transformed*, 50.

[23] See ibid., 50–51.

[24] Conversely, begging for pity, even though it presupposes innocence, entails vulnerability and self-abasement. Konstan notes that warriors rarely ask for pity, which is rather requested for vulnerable people, such as women, children, and the elderly (*Pity Transformed*, 79).

[25] Nussbaum, *Therapy of Desire*, 87; she emphasizes the vulnerability that emotions entail for Aristotle: they imply that significant elements exist outside myself, which I do not fully control, and to which I make myself vulnerable, in case I lose them. See also Nussbaum, *Upheavals of Thought*, 315–21. Konstan notes that Aristotle's definition of pity entails a "principle of vulnerability"—the possibility to be afflicted by a similar suffering (*Pity Transformed*, esp. 49–50).

[26] Marincola, "Beyond Pity and Fear," 290.

[27] For the translation of *Ant.* 2.148, see the important correction offered by Sarah Judith Pearce in her response to this article (p. 858 below).

good man, not worthy [οὐχὶ δίκαιος] of such trials" (2.149), and wraps up with, "let pity [ἔλεος] toward him be more powerful than our wickedness" (2.151). Pity has no place for a deserved misfortune: the brothers, Judah recognizes, have behaved wickedly and are not worthy of Joseph's pity. It is rather on the elderly father that Joseph should have pity. Innocent, the father is already suffering from the loss of one of his sons; now he is threatened with the loss of another child. Pity is thus based on the assessment that the victim is unjustly affected by suffering.[28] Granting pity also involves power: here the appeal to pity, even on behalf of someone else, reinforces the power of the one who is entreated.

The second element of Aristotle's definition concerns the likelihood of suffering a similar misfortune. An example is found in Josephus's interpretation of Exod 23:9: "You will not oppress a resident alien, for you know the life of a resident alien, since you were resident aliens in Egypt." The common experience of residing in a foreign country justifies the nonoppression of resident aliens. In Josephus's summary of the Jewish constitution, as he calls it, the similarity of experience implies more than a negative command, which becomes a call to provide others with providence and pity:

> For it is proper for you, having experienced afflictions in Egypt and in the wilderness, to show providence to those in similar circumstances and, having obtained abundance through God's pity [ἐλέου] and providence [προνοίας], to apportion the same, from a similar emotion [ἐξ ὁμοίου πάθους], to those who need it. (*Ant.* 4.239)

The call to pity is based on the experience of a similar suffering and benefaction: it is because the Israelites have experienced afflictions in their past and have benefited from divine pity, that they now ought to have pity on others, here resident aliens. Pity is based on the memory of one's own vulnerability. Pity is also the emotion (πάθος) from which providence or care is to be provided, again as a way to give to others what has been received from the divine. The Israelites are now able to act toward others as the divine acted toward them; they are in a divine-like position. Memory of past vulnerability therefore allows present privilege and obligation.

Josephus, however, makes free use of this rhetorical framework, as he often presents his readers with Jewish ancestors who exceeded rhetorical pity. A few examples will illustrate this adaptation. Abraham, just before entreating God about the Sodomites' planned destruction, "felt grief [ἤλγησεν] for the Sodomites" (*Ant.* 1.199). The addition may aim at correcting the perceived hostility of the Jews toward non-Jews.[29] It also strikingly expands the conditions for sharing the suffering of others: the Sodomites are in no way deserving of such grief. It is true that, in Josephus's version, Abraham has a history of friendship with the Sodomites (*Ant.*

---

[28] See also *Ant.* 2.26, where Reuben attempts to convince his brothers to spare Joseph's life, "who has not done anything wrong against them, and whose weak age demands rather pity [ἔλεον] and solicitude from us."

[29] See Feldman, *Judean Antiquities 1–4*, 75.

1.176), but Josephus has just reported their insolence, impiety, and hatred of strangers (*Ant.* 1.194). Besides, the root ἀλγ-, which primarily refers to physical pain, involves a lesser cognitive component and greater immediacy, as it is often used, in Classical Greek, for pain felt at the suffering of relatives.[30] By feeling pain for the Sodomites, Abraham shows himself superior in virtue; the patriarch is thus portrayed, by his emotion, in a powerful position over the enemy people.

The encounter between the necromancer of Ein Dor and King Saul, as retold by Josephus (*Ant.* 6.329–42, retelling 1 Samuel 28), displays another expansion of rhetorical pity. Here, the emotional response to the one in pain is accompanied by an inversion of power dynamics, which contributes to elucidating the function of the emotion. At the end of the meeting, as Saul is left "speechless out of grief," the woman prepares for him the calf she had in her house, "her single possession." Josephus insists on her humanity and generosity, which is all the more praiseworthy in that it does not follow or anticipate any favor to her but is purely gratuitous.[31] Josephus also supplies the emotional response of the necromancer to the king's distress: the woman "sympathized [συνεπάθησε] and comforted him [Saul]" (6.341). The emotional meaning of the root is relatively novel, though not unique. Polybius, Diodorus Siculus, and Dionysius of Halicarnassus used the term as an emotional response to others' pain, especially as a reinforcement of either οἶκτος (Diodorus Siculus 3.40.8) or ἔλεος (Polybius 2.56.7; Diodorus Siculus 12.24.5; Dionysius of Halicarnassus, *Ant. rom.* 8.42.1).[32] In Josephus, the root is rare in the *Antiquities*, used only one other time in the section considered here, in the description of David's lament for his son Absalom (συμπαθῶς εἶχεν, 7.252).[33] The medium's feelings for Saul are therefore expressed by the same root as the grief of a father for his dead son.

The necromancer's sympathy goes far beyond pity; she has never seen the king before (6.340) and is not related to him in any way—on the contrary, Saul has declared her livelihood illicit. Besides, Saul does not deserve her sympathy; Samuel, whose oracle she has just transmitted, has clearly stated that God has deserted the king because of his disobedience when fighting against the Amalekites (*Ant.* 6.335–36). Unlike Abraham, the necromancer is not a revered ancestor of the Jewish nation, which suggests that Josephus's intent goes beyond apologetic concerns. The fact that the woman feeds the king situates her sympathy alongside care, as the two sides of her response. Tending to the basic needs of the king was somehow not enough; the woman, for Josephus, had to share the pain of Saul emotionally to become a moral exemplar. The feeding also emphasizes the vulnerability of the

---

[30] See Konstan, *Emotions of the Ancient Greeks*, 244–58.

[31] See Feldman, *Judean Antiquities 1–4*, 193. See also Cheryl A. Brown, *No Longer Be Silent: First Century Jewish Portraits of Biblical Women* (Gender and the Biblical Tradition; Louisville: Westminster John Knox, 1992), 200–203.

[32] See also Konstan, *Pity Transformed*, 58; as well as Mirguet, "Compassion in the Making."

[33] The root συμπαθ- is found also in *Ant.* 13.233; 16.102, 329, 404; 19.330; *War* 1.442, 580; 2.579; 6.211.

king. The necromancer does not have much; however, with her single calf, she is still in a position to help the desperate king. The reversal of gender and power hierarchies emphasizes Saul's demise: the woman, an outlaw by the very word of the king, is now providing him with food and sympathy. By her emotion, the "sympathizer" confirms the distress of the one in pain; by her care, she shows that she possesses more, even if only a little, and is in a position to help. Sympathy and care thus convey privilege and superiority.

Josephus's comments on a case of schadenfreude[34] (which he himself inserts into the scriptural account) further illustrate the shift from the rhetorical tradition, while at the same time suggesting Josephus's conscious adaptation of his model. When concluding his account of the tragic end of Korah and his followers, Josephus states:

> One can lament them, not only for their misfortune, in itself deserving of pity [οἴκτου], but also because, while they were suffering such things, their relatives exulted [ἐφήσθησαν]…; they confirmed the judgment and did not grieve [οὐδ' ἐλυποῦντο], deeming that those around Dathan had perished as villains. (*Ant.* 4.53)

The passage is a good example of what has been called by David Levene "analytic emotions"; the historian is trying to arouse in readers an emotional response that is different from the characters' reaction and is based, rather, on a critical appraisal of the narrated events.[35] This difference is the occasion for Josephus to stage the shift we just observed, thus showing himself aware of the transformation he introduces. Korah's relatives, on the one hand, personify the rhetorical view of pity: they do not grieve, since the victims had deserved their punishment. Josephus, on the other hand, asserts his own emotional rule, or the emotional rule of his time: all calamity, whether deserved or not, is worthy of pity. Having others rejoice at one's suffering especially deserves compassionate feelings. What is the function of this addition to the scriptural account, which mentions neither the relatives' rejoicing nor the invitation to lament? Schadenfreude accentuates the terrible fate of Korah's men; for Josephus, emotionally responding to the pain of others, even those who are dead, does affect that pain—schadenfreude makes it worse! The passage thus highlights not only the emotional shift, but also the conviction that emotional responses to others' pain do affect, if not the experience, at least the social perception of that pain.

To conclude, we observe that Josephus develops his characters' emotions toward others' pain on the basis of the rhetorical tradition—which is unsurprising in light of the influence of Aristotle's *Rhetoric* on historiography—but with expanded conditions. Pity relies on a cognitive assessment and a possibility of relating to the other's suffering. The conditions for pity are extended, as pity or other emotional

---

[34] Other instances of schadenfreude are found in *Ant.* 7.255; 13.119; 15.163.
[35] See Levene, "Pity, Fear and the Historical Audience"; Marincola, "Beyond Pity and Fear," esp. 294.

responses often apply to deserved suffering. Pity thus becomes a hallmark of moral character. For example, Abraham's grief for the Sodomites and the Ein Dor necromancer's sympathy for Saul contribute to their moral portraits. Josephus seems aware of the shift, which he stages in the episode of Korah's demise. A certain willingness to "do better" may be discernible: Josephus may indirectly suggest that the emotional discourse by which he and his community abide is "better"—more humane and benevolent—than previous emotional rules, either Greek or Hebrew. The reasons do not have to be apologetic, especially since such a shift in the understanding of pity is not limited to Josephus or Judeo-Hellenistic authors.[36] It may be characteristic of a cultural environment where excellence was a requirement. As Steve Mason writes about Josephus's milieu, "It was crucial to show that one was the best in all areas of life; hence the abundant superlatives in documents and inscriptions from this period."[37]

The omnipresence of emotional response to others' pain suggests a social discourse where suffering is constructed by the emotional response it elicits in others. Schadenfreude, especially from relatives, can worsen an already miserable fate. The emotional response appears essential to the social perception of suffering. Pity or compassion constitutes here the privilege not only to help but also, and perhaps even more powerfully, to designate and validate suffering. Besides, a look at the identity of the "others" in pain, in the different passages examined, reveals some commonality: except for the elderly father of the first example, all suffering others are potentially threatening. The resident aliens, the Sodomites, King Saul, and Korah represent different aspects of danger to the self: strangers at home, strangers at the border, power, and internal disorder. Constructing the self's relation to (potentially) threatening others while they are in a situation of suffering may constitute a safe way to position the self toward them, even if only in a fictional way. By this ability to acknowledge suffering, and to respond to it with the proper emotions, the compassionate self displays not only its well-being but also its moral superiority, its social propriety, and its empowerment over others.

II. The *Testament of Zebulun*: Compassion as Vulnerability

I turn now to our second text, the *Testament of Zebulun*, for another construction of the emotion felt for the pain of others. Whereas in Josephus the emotion

---

[36] See Konstan, *Pity Transformed*, 75–104.

[37] Mason, *Life of Josephus: Translation and Commentary* (Leiden: Brill, 2001), xli. See also Françoise Mirguet, "Flavius Josèphe construit son image: Quelques postures d'auteur dans la *Vie*," in *Écritures et réécritures: La reprise interprétative des traditions fondatrices par la littérature biblique et extra-biblique. Cinquième Colloque internationale du RRENAB, Universités de Genève et Lausanne, 10–12 juin 2010* (ed. Claire Clivaz et al.; BETL 248; Leuven: Peeters, 2012), 35–48.

functions as an expression of privilege and power, the *Testament* constructs it as a recognition of vulnerability. In fact, the text resists any empowerment of the self over suffering others. The *Testament of Zebulun* constitutes one section of the *Testaments of the Twelve Patriarchs*, a collection of pseudepigraphic deathbed discourses attributed to the twelve sons of Jacob. The *Testaments* combine several literary genres: narrative, paraenesis, and apocalyptic writing.[38] The patriarchs give their descendants moral recommendations, loosely based on events in their own lives, as recorded in the book of Genesis. Each testament deals with one or two virtues or emotions in particular; the *Testament of Zebulun* focuses on pity and compassion.

There is an ongoing debate as to the origin and date of the *Testaments of the Twelve Patriarchs*. While most scholars concur that the text developed from a Jewish core and has been expanded by Christians, they disagree on how to appraise the current text. One strand of scholarship argues that the text is essentially Jewish and predates the first century c.e. except for the most obvious Christian additions, which usually do not affect its core content.[39] For others, and especially Marinus de Jonge, the text in its present state mainly reflects its Christian edition and is to be dated around the second or early third century c.e. For those who hold this view, there is no possible access to the pre-Christian form of the text.[40] A third option is

---

[38] For a definition of the genre paraenesis ("transmission of ethical norms"), see Johannes Thomas, "The Paraenesis of the Testaments of the Twelve Patriarchs: Between Torah and Jewish Wisdom," in *Early Christian Paraenesis in Context* (ed. James Starr and Troels Engberg-Pedersen; BZNW 125; Berlin: de Gruyter, 2004), 157–90, as well as the special issue *Semeia* 50: *Paraenesis: Act and Form* (ed. Leo G. Perdue and John G. Gammie; Atlanta: Society of Biblical Literature, 1990).

[39] See, e.g., Friedrich Schnapp, *Die Testamente der Zwölf Patriarchen* (Halle: Niemeyer, 1884); Wilhelm Bousset, "Die Testamente der zwölf Patriarchen: I. Die Ausscheidung der christlichen Interpolationen," *ZNW* 1 (1900): 141–75; idem, "Die Testamente der zwölf Patriarchen: II. Composition und Zeit der jüdischen Grundschrift," *ZNW* 1 (1900): 187–209; R. H. Charles, *The Greek Versions of the Testaments of the Twelve Patriarchs: Edited from Nine Mss. together with the Variants of the Armenian and Slavonic Versions and Some Hebrew Fragments* (Oxford: Clarendon, 1908); Jürgen Becker, *Untersuchungen zur Entstehungsgeschichte der Testamente der zwölf Patriarchen* (AGJU 8; Leiden: Brill, 1970); Howard Clark Kee, "The Ethical Dimensions of the Testaments of the XII as a Clue to Provenance," *NTS* 24 (1978): 259–70; Jarl Henning Ulrichsen, *Die Grundschrift der Testamente der zwölf Patriarchen: Eine Untersuchung zu Umfang, Inhalt und Eigenart der ursprünglichen Schrift* (Acta Universitatis Upsaliensis, Historia Religionum 10; Stockholm: Almqvist & Wiksell, 1991).

[40] This branch of scholarship is connected with the University of Leiden, and especially Marinus de Jonge. Among his abundant publications on the topic, see Harm W. Hollander and de Jonge, *The Testaments of the Twelve Patriarchs: A Commentary* (SVTP 8; Leiden: Brill, 1985); de Jonge, *Pseudepigrapha of the Old Testament as Part of Christian Literature: The Case of the Testaments of the Twelve Patriarchs and the Greek Life of Adam and Eve* (SVTP 18; Leiden: Brill, 2003), esp. "Defining the Major Issues in the Study of the Testaments of the Twelve Patriarchs," 71–83 (with a complete bibliography). See also Robert A. Kugler, *The Testaments of the Twelve Patriarchs* (Guides to Apocrypha and Pseudepigrapha; Sheffield: Sheffield Academic Press, 2001),

to situate the text in a common "Jewish Christian" milieu, composed by Christians of Jewish descent who still observe the totality of the Jewish law.[41]

The character of the paraenetic material of the *Testaments* is an issue as much debated as their origin. Some scholars defend a Stoic influence,[42] while others highlight the continuity with Israelite tradition.[43] Katell Berthelot's study of exhortations to love in the *Testaments* strongly suggests the Jewish origin of this material, in line with Israelite wisdom literature.[44] In regard to the structure and style of the paraenetic material of the *Testaments*, Johannes Thomas also shows its dependence on Jewish wisdom literature.[45] For de Jonge, however, the presence of the Christian editors can never be excluded. The *Testaments*, rather, suggest the continuity between Judeo-Hellenistic and Christian paraenetic discourses.[46] It is because of this continuity that I include the *Testaments* in this research, as an important witness to the development of the Judeo-Hellenistic, and therefore also Christian, discourse on pity and compassion.

The *Testament of Zebulun* presents a complex treatment of compassion, characterized by several shifts. Some manuscripts include the title Περὶ εὐσπλαγχνίας καὶ ἐλέους,[47] terms that recur in the text. While ἔλεος has been discussed above,

---

31–39; idem, "The Testaments of the Twelve Patriarchs: A Not So Ambiguous Witness to Early Jewish Interpretive Practices," in *A Companion to Biblical Interpretation in Early Judaism* (ed. Matthias Henze; Grand Rapids: Eerdmans, 2012), 337–60. Though following de Jonge's conclusions, Kugler demonstrates that the *Testaments*, in both their ethical and eschatological passages, are rooted in the Hebrew Bible.

[41] See Joel Marcus, "The *Testaments of the Twelve Patriarchs* and the *Didascalia Apostolorum*: A Common Jewish Christian Milieu?" *JTS* 61 (2010): 596–626.

[42] Kee, "Ethical Dimensions of the Testaments of the XII."

[43] Dixon Slingerland, "The Nature of *Nomos* (Law) within the *Testaments of the Twelve Patriarchs*," *JBL* 105 (1986): 39–48. See also Matthias Konradt, "Menschen- oder Bruderliebe? Beobachtungen zum Liebesgebot in den Testamenten der Zwölf Patriarchen," *ZNW* 88 (1997): 296–310.

[44] See Berthelot, "Les parénèses de la charité dans les Testaments des douze patriarches," *MScRel* 60 (2003): 23–39.

[45] Thomas, "Paraenesis of the Testaments of the Twelve Patriarchs."

[46] Marinus de Jonge, "Die Paränese in den Schriften des Neuen Testaments und in den Testamenten der Zwölf Patriarchen: Einige Überlegungen," in *Neues Testament und Ethik: Für Rudolf Schnackenburg* (ed. Helmut Merklein; Freiburg: Herder, 1989), 538–50.

[47] The title is present in mss *blef*; ms *g* has περὶ ἐλεημοσύνης; mss *dm* have περὶ εὐσπλαγχνίας καὶ ἐλεημοσύνης. See Marinus de Jonge, *The Testaments of the Twelve Patriarchs: A Critical Edition of the Greek Text* (PVTG 1.2; Leiden: Brill, 1978). The text has two recensions, a long one (mss *bdglm*) and a short one (mss *acefhij*) that is displayed in the Armenian and Slavonic versions. In the short recension, the section containing 6:4–8:3 is missing, except for 6:7a and 6:8. Most materials on human compassion are therefore missing in the short text. Two manuscripts of the short recension (*e* and *f*), however, are still preceded by the title, which leads de Jonge to regard the short text as an abbreviation of the long one, which is therefore viewed as original. The short recension would constitute "an attempt to avoid some of the more extravagant examples of Zebulun's compassion" (Hollander and de Jonge, *Testaments of the Twelve Patriarchs: A Commentary*, 254). See also Marinus de Jonge, *Studies on the Testaments of the Twelve Patriarchs: Text*

εὐσπλαγχνία and connected terms deserve some attention. The noun εὐσπλαγχνία is formed on the plural σπλάγχνα, which, in classical literature, originally designated the inner parts of a sacrificial victim (Herodotus, *Hist.* 4.61). The use was then extended to human inner organs, including the womb (Pindar, *Nem.* 1.35; Plutarch, *Am. prol.* 496d). The σπλάγχνα also refer to the inner organs as a seat of passions, for example, anger (Aristophanes, *Ran.* 844), anxiety (Aeschylus, *Ag.* 995), and love (Theocritus, *Id.* 7.99). In Judeo-Hellenistic literature, the word σπλάγχνα likewise designates the inner organs (most occurrences are in Philo, e.g., *Abr.* 241, or *4 Macc.* 5:30), as well as the seat of different passions (*T. Abr.* 3:9 [L]; *Jos. Asen.* 6:1 [S]),[48] in particular, parental affection (*4 Macc.* 14:13; *T. Benj.* 3:7). The term is also invested with a new meaning: the seat of compassion (e.g., *T. Sim.* 2:4; *T. Zeb.* 7:3). Similarly, the verb σπλαγχνίζομαι, which originally meant "to take part in a sacrifice" (2 Macc 6:8), comes to express exclusively the experience or display of compassion, with both a human (*T. Zeb.* 4:2; with the particle ἐπί, Prov 17:5 LXX) and a divine subject (*L.A.E.* 9:3; 27:2; *Apoc. Sedr.* 13:3).

There are different ways to account for the association of σπλάγχνα with compassion. On the one hand, a fragment from Chrysippus associates the root σπλαγχν- with compassion: in this fragment, conserved by Galen, the Stoic philosopher wonders whether ἄσπλαγχνος should be defined as "not having any compassion [συναλγοῦν] in one's inner parts" (frag. 904).[49] The evidence is thin but could suggest that the root σπλαγχν- was already associated with compassion in the Hellenistic world and that Jewish writers expanded an existing use.

On the other hand, σπλάγχνα as compassion could also constitute a Hebraism. The noun σπλάγχνα shares a number of characteristics with the Hebrew רחמים, also a plural form. The singular רחם designates the womb (Gen 20:18; 29:31; etc.), while the plural form refers to brotherly or motherly love (Gen 43:30; 1 Kgs 3:26)— two possible meanings of σπλάγχνα. The plural form רחמים and the verb רחם ("to have compassion") are used mainly with a divine subject, while the root σπλαγχν-, by contrast, is used for both divine and human compassion. It should also be noted that the Hebrew רחם is usually translated by ἐλε- or οἰκτ- in the LXX; it is only rendered by σπλάγχνα in LXX Prov 12:10.[50] Therefore, if indeed the term σπλάγχνα has been associated with the meaning "compassion" under the influence of the

---

and Interpretation (SVTP 3; Leiden: Brill, 1975), esp. "Textual Criticism and the Analysis of the Composition of the Testament of Zebulun," 144–60.

[48] The letters L and S in references to primary sources designate, respectively, the long and short recensions of the quoted texts.

[49] Fragment 904 in Chrysippe, *Œuvre Philosophique: Textes traduits et commentés*, vol. 2 (ed. Richard Dufour; Collection Fragments 4–5; Paris: Les Belles Lettres, 2004). The adjective ἄσπλαγχνος is rare before the Christian era but refers to lack of courage in Sophocles, *Aj.* 472.

[50] The root σπλαγχν- occurs in 2 Macc 6:7, 8, 21; 7:42; 9:5, 6; *4 Macc.* 5:30; 10:8; 11:19; 14:13; 15:23, 29; *Odes Sol.* 9:78; 12:7; Prov 12:10; 17:5; 26:22; Wis 10:5; 12:5; Sir 30:7; 33:5; Sol 2:14; Jer 28:13; Bar 2:17. Only four of those occurrences have a Hebrew source text: Jer 28:13 (where σπλάγχνα translates an unrelated Hebrew word, בצעך, "your unjust gain"); Prov 17:5 (the segment

Hebrew רחמים, it was probably toward the end of the process by which the Hebrew Bible was translated into Greek.[51]

Let us now return to the *Testament of Zebulun*. The motif of compassion is anchored in the scriptural scene where Joseph is sold into slavery. Zebulun, the pseudepigraphic speaker, begins his deathbed discourse by stating:

> I do not know ... that I have sinned in my days, except in thought; neither do I remember that I have done any lawlessness, except the mistake (by ignorance) [ἄγνοιαν] that I did against Joseph, because I covered my brothers and did not tell my father what had happened. And I cried a lot in secret, for I was afraid of my brothers.... (*T. Zeb.* 1:4–6)

Zebulun has only one sin to confess: having stayed silent about the selling of his younger brother Joseph out of the fear of his other brothers. The *Testament*, though, does not focus on the sin but develops what Zebulun did instead—or, rather, what he *felt*. Compassion appears in the very next chapter. Jacob's sons are about to murder Joseph, who begs for their pity. Zebulun describes his own reaction:

> As he was saying those words, I was moved to pity [οἶκτον], and I began to cry, and my livers were pouring out within me, and all the foundation of my inner parts [σπλάγχνων] became porous in my soul. And Joseph cried, and I with him, and my heart was humming, and the joints of my body were shaken, and I was not able to stand. And, when [Joseph] saw me crying with him, and them coming to kill him, he fled behind me, fearing them. (*T. Zeb.* 2:4–6)

This short passage, loaded with pathos, graphically renders the experience of pity or compassion felt in the σπλάγχνα. The physical reactions alluded to—internal confusion, weakness, elevated heart rate—suggest that Zebulun is experiencing the physical symptoms of the terror affecting his brother Joseph, as if he himself were threatened. Compassion is thus pictured as the physical experience of an emotion felt by another person.[52]

The suffering other here is Joseph, Zebulun's younger brother. He is defenseless, endangered by his brothers, among whom is Zebulun. The relationship between the one in pain and the provider of compassion is thus different from the examples studied in Josephus, where the distressed ones are often potentially threatening. In addition, we note that Zebulun is unable to protect Joseph, who is

---

where σπλάγχνα occurs does not have an equivalent in Hebrew); Prov 26:2 (σπλάγχνα translates בטן, "belly"); Prov 12:10 (see above).

[51] See Mirguet, "Compassion in the Making."

[52] In the same way, Gregory of Nyssa would later describe pity (ἔλεος) in terms of "loving self-identification [ἀγαπητικὴ συνδιάθεσις] with those vexed by grievous events" (*De beat.* 126.24 [1252.38]; translation by Stuart George Hall, in *Gregory of Nyssa, Homilies on the Beatitudes: An English Version with Commentary and Supporting Studies. Proceedings of the Eighth International Colloquium on Gregory of Nyssa, Paderborn, 14–18 September 1998* (ed. Hubertus R. Drobner and Albert Viciano; VCSup 52; Leiden: Brill, 2000), 59. Thanks to David Konstan for letting me know about this passage.

hiding behind him. On the contrary, Zebulun, already "afraid of his brothers" (1:6), is "unable to stand" (2:5). It is rather another brother, Reuben, who intervenes, in order to avoid direct bloodshed (2:7–8). Compassion is pictured as emotional turmoil, which seizes the self at the expense of action; the compassionate person does not have the ability, or the power, to assist the one in need.

Another narrative section of the *Testament of Zebulun* nuances those observations and reveals another aspect of compassion. Here Zebulun describes the compassion he provided when he was a fisherman. "Having compassion [σπλαγχνιζόμενος]," he was sharing his catch with every stranger (6:4); "having sympathy [συμπάσχων]," he prepared fish for any stranger and any ill or aged person (6:5). In this case, the two verbs, σπλαγχνίζομαι and συμπάσχω, are combined to suggest compassion, without the graphic descriptions of the physical turmoil that we found in the previous section. Less emotional involvement seems to leave more room for action, which reveals the other face of compassion: care, here in the form of sharing food.

In the next chapter, Zebulun tells about two acts of compassion that he performed. The first one concerns a stolen garment given to someone in need:

> I saw someone oppressed by nakedness, in the winter; having compassion [σπλαγχνισθείς] for him, I stole [κλέψας] a garment [ἱμάτιον] from my house,[53] and gave it secretly [κρυφαίως] to the oppressed person. (*T. Zeb.* 7:1)

Why is Zebulun stealing the garment, and why is he acting secretly? The anecdote could suggest that the requirement of compassion supersedes the prohibition of theft, but that explanation is hardly satisfying. Theft and secrecy seem to reinforce the powerlessness of the compassionate person, who does not have more than the person in need and has to steal in order to help.[54] Zebulun's second act of compassion again emphasizes the powerlessness of the compassionate person, in an even more extreme way:

> Εἰ δὲ μὴ ἔχετε πρὸς καιρὸν δοῦναι τῷ χρήζοντι, συμπάσχετε ἐν σπλάγχνοις ἐλέους. Οἶδα ὅτι ἡ χείρ μου οὐχ εὗρε πρὸς τὸ παρὸν ἐπιδοῦναι τῷ χρήζοντι, καὶ ἔτι ἑπτὰ σταδίους συμπορευόμενος αὐτῷ ἔκλαιον. Καὶ τὰ σπλάγχνα μου ἐστρέφετο ἐπ' αὐτῷ εἰς συμπάθειαν.

> And if, at one time, you do have nothing to give to the one in need, suffer [with him] in inner feelings of pity. I know that my hand did not find anything available to give to the one in need; for seven stadia, walking with him, I cried and my inner parts turned towards him in sympathy. (*T. Zeb.* 7:3–4)

---

[53] Manuscripts *ldm* add τοῦ πατρός.

[54] Zebulun's compassion could also be vicariously addressed to Joseph. When the brothers are about to sell Joseph, they take off Joseph's tunic and replace it with "an old slave's garment [ἱμάτιον]" (4:10). As for the theme of secrecy, it harks back to Zebulun's confession that he "cried a lot in secret [ἐν κρυφῇ]" (1:6). Zebulun would then provide the stranger with the garment he could not offer to his brother, as a possible reparation for his "only sin" (1:4–5).

The three verbs with the prefix συν- hint at the point of the anecdote. Compassion, here, is not about giving help but about sharing the condition of the one in need. The compassionate person does not have anything to offer. Zebulun's intense emotions somehow take the place of the actions that he cannot perform; a crying hero substitutes for a wealthy benefactor. The impossibility of action is compensated for by intense emotional involvement. Compassion is treated according to its component of vulnerability: being compassionate, here, means sharing both the predicament and the emotion of the one in pain.

Chapter 8 of the *Testament of Zebulun* wraps up what comes before; in doing so, it situates the discourse on compassion in a larger context. The patriarch gives his descendants his final recommendations:

> Καὶ ὑμεῖς οὖν, τέκνα μου, ἔχετε εὐσπλαγχνίαν κατὰ παντὸς ἀνθρώπου ἐν ἐλέει, ἵνα καὶ ὁ κύριος εἰς ὑμᾶς σπλαγχνισθεὶς ἐλεήσῃ ὑμᾶς, ὅτι καίγε ἐπ' ἐσχάτων ἡμερῶν ὁ θεὸς ἀποστέλλει τὸ σπλάγχνον αὐτοῦ ἐπὶ τῆς γῆς, καὶ ὅπου εὕρῃ σπλάγχνα ἐλέους, ἐν αὐτῷ κατοικεῖ. Ὅσον γὰρ ἄνθρωπος σπλαγχνίζεται εἰς τὸν πλησίον, τοσοῦτον κύριος εἰς αὐτόν.

> You also, my children, have compassion for every human being, in pity, so that also the Lord, having compassion for you, may pity you. Because, also in the last days, God will send his compassion on the earth, and where he finds feelings of pity, in him he dwells. For in the degree in which a human being has compassion for the neighbor, so in the same degree the Lord for him. (8:1–3)

Zebulun turns the tables, so to speak, as the discourse comes full circle: the provider of compassion now becomes the recipient. The motif of the divine "dwelling on earth" suggests a Christian context;[55] however, the idea of justifying compassion as a means to receive divine pity is already found in LXX Prov 17:5. Compassion, which, at the beginning of the text, was felt for a brother in danger, is now to be practiced toward all other human beings. It is also part of the exercise of piety and addresses human beings in their relation to the divine. In the background lies the belief that humans need divine compassion and have to behave with their fellow human beings in a way that will win them divine favor. The human being is thus seen as fundamentally vulnerable when facing the divine, and ethical behavior finds its justification as a way to deal with that vulnerability. The innocent victim or despondent neighbor of the previous examples is thus identified with the self, not in its human interactions but in its relation to the divine.

The principle of reciprocity between human and divine compassion is expanded in the next verse, which returns to the fictional setting of the *Testament*:

> Ὅτε γὰρ κατήλθομεν εἰς Αἴγυπτον, Ἰωσὴφ οὐκ ἐμνησικάκησεν εἰς ἡμᾶς, ἐμὲ δὲ ἰδὼν ἐσπλαγχνίσθη. Εἰς ὃν ἐμβλέποντες καὶ ὑμεῖς ἀμνησίκακοι γίνεσθε, τέκνα μου.... Ὁ γὰρ μνησίκακος σπλάγχνα ἐλέους οὐκ ἔχει.

---

[55] See Hollander and de Jonge, *Testaments of the Twelve Patriarchs: A Commentary*, 269.

For, when we went down into Egypt, Joseph did not remember wrongs we had done to him; seeing me, he had compassion. Considering this, you also do not remember wrongs done to you, my children.... For he who remembers wrong done to him has no feelings of pity. (*T. Zeb.* 8:4, 5a, 6b)

This passage once again reframes the discourse of compassion. Being compassionate is equated to "not remembering wrongs done to the self" [μνησικακέω], according to the verb's etymological meaning (and LSJ's definition). Basically, compassion corresponds here to a refusal to seek revenge. This constitutes a profound departure from Aristotle's pity, which, as noted by Konstan, always assumes innocence.[56] There is also a clear shift from the preceding instances of compassion; the recipients are not innocent victims or destitute neighbors, but, in the case of Joseph's brothers, wrongdoers. Compassion is not about helping those in need, or even sharing their despondency; it is about renouncing revenge toward offenders. This semantic shift, I suggest, can be explained by the change in the identity of the compassionate character, which was first Zebulun, then Joseph, and ultimately the divine. In the background of the text, we therefore find the conception of the human being as wrongdoer, in need of divine compassion—which takes on the characteristics of mercy.[57] Compassionate attitudes toward fellow human beings—whether victims, destitute neighbors, or past offenders—are ways to give oneself the assurance, or at least the hope, of receiving divine grace.

The *Testament of Zebulun* resists any empowerment of the self over suffering others. Far from being an ethical attitude that enhances the portrait of an exceptionally moral character, as in Josephus, compassion is here the expression of a basic human need, stemming from the recognition of one's own vulnerability. Human beings must have compassion on their neighbors in need, and even past offenders, not as a manifestation of their superiority but because they are themselves just as powerless and destitute. In a certain sense, the poor neighbor and past offender are metaphors of everyone's condition. It may not be a coincidence that Zebulun is a minor character in scriptures; in the *Testament*, he is not supposed to be an exceptional hero but rather a stand-in for all human beings, in their fragility and powerlessness. The embodied depiction of compassion is probably part of a larger discourse on emotions. However, understanding compassion as a physical and emotional experience is characteristic of the text's view of human beings: not ethical heroes in full mastery of their emotions and impulses, as with Josephus's compassionate characters, but vulnerable human beings trapped in their bodies and emotions. Beholding suffering in others prompts a repositioning of the self,

---

[56] See Konstan, *Pity Transformed*, 27–48.

[57] For a definition of mercy in relation to compassion, see, e.g., Nussbaum, *Upheavals of Thought*, 397–98. The connection between compassion and mercy is found also in *L.A.E.* 9:1–3; see David Konstan, *Before Forgiveness: The Origins of a Moral Idea* (Cambridge: Cambridge University Press, 2010), 92–94.

though not in terms of empowerment but toward a recognition of its own vulnerability in the pain affecting others. This vulnerability is reinforced by the need for divine pity; the presence of the divine in the text seems to prevent any attempt of empowerment over others.

III. Conclusion

Josephus's *Antiquities* 1–11 and the *Testament of Zebulun* are both Judeo-Hellenistic texts based on the Hebrew scriptures, either rewriting (Josephus) or expanding (*Testament of Zebulun*) scriptural narratives. They present a common insistence on emotional responses to others' pain. They both portray characters being emotionally affected by the suffering of others, even though those reactions are absent in the corresponding scriptural texts. This common emphasis suggests the importance of emotionally responding to others' pain at a certain time in Jewish (and early Christian) history, and possibly in the wider social context. This emphasis seems to have pervaded very disparate discourses, which have developed the motif in different ways and under specific influences. I examine here how both texts construct the emotional responses to others' pain, and use it to imagine different modalities of the self's relation to others, between the poles of power and vulnerability.

Josephus uses words from Classical Greek literature (ἔλεος, οἶκτος, ἀλγέω), or words used by contemporary historians (συμπαθέω). He develops his own discourse within and in reaction to the rhetorical tradition. Pity is often conditioned on suffering to which the self can relate and which is not deserved—though Josephus tends to detach pity from these two conditions. Consistent with the cognitive aspect of classical pity, responses to others' pain are for Josephus a matter of choice: the self is in control of one's emotions. Emotionally responding to others' pain is characteristic of high moral character, especially in relation to enemies. Pity, grief, and sympathy are represented only by single words; the experiences are not further described. The response is an emotion but not necessarily the emotion felt by the person in pain.

The *Testament of Zebulun* also uses a variety of Classical Greek terms but favors the root σπλαγχν-, which is typical, in its emotional sense, of Judeo-Hellenistic literature and may be rooted in the Hebrew רחמים. The root suggests the embodied character of the emotion and is often used in vivid descriptions of experienced compassion. Here the compassionate person embraces the emotions of the distressed person; compassion affects the self in a way similar to that of the pain affecting the other.

I have examined emotional responses to others' pain with a particular lens: the way the self positions itself, in imagination or in reality, toward suffering others. Confrontation of others' pain constitutes a privileged place for the self to reflect on, imagine, and enact its relationships to fellow human beings. Their vulnerability provides the self with an array of possibilities to position itself, illustrated by the texts examined here, in two different directions: as an occasion to convey power, or as an imperative to share vulnerability.

In Josephus, the ubiquity of emotional responses to suffering suggests that they are constitutive of the experience of pain. The beholders' emotions acknowledge or validate the pain; they can also be a way for them to dissociate themselves from the sufferers. They affirm their well-being and display their moral characters. Suffering others, in the different passages studied, frequently represent some threat to the self. Emotionally responding to others' pain, therefore, appears as a way to assert oneself toward fellow human beings, especially if they are potentially endangering. Appropriate emotions to others' pain redefine, in an empowered way, the self's position in society. In all of these aspects, power dominates in this construction of pity and sympathy.

The *Testament of Zebulun*, by contrast, roots its discourse in the compassion experienced by the pseudepigraphic voice of the text, Zebulun, for his younger brother, Joseph. The suffering other, in this initial scene or throughout the text, is in no way threatening but defenseless. On the contrary, Zebulun is the one who is potentially endangering, as he is initially among those who are planning Joseph's murder. The imbalance of power is dealt with by way of divestment: Zebulun does not act—his silence constitutes his only sin—but makes himself as vulnerable as his younger brother. Brotherly compassion is then expanded to include all human beings, while the emotional construction of compassion remains present. Compassion may be accompanied by care, but the inability to provide help is explicitly considered, with heightened emotional involvement compensating for lack of action. The introduction of a divine transcendence guarantees this shared vulnerability. The boundaries are blurred between the provider and recipient of compassion, as the latter functions as a figure of the former in its relation to the divine. The suffering of others and the compassion of the self may, here too, result in the self's repositioning, but this time toward a shared vulnerability, as if the text was invalidating any form of empowerment based on human relations.

Both discourses adopt the perspective of the compassionate person, not of the one in pain; they deal with given, not received, compassion. Responding emotionally to others' pain ultimately concerns the self and its position toward others. It is constructed either as a moral attitude, which reveals the self's advantage and superiority over the one in pain, or, conversely, as a vulnerable attitude, tending toward identification with the sufferer. The two discourses suggest that confronting others' suffering questions the self in its relationships to others and prompts its repositioning. It also offers a safe opportunity to negotiate such relationships, either toward an empowerment of the self over others, or toward the perception of a common vulnerability.

Pity and Emotion in Josephus's Reading of Joseph

SARAH JUDITH PEARCE
S.J.Pearce@soton.ac.uk
University of Southampton, Southampton 5O17 1BF, United Kingdom

Pity must be directed toward a harm that is not deserved, following Aristotle (*Rhet.* 2.8, 1385b.13–16). In her analysis of Josephus's construction of pity in his paraphrase of Genesis, Françoise Mirguet demonstrates how this principle is exemplified in Josephus's account of Judah's appeal to Joseph to release Benjamin for the sake of their father, Jacob (*Ant.* 2.140–59; cf. Gen. 44:18–34). Here, Judah's speech endorses the view that only the innocent (the brothers' father, Jacob) deserves pity and that this should outweigh the punishment justly deserved by the brothers: that Joseph "graciously give [χάρισαι] to our father" what justice demands for the brothers' wrongdoing, and that he "let pity for [Jacob] be more powerful (δυνηθήτω ... ἔλεος) than our wickedness" (*Ant.* 2.151). In what follows, I suggest that Judah's appeal, as constructed by Josephus, is interesting also in other ways for thinking about the significance of pity and the subversion of its construction in Aristotle's *Rhetoric*.

Questions of guilt, pity, and power are not straightforward in Josephus's account of Judah's appeal. While Joseph demands punishment only of Benjamin (framed for stealing Joseph's cup), it is Judah who insists that the brothers' collective punishment is "just" (*Ant.* 2.140, interpreting Gen 44:10, 16; cf. 2.155).[1] And it is Judah, according to Josephus, who argues that the brothers' appeal for clemency is not based on their pitying (ἐλεοῦντες) *themselves* but is because *they* have compassion (οἰκτείροντες) on their father's old age (*Ant.* 2.148).[2] While appealing to Joseph's

---

[1] The same point is made by Reuben: *Ant.* 2.107, interpreting Gen 42:22.
[2] Judah's words also imply that pity might be expected (though not by themselves) for the brothers, on account of their youth (*Ant.* 2.148; cf. 2.156, of Benjamin; and, in other contexts, *Ant.* 6.138; 10.202; 14.480).

power, Judah aims to influence, even to control that power by defining what is just vis-à-vis guilt and pity.

Judah's appeal to reason. In his epitaph for Joseph, Josephus praises the patriarch for his extraordinary virtue; he is to be remembered as a man who controlled everything by the use of "reason," using his authority sparingly (*Ant.* 2.198). The appeal to Joseph as a man of *reason* also plays a major part in Josephus's account of Judah's appeal. Just before the appeal begins, Joseph rejects the brothers' offer to put themselves forward for punishment in place of Benjamin: it is not "reasonable" (σώφρον), argues Joseph, to release Benjamin for the sake of those who have done nothing wrong, nor to punish them together with Benjamin, the only one of the brothers to be convicted of stealing Joseph's cup (*Ant.* 2.138). This statement represents a significant expansion of Gen 44:17, in which Joseph rejects outright Judah's offer to have all the brothers submit to punishment. Against this background, Josephus makes Judah appeal to Joseph's reasoning powers (λογισμός) (*Ant.* 2.151; cf. 157) to persuade him of the grounds on which he should grant pity. Judah begins by appealing to Joseph's superiority in *virtue*: to his "goodness" (χρηστότης) (2.140; cf. 157); to his superiority over lesser men in following "virtue" instead of "wrath"; to be "high-minded" (μεγαλόφρων), not mastered by wrath (2.141); to continue the gracious generosity and benefactions that had saved the brothers' lives up to now (2.142–57).[3] These are the virtues expected of a king, a thought perhaps directly inspired by Judah's opening words to Joseph, "Be not impatient with your servant, you who are the equal of Pharaoh" (Gen 44:18 JPS). This is a God-given opportunity for Joseph to show himself the best kind of ruler; by exercising his authority as a "humane" (φιλάνθρωπος) leader, Joseph's superiority is distinguished by extending his humaneness even to those who deserve the severest punishment (*Ant.* 2.145–46). In this respect, Josephus reflects a principle encapsulated within Greek-speaking Jewish tradition in the *Letter of Aristeas*. As a fundamental witness to the ideology of kingship in the Hellenistic world, *Aristeas* offers abundant advice—mediated by the fictional dialogue of King Ptolemy II Philadelphus with representatives of Jewish wisdom—including the idea that to grant "pity" is the work of the best kings. Thus, to the question posed by Ptolemy, "How might [the king] be humane [φιλάνθρωπος]?," the Jewish sage responds:

> By observing that the race of man comes to maturity and even to birth at the cost of much time and suffering; one must therefore not punish men on slight provocation nor inflict injuries upon them, realizing that human life is comprised of pains and penalties. Taking all things into consideration, then, you will turn to mercy [πρὸς τὸν ἔλεον], for God too is merciful [ἐλεήμων]. (*Let. Aris.* §208)[4]

---

[3] For terms expressing the idea of gracious favor in this section, see ἐχαρίσω (*Ant.* 2.142), εὐεργεσία (2.143), χάρις (143, 153), χαριζόμενος (147, 151, 157), χάρισαι (151).

[4] Moses Hadas, *Aristeas to Philocrates: Letter of Aristeas* (Jewish Apocryphal Literature; New York: Published for the Dropsie College for Hebrew and Cognate Learning by Harper and Brothers, 1951), 181–82.

Josephus endorses the same principle in his portraits of Israelite kings and, indeed, in his own depiction of Ptolemy II Philadelphus as exercising "pity" in releasing Jewish slaves in the Ptolemaic kingdom of Egypt.[5]

The model of divine pity and compassion. Returning to Judah's appeal to Joseph, it is the prerogative of the ruler to show pity in such cases, but it is also, as Josephus's account of the speech makes explicit, an attribute of God's nature to do so (*Ant.* 2.146). The appeal to pity is rooted not only in the thought of Jacob's undeserved suffering, vividly conjured up by Josephus on the basis of Genesis 44, but also in piety: in showing pity (οἶκτον λαβών) toward the brothers' father, Joseph will demonstrate his piety toward God (*Ant.* 2.152). Though he has the power to take God-given life, Judah argues, it is for Joseph to give (δοῦναι) and to match God in kindness (χάρις) by saving the guilty (indeed, as many as possible of them), not by destroying them (2.153). Josephus's emphasis on God as the model of compassion in this context points to several influences. That God should be merciful toward Benjamin, on whose fate rests that of Jacob, is Joseph's expressed wish in his first encounter with Benjamin in Egypt: "May God be gracious to you" (Gen 43:29; cf. LXX ὁ θεὸς ἐλεήσαι σε); in Josephus's version of the same meeting, Joseph affirms God's universal care, "that God presides [προστάτης] over all" (*Ant.* 2.122). The power to grant pity, then, is ultimately a power that belongs to God, the universal ruler.

In the wider context of the Pentateuch, the idea of God as merciful to all, including sinners, is fundamental.[6] The way in which this is expressed in the Greek Pentateuch may have shaped what Josephus says about pity in Judah's speech.[7] We may compare to the language of "pity" employed by Josephus in Judah's speech (ἐλεοῦντες, οἰκτείροντες, ἔλεος), terms highlighted in Mirguet's analysis, the

---

[5] Josephus's depictions of Israelite kings include, for example, that of Saul as corrupted by power and showing no pity for infants or children (*Ant.* 6.262–68), and that of David as a merciful king who forgave wrongs done to him and spared his enemy (*Ant.* 7.265; cf. 2 Sam 19:23). On Ptolemy II Philadelphus as granting pity to the Jews of Egypt and release from their enslavement, see Josephus, *Ant.* 12.30, interpreting *Let. Aris.* §§22–25. See also the valuable comments of Tessa Rajak on Josephus's construction of the emperor Titus: "by making compassion (tempered with firmness) into one of Titus's principal attributes, Josephus was ascribing to him what was the monarch's virtue *par excellence*" (*Josephus: The Historian and His Society* [2nd ed.; London: Duckworth, 2002], 212).

[6] See, for example, Josephus's statements about God by nature exercising "pity" (ἔλεος) as the motive for humans showing "pity" in Mosaic laws dealing with the care of the destitute (*Ant.* 4.239, on which see Mirguet's analysis in this volume; 4.269), or as the motive for pleas for God's compassion (οἶκτος, *Ant.* 1.188; 2.211; 4.40).

[7] On Josephus's knowledge and use of the Greek Bible, see Tessa Rajak, *Translation and Survival: The Greek Bible of the Ancient Jewish Diaspora* (Oxford: Oxford University Press, 2009), 252–54, esp. 253: "It is implausible that [Josephus's] use of the Greek will have been other than direct."

self-revelation of Israel's God as mediated in Greek Exodus: "the God who is compassionate and merciful [οἰκτίρμων καὶ ἐλεήμων], long suffering and very merciful [πολυέλεος] and truthful, and ... exercising mercy [ποιῶν ἔλεος] toward the thousandth generation, forgiving iniquities" (LXX Exod 34:6–7).[8]

Philo's Joseph is perhaps a further influence on Josephus's construction of pity in Judah's encounter with Joseph. Other kinds of connections have been made in previous studies of the relationship between the Joseph of Josephus's *Antiquities* and the slightly earlier construction of Joseph in Philo's life of the patriarch, *On Joseph* (*Ios.*).[9] Here, as in many other contexts, Josephus may have known and drawn on Philo's interpretation of the Pentateuch.[10] As in Josephus, so too in Philo, the treatment of Joseph's reconciliation with his brothers emphasizes the appeal to pity in Judah's speech: thus, Judah begs Joseph not to yield to wrath (*Ios.* 222); "to have compassion [οἶκτον λαβεῖν]" for the aged Jacob (227); "to take pity [ἔλεος] ... on the old age of a man who has labored throughout his life in the ordeals of virtue" (230).

Josephus's Joseph and emotion: Mirguet's analysis of Josephus's *Antiquities* opens up a rich resource for the study of emotion in which, as she puts it, Josephus "often enriches the emotional life of his characters," creating "an omnipresence of emotions" (p. 841). Her study proves this very well. And yet, in the case of the figure of Joseph, the picture is curiously rather different. Emotions are prominent in the Genesis narrative of the reunion of Joseph and his brothers and father (Genesis 42–50). Joseph weeps throughout: at their first meeting, on overhearing the brothers admit their guilt for the loss of Joseph, he turns away and weeps (Gen 42:24); on meeting Benjamin, Joseph runs from the room to break down (43:29–30); on hearing Judah's appeal, Joseph's sobs are so loud they can be heard in the palace (45:1–2); Joseph embraces and weeps on all his brothers (45:14–15); Joseph weeps over his father Jacob, on meeting him, and on his death (46:29; 50:1); and, finally, as the brothers tell Joseph of their late father's plea that Joseph forgive his brothers for all their wrongs against him, Joseph weeps again: he "was in tears as they spoke to him" (50:15–17).

---

[8] Cf. Exod 33:19, καὶ ἐλεήσω ὃν ἂν ἐλεῶ, καὶ οἰκτιρήσω ὃν ἂν οἰκτίρω; and Deut 4:31, θεὸς οἰκτίρμων κύριος ὁ θεός σου. Among the many LXX parallels to the presentation of the divine nature as οἰκτίρμων καὶ ἐλεήμων (Exod 34:6), see 2 Chr 30:9; 2 Esdr 19:17, 31; 1 Macc 3:44; multiple examples in the Psalms (esp. Pss 85:15; 102:8; 144:8); Sir 2:11; Joel 2:13; Jonah 4:2; etc.

[9] Maren Niehoff, *The Figure of Joseph in Post-Biblical Jewish Literature* (AGJU 16; Leiden: Brill, 1992), 100: "Philo basically shares Josephus's interpretation of Joseph" (p. 100); see further her analysis, pp. 54–110.

[10] On the likelihood that Josephus knew and used Philo's writings on the interpretation of the Pentateuch, see Gregory E. Sterling, "'A Man of the Highest Repute': Did Josephus Know the Writings of Philo?" *Studia Philonica Annual* 25 (2013): 101–14.

Josephus makes Joseph, the man of reason, a figure more in control of his emotions than the Joseph of Genesis.[11] Josephus closely follows Genesis in reporting the tears of emotion wept by Joseph on first meeting his brothers and on being reunited with Benjamin (*Ant.* 2.109, cf. Gen 42:24; *Ant.* 2.123, cf. Gen 43:29–30). In Josephus's version of events, however, this is the end of Joseph's tears. Thus, when Joseph reveals his true identity, there are no tears from Joseph, no loud sobs that penetrate the palace walls (Gen 45:1–2); in Josephus's terms, Joseph is merely "exposed by his emotion" and drops his pretense of anger toward the brothers (*Ant.* 2.160). Following Joseph's speech of forgiveness and reconciliation with the brothers, Joseph embraces them but, contra Gen 45:14, does not weep (*Ant.* 2.166).[12] On being reunited with Joseph, Jacob nearly dies of joy,[13] but Joseph revives him. In this context, toward the end of his story, Josephus makes explicit the contrast between Joseph's self-control and the emotions of others: Joseph, we are told, while unable to master the same emotion of joy, "was not, like his father, overcome by it" (*Ant.* 2.184). Finally, on Jacob's death, nothing is said of Joseph's emotion. In the wider context of the *Antiquities*, such restraint befits Joseph, the man of virtue, who controlled all things by the use of "reason" (*Ant.* 2.198).

---

[11] See Louis H. Feldman, *Flavius Josephus: Translation and Commentary*, vol. 3, *Judean Antiquities 1–4* (Leiden: Brill, 2000), 181 n. 518.

[12] All the brothers except Joseph weep profusely at this point (*Ant.* 2. 166); in Genesis, only Benjamin is said to have wept "on [Joseph's] neck" (Gen 45:14). In Josephus's version of events, the brothers betray more emotion than in the Genesis narrative, and certainly more emotion than Joseph: see, for example, the report of Judah's tears, with no basis in the equivalent passage in Genesis (*Ant.* 2.159).

[13] Presumably, this statement is based on Gen 46:30, "Now I can die, having seen for myself that you are still alive" (JPS); see further Feldman, *Judean Antiquities 1–4*, 181, noting that Josephus "adds greatly to the emotion of the scene."

Pain and Pity in Two Postbiblical Responses to Joseph's Power in Genesis

DONALD LATEINER
dglatein@owu.edu
Ohio Wesleyan University, Delaware, OH 43015

Josephus's first-century rewrite of ancient Jewish biblical legend and "history" (*Ant.* 1.17: "neither adding nor omitting anything") and the brief, anonymous, somewhat chronologically unanchored *Testament of Zebulun* both address Joseph and his brothers. Both attribute unforgiving and compassionate responses by Joseph and his many brothers to others' pain in the original biblical narrative. Françoise Mirguet's essay innovatively pairs these two works conceived in different genres and flowing from divergent cultural expectations.

The Jewish historian wrote his narrative in Aramaic, then translated it with help into Greek for the educated, wealthier Mediterranean classes thriving under Roman rule (*War*, praef.; cf. *Ant.* 20.11). This was two decades after he had promised an "archaeology" and finished his polemical *Jewish War*. On occasion, Josephus foregrounds pity and presents examples of the emotion in a manner familiar to readers of Aristotle's *Rhetorics* and *Poetics*. There, pity (if an emotion at all, as Mirguet notes [p. 843]) follows someone's appraisal from safety and emerges from a sensed superiority to the situation of the pitiable person. In contrast, and possibly enriched by Christian contaminations, *Testament of Zebulun* (Jewish or Jewish-Christian in origin and apparently written in Greek), foregrounds human vulnerability as an unavoidable, universal trait, and compassion, consequently, as a universally desirable response. The relatively insignificant sixth son of Jacob narrates events of his life that invite or require his deathbed meditation on mercy and compassion (surely motivating early Christians' interest).

Josephus's Joseph, desperately appealing for supportive action and practical assistance, evokes pity in a situation far from any Hellenic theatrical stage but in the context of postclassical Hellenic values and expectations. In *Testament of Zebulun*, however, the pitier who is helpless to help can still show pity (emotional support) by intensifying his or her emotional display, however ineffectual. The self in these two texts calibrates its reaction toward others' suffering differently, depending on one's own situation and on one's view of the extent to which cognition and judgment of suffering are essential to feeling pity.

Hellenists will worry that Mirguet inadequately explains or explores the vague and capacious Hellenic "rhetorical tradition." Just what was "the influence of Aristotle's *Rhetoric* on [Josephus's] historiography" (p. 847)? Mirguet looks no further than Herodotus for the literal meaning of σπλάγχνα, the inner organs of sacrificial animals, but the noun appears earlier, in both the *Iliad* (1.464) and the *Odyssey* (3.461). She then traces the metaphorical meaning, "gut-felt compassion (root σπλάγχν-)" (p. 839)—whether anger, anxiety, or love—to its appearances in the dramatists and Theocritus, the poet of love idylls (p. 851). There the word provides the seat of erotic passion (7.99), part of the Hellenistic poets' eroticization of all sorts of figurative vocabulary.

Josephus, like previous "Hellenistic" historians, features emotions in his accounts—characters' feelings and passions that agitated susceptible readers supplement, if not displace, dryer accounts of battle strategies, assembly debates, and partisan bickering. Such matters of state earlier filled more of the pages of Thucydides, although Herodotus's narrative before, and Xenophon's later, found greater room for scenes of *pathos*. Like these distant fifth-century congeners, Josephus claims a dedication to truth, not to entertainment or distortion from prejudice (*Ant.*, praef.; *War*, praef.). Nevertheless, he also proudly proclaims himself the successful deceiver in tight quarters of many contemporaries (*Ant.*, praef. 3.14, 26), so his own words call into question this rhetoric posturing about his dependability. Meanwhile, he faults those scurrilous compatriots who write garbled accounts designed to flatter or abuse, or who commemorate, he alleges, from ignorance, zealotry, or hearsay.

If one wishes to evaluate properly Josephus's emotional or dramatizing quotient in narratives, the better comparand would be his own lively account of the Roman war with the Jews. Otherwise, one might compare contemporary historiographers such as the Romans Tacitus or Pliny the Elder (mostly lost) or the biographers, both Greek Plutarch and the nearly contemporary North African Latinist Suetonius, who had access to the Roman imperial archives. The severely senatorial and savage critic of the emperors, Cornelius Tacitus, is famous—infamous really—for his stereotypical if laconically expressed disclaimer of bias, "without anger or partisanship" (*sine ira et studio*, *Ann.* 1.1). His harsh animus, however, is painfully clear—prejudice against Jews, Christians, freedmen, emperors, Germans, or anyone else you might name.

The retelling of the distant *Antiquities of the Jews* invited, actually demanded, a reconstructive method different from that of the *Jewish War*. Josephus himself saw the catastrophic events unroll, to his dismay, and he played a significant (indeed, notorious [*War* 3.26]) part in them as reluctant commander and wily survivor. The *Antiquities* certainly makes no claim to autopsy since the events occurred, if they did at all, as many as five millennia earlier. Those he attributes to

Moses himself as recorder were still two millennia earlier than the reign of Titus, his patron and, of course, the destroyer of the temple at Jerusalem.

Yosef ben Matatyahu, the self-proclaimed boy genius (*Vit.* 2), Pharisee, and prophet, was usually without honor from his coreligionists. He was simultaneously the Roman citizen and apologist Flavius Josephus to his imperial, polytheistic or lightly philosophical pension grantors. He tries to re-present Hebrew Scripture in terms that Hellenically educated philosophers, educators, and administrators can swallow, digest, and respect. His own previous tightrope-walking success between two hostile cultures and power systems made him seem to himself the right acrobat for the job. The *Antiquities* is not sui generis in Greek literature. Hellenized ethnics—for example, Berossos, Manetho, and Strabo—had already presented their fellows to the dominant culture, but Josephus elected to provide one unique element. He made visible and audible the emotions that were only latent in the narratives of "primitive" Hebrew Scripture. Cosmopolitan men of the Roman *oikoumenē*, educated on the Attic tragedians and Greek philosophers, expected a narrative adjusted to their values. Like anyone presenting old foreign stories to a new audience steeped in a different language and culture, Josephus provided a more appealing version with contemporary and familiar motives. He wanted to render his peculiar and distant desert "tribe's" legends respectable and comprehensible to his pan-Mediterranean, skeptical (toward Jews), literate public. So one meets "groans and lamentations and rending of garments" (*Ant.* 2.134) where Gen 44:13 "records" only the last item. In other words, he had to invent.

Mirguet contrasts the emotion one experiences with the emotion one is expected to feel and show when brought face to face with suffering (p. 840). A self-proclaimed historian faces this issue differently from a writer imagining a deathbed sermon or exhortation. Like David Konstan, the cited social constructionist classicist and pioneer in the study of Hellenic emotions, Mirguet identifies compassion, or sympathy, with a three-part experience: a sensation, an act of cognition (a considered judgment, for example, does the abandoned noncombatant Philoktetes deserve our pity?), and a feeling of anxious concern—experienced at a distance from the sufferer. As the cool Aristotle notes, we well-educated, comfortable folks can feel pity for tragic Oedipus, because (a) he is not us, or (b) even our cousin, but (c) he is "like us" and "it" could happen to us—we and our friends are fragile. In fact, Aristotle "wrote the book" about creating emotionally agitating narratives (*Rhet.* 1385b–86b; *Poet.* 1452b37–53a10): to make the suffering of ten thousand years past excite pity, he says, add gestures, voice, dress, objects, and actions to intensify the pity effect (ἐλεεινοτέρα).

Whether one must construct a history for pity (as another title of Konstan's claims for forgiveness and Mirguet's claims here), or whether jealousy has histories, or whether distinct cultures (contemporary or later) perceive undeserved misfortunes in different although overlapping ways remain questions for another day. Josephus and *Testament of Zebulun* riff on a Hebrew masterpiece, Gen 44:18–34, Judah's affecting and pathos-filled speech supplicating for his brother's life in order to save that of their father, Jacob. Josephus's Judah appeals to Joseph to pity Benjamin's father (*Ant.* 2.140–58), who faces death caused by the pain of losing another son (besides Joseph, still in local disguise and whom his brothers think to be long dead). Josephus has Judah eloquently appeal to pity by emphasizing Joseph's power (to abort the Egyptian execution) and his anger (as a robbed host) before appealing to his compassion. It is "more like a ruler" to save a life (ἡγεμονικώτερον δὲ σῶσαι).

Elsewhere, too, in this *Hebrew Bible for Pagans*, Josephus invites his readers/listeners to respond with pity, even when characters within his story do not. Moses indicts the wicked Korah and his family, children included. God has the earth immediately swallow Korah with his miscreant and innocent followers—corporate guilt (Num 16:31; *Ant.* 4.53). Josephus, embellishing this moment of Hebrew Scripture, asserts that some even rejoiced and denies that those whom God spared experienced any grief or pity. Josephus in effect chastises them for their deficiency of pity. "All calamity … is worthy of pity" for Josephus, and, in Mirguet's view of the Jewish writer, feeling pity is "a hallmark of moral character" (pp. 847–48). Flavius Josephus expected tears from his own perspective, or he expected his current Jewish and Hellenic readers to expect them from the Bible's internal Hebrew audience. He thus moralistically annotates Scripture from the perspective of his own age, and he blends Hebrew and Greek views of piety and fate (*Ant.* 16.118).

Instead of having Judah appeal to Joseph's power and privilege to spare their brother Benjamin, Zebulun in the *Testament* praises compassion in general based on all humans' shared vulnerability. The *Testament of Zebulun*'s presumably knowledgeable audience is assumed to be conversant with Judah's speech. The narrating "I" in the *Testament*, on his deathbed, can discover but one fault committed in his lifetime—and that a mistake, not a sin—fearful crying at the thought of what his brothers might have done to him, if he had defended Joseph and "snitched" to his father about his brothers' behaving badly. Defenseless Joseph had sought assistance from his brother Zebulun against his ill-intentioned brothers, but failed to get it. Joseph, later, although a big man in Egypt, renounced revenge. He could have remembered the wrongs he had suffered and exacted retribution (*T. Zeb.* 8:4–6).

The implication that Zebulun draws: even guilty parties deserve pity from their victims! In other examples of pity, bizarre by more demanding Aristotelian ideas of pity, poor Zebulun stole a garment in his compassionate desire to aid a naked stranger in winter (*T. Zeb.* 7:1 κλέψας … σπλαγχνισθείς). Zebulon recommends fellow feeling, weeping, and sympathizing, at least when one lacks other, more practical resources (*T. Zeb.* 7:3-4). His heart melts and "all his bowels' substance is loosened" in merciful compassion for sufferers.[1]

---

[1] Greek words for inner organs of the body as seat of the emotions, for example, ἥπατα [here], ἔντερα, καρδία, κοιλία, and σπλάγχνα, supply metaphors for various gut-wrenching

Divine compassion fortunately lurks in the background; humans need that supernal favor to compensate for their endless vulnerability to pain and injustice. Insignificant Zebulun's "ideology of the feeble" excuses his incapacity to vindicate or protect the powerless. "Intense emotions somehow [substitute for] actions that he cannot perform" (p. 854). His sorrow and pity would not persuade or impress Aristotle or Josephus. That is Mirguet's good distinction.

Readers might note that reactions to others' pain, their feelings and emotional displays, include a wider spectrum than Mirguet considers. One person's pain can be another person's pleasure, sadistic joy, or curiosity. In Rome of Josephus's age, lunchtime snackers gladly watched defeated gladiators, prisoners of war, and defenseless criminals thrown to the beasts, crucified, or burned to death.[2] The student of emotions in antiquity, furthermore, faces conflicting lists of which "feelings" count as emotions. One can expect to find "disparate discourses" (p. 856) reacting to undeserved suffering in each author's expected audience and milieu. One must distinguish the crowd in the classical *polis* from the Hellenistic philosophers, when they analyze overlapping concepts like οἶκτος, ἔλεος, ἄλγος, συμπάθεια, εὐσπλαγχνία, κ.τ.λ. Both groups would differ in judgment from the sophisticated Pharisaic refugee formerly of Flavian-desolated Jerusalem, or from a Christian expander of Hebrew holy writ explaining the proper place of pity in Judean villages, if that is who the author of the *Testament* was.

Confronting the pain and suffering of others is rarely easy in real life. Drama, art, and fictions, however, offer less-threatening imaginary options where one can safely choose to do the right thing. The hellenizer Josephus presents his pitiers as "top-down" strategists. Like Aristotle's *megalopsychos*, his biblical characters wield compassion as a gift for deserving, suffering souls. If it is "a way to assert oneself" (p. 857), then it constitutes, or perhaps justifies, at least one form of condescension.

The author of the *Testament of Zebulun*, in contrast, as Mirguet explains the authors' goals, exhorts humans to be sym-pathetic; that is, he or she will not merely recognize and acknowledge your pain, whether you are innocent or not, but *feel it with* you—an emphatic gut reaction, even if she or he can do nothing about it. This compassion blurs boundaries and hierarchies between the pitier and pitied because it is grounded in shared vulnerability. This is a safer, less expensive, less discriminatory pity. Mirguet does not examine Pentateuch pity, the yardstick for later Jewish meditations, or classical Hellenic instances,[3] when

---

passions (e.g., Song 5:4). English now translates them as "innards" rather than as obsolete "bowels" or overprecise "livers" (p. 852).

[2] The gentle Titus celebrated his brother's birthday with lethal amusements at Caesarea (*War* 7.3), during which more than twenty-five hundred Jews died. Donald G. Kyle presents well all aspects of this discomfiting pleasure in death for amusement, with a final chapter entitled "Christians: Persecution and Disposal" (*Spectacles of Death in Ancient Rome* [London: Routledge, 1998]).

[3] Rachel Hall Sternberg edited a relevant collection of essays from a Rutgers University conference: *Pity and Power in Ancient Athens* (Cambridge: Cambridge University Press, 2005),

she examines, if briefly, Aristotle's later observations on the nature of this emotion and its intentional evocation responding to pain and anguish. I congratulate Professor Mirguet for addressing the treatment of emotions as a profitable intersection between one group's ancient religious exhortation and another's secular narrative "translating" a third's chronologically organized, oblique religious understanding.

---

for which both David Konstan and I wrote essays, his on pity in Athenian politics and drama (pp. 48–66) and mine on pity in fifth-century Hellenic historiography (pp. 67–97). See also my "Tears and Crying in Hellenic Historiography," in *Tears in the Graeco-Roman World* (ed. Thorsten Fögen; Berlin: de Gruyter, 2009), 105–34. Although I discuss in an appendix the weeping sprinkled in Plutarch, Josephus (e.g., *War* 3.14; 5.9) exceeded my available space.

The Varieties of Pity

DAVID KONSTAN
david_konstan@brown.edu
New York University, New York, NY 10012

If the quarrel over whether emotions are innate and universal or culturally constructed and subject to historical change has now been superseded, it is in large part thanks to meticulous investigations into how specific emotions are construed in different social contexts. Françoise Mirguet's study of ἔλεος in two Hellenistic Jewish texts is a model of what can be achieved in this regard.

Human beings everywhere are capable of responding emotionally to the suffering of others—in this respect we may speak of a common or fundamental human sentiment, though it is not usually included in modern inventories of basic emotions—but such feelings are shaped by social life and beliefs and may assume quite varied forms. Sometimes such differences are reflected in distinctions of vocabulary. For example, in the semantic sphere that we may loosely define as sorrow for a past action, modern English distinguishes between regret, remorse, and repentance, whereas in classical Greek or Latin all these senses, as well as a simple change of mind, may be expressed by the single term μετάνοια or *paenitentia*. The difference in terminology is significant and reflects a particular conjunction of moral and religious ideas, but this is not to say that the Greeks and Romans were incapable of making the relevant discriminations: just what μετάνοια or *paenitentia* may connote depends on the wider context, and philological rigor is required to determine whether, for example, the words acquired radically new meanings over the course of time or under the pressure of Jewish and Christian conceptions (which may themselves have evolved historically).

The question has an important bearing on our understanding of Jesus' mission in the NT, for in recent translations of the Bible, μετάνοια is sometimes rendered as "conversion" (that is, a change of heart) rather than as "repentance." To take just a few examples, whereas the *Spanish Nueva Versión Internacional* renders Luke 3:3 as "Juan recorría toda la región del Jordán predicando el **bautismo de arrepentimiento** para el perdón de pecados," and *La Biblia de las Américas* offers "él fue por toda la región contigua al Jordán, predicando un **bautismo de arrepentimiento** para el perdón de los pecados," the *La Palabra* version reads, "Comenzó Juan a recorrer las tierras ribereñas del Jordán proclamando **un bautismo como signo de conversión** para recibir el perdón de los pecados," and the *Traducción en Lenguaje Actual* gives "Juan fue entonces a la región cercana al río Jordán. Allí le decía a la gente: '**¡Bautícense y vuélvanse a Dios!** Sólo así Dios los perdonará.'" The Italian *Nuova Riveduta 2006* opts for "repentance": "Ed egli andò per tutta la regione intorno al Giordano, predicando **un battesimo di ravvedimento** per il perdono dei peccati"; however, the *Conferenza Episcopale Italiana* version gives "Ed egli percorse tutta la regione del Giordano, predicando **un battesimo di conversione** per il perdono dei peccati." Luther rendered the verses as "Und er kam in alle Gegend um den Jordan und predigte **die Taufe der Buße** zur Vergebung Sünden," that is, "penance", but the *Gute Nachricht Bibel* has "Da machte er sich auf, durchzog die ganze Gegend am Jordan und verkündete: '**Kehrt um und lasst euch taufen,** denn Gott will euch eure Schuld vergeben!'" In Lothar Coenen and Klaus Haacker's *Theologisches Begriffslexikon zum Neuen Testament* (Wuppertal: Brockhaus, 1967), there is a joint entry under the lemma "Busse/Bekehrung," as also in Xavier Léon-DuFour's *Wörterbuch zur biblischen Botschaft* (Freiburg: Herder, 1967) ("Busse-Bekehrung"), which only highlights the nature of the problem.

When it comes to our responses to the misfortunes of others, English today distinguishes between pity, sympathy, and empathy. There is also the related notion of mercy, which shades over into the ideas of clemency and pardon, or even forgiveness, terms that imply sensitivity to another person's condition but place the emphasis more on leniency in response to an offense rather than to adversity per se. There is no ancient Greek or Latin word that quite corresponds to "mercy": the term that is commonly rendered as such in translations of the Bible is the same as that for pity, that is, ἔλεος or in Latin *misericordia*. Today, pity is out of fashion as an emotion, in part because it carries overtones of condescension or at least the relative superiority of the pitier in relation to the pitied. In the classical lexicon, however, pity was one of the primary emotions, and there were no compunctions about recognizing that one felt it for someone worse off than oneself. To be sure, pity presupposed one's own vulnerability to a comparable misfortune—but vulnerability implies that one is not at the moment in trouble. That is why Aristotle says that those who are wholly wretched are as immune to pity as those who, like the very rich and gods, are confident that they will never suffer a like distress. This difference in the station of the pitier and the pitied brings it closer to mercy; nevertheless, the stipulation, frequently insisted upon by classical writers, that pity is elicited only by undeserved misfortune augments the gap between pity and mercy, to the extent that mercy is analogous to pardon or forgiveness, which are responses precisely to wrongdoing or sin.

Once again, it is a delicate matter to decide how to render ἔλεος or *misericordia* in various passages of the NT (and the corresponding terms in the Hebrew Bible as well). God is presumably invulnerable to misfortune, and yet God is understood to experience ἔλεος in regard to human suffering; at all events, one may beseech

God's pity. What is more, if ἔλεος was an ordinary emotion, then it was suspect, since according to the Stoics, the wise were not subject to such passions. Jewish and Christian thinkers writing in Greek or Latin had to wrestle with this problem, which was implicit in their vocabulary.

In the ancient Greek novels, characters did indeed implore the gods to show pity, without apparently entering into the theological issue of whether such a sentiment would imply the gods' susceptibility to similar hardship; but they insist on their innocence as a condition for the gods' consideration. To take just one example, in the beginning of the *Ephesiaca*, Xenophon affirms that Habrocomes, the hero, was so proud of his beauty that he denied that Eros was a god (1.1.5). Eros responds by causing him to fall in love with Anthia, and this leads to the various trials and tribulations that typically beset the protagonists of these novels. Yet nowhere does Habrocomes confess to having done wrong, and when he is bound to a cross as a result of another woman's false testimony, he proclaims his innocence as he prays to the Nile, and the god takes pity on him. Later, Anthia appeals to Apis, who is, she says, the most humane (φιλάνθρωπος) of gods and one who takes pity on all strangers, and she begs him to pity her too in her misfortune (5.4.10). Here, we may perhaps see a hint of the extension of the idea of pity beyond desert, and its approximation to a broader sense of compassion or benevolence toward all. This would be analogous to the usage that Mirguet detects in Josephus's treatment of the revolt of Korah against Moses, in which the misfortune that afflicts even an enemy of God can inspire a certain kind of pity or sympathy.

There is a marked contrast between the classical novels and the novelistic text in the Judeo-Christian tradition known as the *Life of Adam and Eve*, composed in Greek sometime during the early imperial period. Whereas the protagonists in the novels nowhere suggest that they might be guilty of some offense against the gods, and hence neither express remorse nor ask for forgiveness, Adam and especially Eve are intensely aware of having sinned against the Lord; and in begging for pity they are simultaneously asking for absolution. The fallen state of mankind is adumbrated in this text, and no one can claim entire innocence in the face of God.

The *Testament of Zebulun* further broadens the idea of pity, employing the compound expressions, εὐσπλαγχνίαν ... ἐν ἐλέει, σπλαγχνισθεὶς ἐλεήσῃ, and σπλάγχνα ἐλέους so as to suggest compassion for all of humankind; this sentiment in turn is the basis for God's mercy toward human beings, who are in need of redemption. As Mirguet writes, "In the background of the text, we ... find the conception of the human being as wrongdoer, in need of divine compassion— which takes on the characteristics of mercy" (p. 855). God's pity would seem to be the model for human sympathy, yet there is an important difference. God's sentiment does not depend on divine vulnerability, and, like the Aristotelian or rhetorical conception of pity that in large measure informs Josephus's conception, it is granted by the more powerful to the less so. Just how God's compassion stands in relation to the human emotion seems to me to invite further investigation.

While the classical languages developed new expressions, such as σπλάγχνα in Greek or the Latin *compassio* (first attested in Tertullian), to denote sensitivity to suffering, or adapted old words to new uses, as with the Greek συμπάθεια, the old vocabulary of ἔλεος and οἶκτος in Greek and *misericordia* in Latin continued to predominate. Sometimes the same word acquired new nuances, whereas different expressions might nevertheless be more or less synonymous. Close studies of such terms reveal both the continuities and the changes, bringing to light abiding features even as they exhibit how emotions vary in accord with social and ideological conditions. I would only add that, in the process, we stand to learn much about our own emotional capacities and the historical conditions to which they respond.

Abingdon ACADEMIC

From Crisis to Christ: A Contextual Introduction to the New Testament
By Paul N. Anderson
9781426751042

Holding Faith: A Practical Introduction to Christian Doctrine
By Cynthia L. Rigby
9781426758140
February 17, 2015

Nuestra Fe: A Latin American Church History Sourcebook
By Justo L. González and Ondina E. González
9781426774263

Me and We: God's New Social Gospel
By Leonard Sweet
9781426757761

Paul: Apostle and Fellow Traveler
By Jerry L. Sumney
9781426741975

A Sense of the Heart: Christian Religious Experience in the United States
By Bill J. Leonard
9781426754906

Abingdon Press

AbingdonPress.com | 800.251.3320

Visit AbingdonAcademic.com to learn more and request an exam copy today.

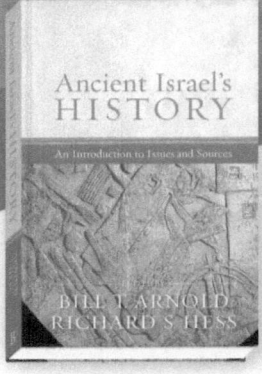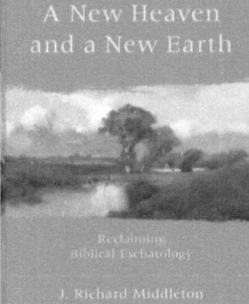

top scholarship from
BAYLOR UNIVERSITY PRESS

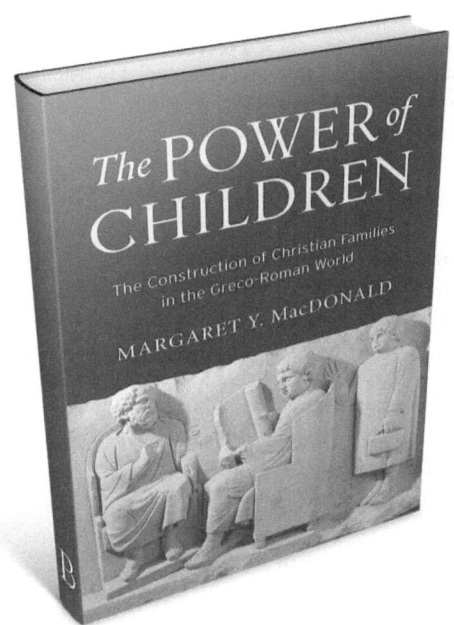

by **MARGARET Y. MacDONALD**

"...the best book available on children, households, and the household codes in early Christianity."

— CAROLYN OSIEK,
Brite Divinity School, Emerita

B
Books for Good | baylorpress.com
use code **BJBL** to order online for 10% off and free domestic shipping

NEW FROM B&H ACADEMIC

CHRISTIAN BIOETHICS
A Guide for Pastors, Health Care Professionals, and Families
C. Ben Mitchell and D. Joy Riley, MD

"Draws on the history and practice of medicine, theological guidelines, philosophical insights, and case studies to help Christians develop awareness about bioethical dilemmas."

—Paige Comstock Cunningham, Executive Director, The Center for Bioethics & Human Dignity

978-1-4336-7114-2 • 224 pgs • paperback • $24.99

TRUTH IN A CULTURE OF DOUBT
Engaging Skeptical Challenges to the Bible
Andreas J. Köstenberger, Darrell L. Bock, and Joshua D. Chatraw

"The authors dismantle the attacks of Ehrman one by one, showing not only that the New Testament is historically reliable, but also that its teachings are coherent and consistent."

— Michael J. Kruger, President and Professor, Reformed Theological Seminary

978-1-4336-8404-3 • 208 pgs • paperback • $19.99

ILLUSTRATED LIFE OF PAUL
Charles L. Quarles

"*Illustrated Life of Paul* is a well-written, beautifully illustrated, and accurate basic introduction to the apostle Paul."

—Douglas J. Moo, Professor of New Testament, Wheaton College

978-0-8054-9453-2 • 300 pgs • paperback • $29.99

INTRODUCTION TO GLOBAL MISSIONS
Zane Pratt, M. David Sills, and Jeff K. Walters

"Pratt, Sills, and Walters have provided their readers with a marvelous overview of global missions. I highly recommend this outstanding, capably researched, and highly applicable volume."

—David S. Dockery, President, Trinity International University

978-1-4336-7875-2 • 288 pgs • hardcover • $34.99

bhacademic.com
bhacademicBLOG.com

OUTSTANDING SCHOLARSHIP FROM CAMBRIDGE

The New Cambridge History of the Bible
Volume 4 - 4
Edited by John Riches
New Cambridge History of the Bible
$190.00: Hardback: 978-0-521-85823-6;
894 pp.

An Introduction to the Medieval Bible
Frans van Liere
Introduction to Religion
$85.00: Hardback: 978-0-521-86578-4;
332 pp.
$28.99: Paperback: 978-0-521-68460-6

Hellenistic and Biblical Greek
A Graduated Reader
B. H. McLean
$115.00: Hardback: 978-1-107-02558-5;
352 pp.
$39.99: Paperback: 978-1-107-68628-1

Psalms
Walter Brueggemann, W. H. Bellinger, Jr
New Cambridge Bible Commentary
$99.00: Hardback: 978-0-521-84092-7;
670 pp.
$39.99: Paperback: 978-0-521-60076-7

David, King of Israel, and Caleb in Biblical Memory
Jacob L. Wright
$80.00: Hardback: 978-1-107-06227-6;
284 pp.
$29.99: Paperback: 978-1-107-67263-5

Cicero and the Rise of Deification at Rome
Spencer Cole
$90.00: Hardback: 978-1-107-03250-7;
216 pp.

Introduction to the Old Testament
Bill T. Arnold
$120.00: Hardback: 978-0-521-87965-1;
436 pp.
$53.99: Paperback: 978-0-521-70547-9

Esther in Ancient Jewish Thought
Aaron Koller
$95.00: Hardback: 978-1-107-04835-5;
274 pp.

Losing the Temple and Recovering the Future
An Analysis of 4 Ezra
Hindy Najman
$90.00: Hardback: 978-1-107-00618-8;
203 pp.

The Ancient Jews from Alexander to Muhammad
Seth Schwartz
Key Themes in Ancient History
$75.00: Hardback: 978-1-107-04127-1;
199 pp.
$29.99: Paperback: 978-1-107-66929-1

The Bible on Silent Film
Spectacle, Story and Scripture in the Early Cinema
David J. Shepherd
$95.00: Hardback: 978-1-107-04260-5;
331 pp.

The Cambridge Companion to Ancient Mediterranean Religions
Edited by Barbette Stanley Spaeth
Cambridge Companions to Religion
$90.00: Hardback: 978-0-521-11396-0;
364 pp.
$32.99: Paperback: 978-0-521-13204-6

The Eschatology of 1 Peter
Considering the Influence of Zechariah 9–14
Kelly D. Liebengood
Society for New Testament Studies Monograph Series
$95.00: Hardback: 978-1-107-03974-2;
262 pp.

The Genre of Acts and Collected Biography
Sean A. Adams
Society for New Testament Studies Monograph Series
$99.00: Hardback: 978-1-107-04104-2;
332 pp.

The Hermeneutics of Christological Psalmody in Paul
An Intertextual Enquiry
Matthew Scott
Society for New Testament Studies Monograph Series
$95.00: Hardback: 978-1-107-05635-0;
240 pp.

Corinthian Wisdom, Stoic Philosophy, and the Ancient Economy
Timothy A. Brookins
Society for New Testament Studies Monograph Series
$99.00: Hardback: 978-1-107-04637-5;
288 pp.

Covenant Renewal and the Consecration of the Gentiles in Romans
Sarah Whittle
Society for New Testament Studies Monograph Series
$95.00: Hardback: 978-1-107-07689-1;
224 pp.

Faith and the Faithfulness of Jesus in Hebrews
Matthew C. Easter
Society for New Testament Studies Monograph Series
$99.00: Hardback: 978-1-107-06321-1;
365 pp.

The Romance between Greece and the East
Edited by Tim Whitmarsh, Stuart Thomson
$110.00: Hardback: 978-1-107-03824-0;
409 pp.

@cambUP_religion   www.cambridge.org/religion   CAMBRIDGE UNIVERSITY PRESS

fp fortress press
scholarship that matters

opening new possibilities

Galilee in the Late Second Temple and Mishnaic Periods, Volume 1
Life, Culture, and Society
DAVID A. FIENSY and
JAMES RILEY STRANGE, editors
The latest scholarship on synagogues, roads, literacy, village life, taxation, households, and much more.
9781451466744   352 pp   pbk $69.00

Jesus the Seer
The Progress of Prophecy
BEN WITHERINGTON III
An extensive, cross-cultural survey of the broader expressions of prophecy in its ancient Mediterranean context.
9781451488876   446 pp   pbk $39.00

Healing in the Gospel of Matthew
Reflections on Method and Ministry
WALTER T. WILSON
Explores how Matthew's narratives of healing expose the distinctive priorities of the evangelist.
9781451470376   240 pp   pbk $39.00

Paul and the Politics of Diaspora
RONALD CHARLES
Applies the insights of contemporary diaspora studies to address much-debated questions about Paul's identity as a diaspora Jew.
9781451488029   192 pp   hc $39.00

Parables Unplugged
Reading the Lukan Parables in Their Rhetorical Context
LAURI THURÉN
Proposes to read the parables "unplugged" from any assumptions beyond those given in the narrative situation in the text.
9780800699796   208 pp   pbk $39.00

Consider Leviathan
Narratives of Nature and the Self in Job
BRIAN R. DOAK
Doak argues that Job is an anthropological "ground zero" for the traumatic definition of the post-exilic human self in ancient Israel.
9781451469936   208 pp   pbk $39.00

Available wherever books are sold or
800-328-4648
fortresspress.com

fresh encounters with Scripture!

Fortress Commentary on the Bible

Six scholar editors and seventy contributors offer concise commentary on key sense units in each book of the Old Testament, Apocrypha, and New Testament exploring the text in its ancient context, it's interpretive tradition, and its contemporary challenges for today. "Very impressive—the best one-volume scholarly commentary on the New Testament available today."
—MARCUS J. BORG, Oregon State University

The Old Testament and Apocrypha
GALE A. YEE, HUGH R. PAGE JR.,
MATTHEW J. M. COOMBER, editors
9780800699161 hc 1,050pp $70

The New Testament
MARGARET AYMER,
CYNTHIA BRIGGS KITTREDGE,
and DAVID A. SÁNCHEZ, editors
9780800699178 hc 700pp $50

2-book set: 9780800699529 hc 1,750pp $120

Mark
DAVID SCHNASA JACOBSEN
Fortress Biblical Preaching Commentaries
"A strikingly refreshing and thought-provoking resource for both scholars and preachers."
—JOHN S. McCLURE, Vanderbilt Divinity School
9780800699239 224pp pbk $22

John
KAROLINE M. LEWIS
Fortress Biblical Preaching Commentaries
"The theological vistas in this volume are breathtaking, and the insights for preaching are stunning."
—THOMAS G. LONG, Candler School of Theology
9780800699246 pb 256pp $22

Available wherever books are sold or
800-328-4648
fortresspress.com

Exploring Our Hebraic Heritage

A Christian Theology of Roots and Renewal

Marvin R. Wilson

"For two thousand years, we have longed for a Christian scholar of Judaism as sensitive and knowledgeable as Marvin Wilson, and his work fulfills our hopes. Insightful and deeply learned, this book is a remarkable example of a Christian theology that affirms Judaism with respect and appreciation."
— Susannah Heschel

"As a historical religion, Christianity must own its Jewish origins and live up to the best of that heritage. Marvin Wilson, a pioneer in evangelical-Jewish relations, makes a compelling argument for renewing Christian faith by recovering our Hebraic heritage."
— David Neff

"A rare literary gem. . . . This book is easily accessible for students and seekers, not just academics; for congregants and parishioners, not just clergy. Jews, atheists, and Gentiles alike can all find their way into and through this truly informative and inspirational work. . . . Here is reading for the mind, the heart, and the soul."
— Rabbi Baruch HaLevi

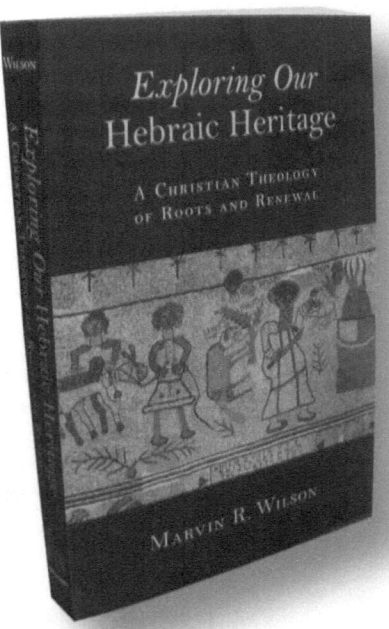

ISBN 978-0-8028-7145-9 • 332 pages • paperback • $22.00

At your bookstore, or call 800-253-7521
www.eerdmans.com

4571

Wm. B. Eerdmans Publishing Co.
2140 Oak Industrial Drive NE
Grand Rapids, MI 49505

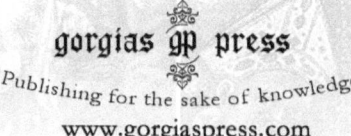

gorgias gp press
Publishing for the sake of knowledge
www.gorgiaspress.com

Conversos in the Responsa of Sephardic Halakhic Authorities in the 15th Century
BY DORA ZSOM
978-1-4632-0239-2

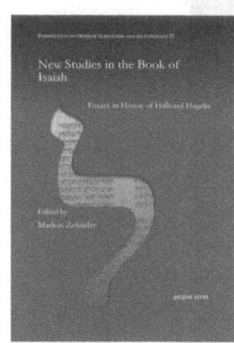

New Studies in the Book of Isaiah: Essays in Honor of Hallvard Hagelia
EDITED BY MARKUS ZEHNDER
978-1-4632-0356-6

Tribe and State: The Dynamics of International Politics and the Reign of Zimri-Lim
BY ADAM MIGLIO
978-1-4632-0249-1

An Introduction to Early Christianity
BY PAU FIGUERAS
978-1-4632-0238-5

"YHWH Fights for Them!": The Divine Warrior in the Exodus Narrative
BY CHARLIE TRIMM
978-1-4632-0271-2

Insiders versus Outsiders: Exploring the Dynamic Relationship Between Mission and Ethos in the New Testament
EDITED BY JACOBUS (KOBUS) KOK & JOHN ANTHONY DUNNE
978-1-4632-0257-6

Scribal Wit: Aramaic Mnemonics in the Leningrad Codex
BY DAVID MARCUS
978-1-61143-904-5

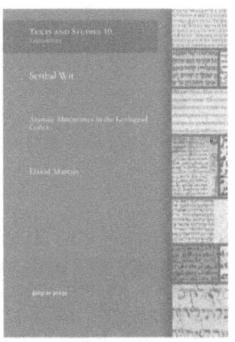

Jews, Christians and Zoroastrians: Religious Dynamics in a Sasanian Context
EDITED BY GEOFFREY HERMAN
978-1-4632-0250-7

Evangelically Rooted. **IVP Academic** *Critically Engaged.*

UNCOVERING FRESH BIBLICAL INSIGHT

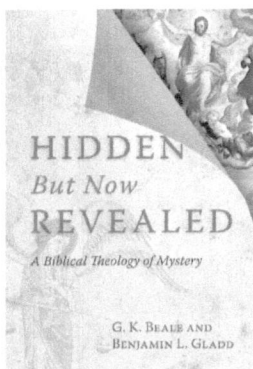

393 pages, paperback,
978-0-8308-2718-3, $27.00

HIDDEN BUT NOW REVEALED
A Biblical Theology of Mystery

G. K. Beale and Benjamin L. Gladd

"In the realm of lay readers, I can hardly think of an area that is more misunderstood than the area of prophecy; in the realm of biblical scholars, I can hardly think of a topic more controverted than the relationship between the Old and the New. At the crosshairs of both discussions is Daniel's term 'mystery.' For the sake of both readerships, I'm grateful that we finally now have a book that reduces the mystery behind 'mystery.'"

Nicholas Perrin, Wheaton College

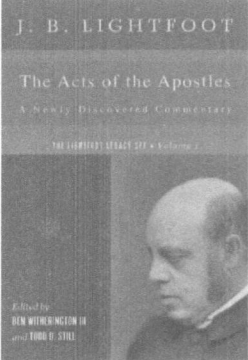

viii + 399 pages, hardcover,
978-0-8308-2944-6, $40.00

THE ACTS OF THE APOSTLES
A Newly Discovered Commentary

J. B. Lightfoot

"The discovery of hitherto unknown exegetical works by J. B. Lightfoot is a rare gift, full of potential for fresh insight both about the man himself (acknowledged worldwide as the leading scholar of his day) and, as he would have wished, about texts which he knew so well and which themselves express the heart of the gospel.... An unexpected and exciting addition to the core library of seminal biblical studies."

N. T. Wright

Visit **ivpacademic.com** to request an exam copy.

Follow us on Twitter   Join us on Facebook   800.843.9487 | ivpacademic.com

Evangelically Rooted. **IVP** Academic *Critically Engaged.*

FRESH INSIGHTS FROM TRUSTED VOICES

288 PAGES, PAPERBACK, 978-0-8308-4063-2, $24.00

384 PAGES, HARDCOVER, 978-0-8308-4035-9, $40.00

THE GOOD SHEPHERD
A Thousand-Year Journey from Psalm 23 to the New Testament
Kenneth E. Bailey

"This book has an abundance of surprises. Again and again I thought, 'Why have I never seen that before?'—as Ken draws on his rich lifetime's experience of Middle Eastern culture to explore biblical texts, and particularly when he shows eye-opening connections between Old and New Testament texts around the shepherd theme."

Christopher J. H. Wright,
international ministries director,
Langham Partnership

A CHANGE OF HEART
A Personal and Theological Memoir
Thomas C. Oden

"Tom Oden is one of the most remarkable Christians of our time. This is the story of how he has lived through, contributed to and helped to overthrow several revolutions during his long and fruitful life. . . . Those of us who know and love this great theologian will be delighted to read the story of his pilgrimage thus far. The whole church will be blessed by it."

Timothy George,
founding dean of Beeson Divinity
School of Samford University

Visit **ivpacademic.com** to request an exam copy.

Follow us on Twitter   Join us on Facebook   800.843.9487 | ivpacademic.com

SBL PRESS New and Recent Titles

MARK, MUTUALITY, AND MENTAL HEALTH
Encounters with Jesus
Simon Mainwaring
Paper $45.95, 978-1-58983-984-7   368 pages, 2014   Code: 060679
Hardcover $60.95, 978-1-58983-985-4   E-book $45.95, 978-1-58983-986-1
Semeia Studies 79

PSALM STUDIES
Sigmund Mowinckel
Translated by Mark E. Biddle
Volume 1
Paper $59.95, 978-1-58983-508-5   504 pages, 2014   Code: 063702
Hardcover $79.95, 978-1-58983-801-7   E-book $59.95, 978-1-58983-509-2
History of Biblical Studies 2

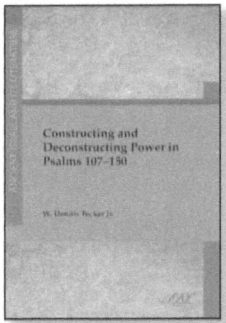

Volume 2
Paper $53.95, 978-1-58983-510-8   424 pages, 2014   Code: 063703
Hardcover $73.95, 978-1-58983-802-4   E-book $53.95, 978-1-58983-511-5
History of Biblical Studies 3

CONSTRUCTING AND DECONSTRUCTING POWER IN PSALMS 107–150
W. Dennis Tucker, Jr.
Paper $28.95, 978-1-58983-972-4   240 pages, 2014   Code: 062619
Hardcover $43.95, 978-1-58983-973-1   E-book $28.95, 978-1-58983-974-8
Ancient Israel and Its Literature 29

NONNUS OF NISIBIS, COMMENTARY ON THE GOSPEL OF SAINT JOHN
Translation of the Armenian Text with Introduction and Commentary by Robert W. Thomson
Paper $64.95, 978-1-58983-987-8   514 pages, 2014   Code: 061901
Hardcover $84.95, 978-1-58983-988-5   E-book $64.95, 978-1-58983-989-2
Writings from the Islamic World 1

SBL Press • P.O. Box 2243 • Williston, VT 05495-2243
Phone: 877-725-3334 (toll-free) or 802-864-6185 • Fax: 802-864-7626
Order online at www.sbl-site.org

SEMEIA

THE SEMEIA PROJECT
1974 – 2014

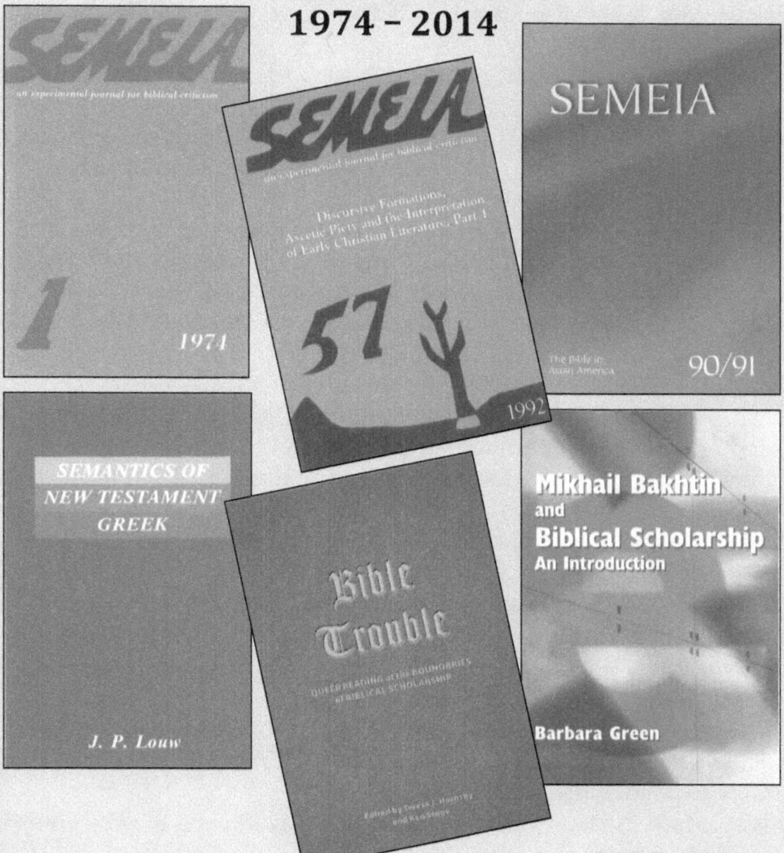

still experimental after all these years

SBL PRESS

Annual Index
Volume 133 (2014)

Aichele, George. *See* Miscall, Peter

Avalos, Hector, "Nebuchadnezzar's Affliction: New Mesopotamian Parallels for Daniel 4," 497–507

Baruchi-Unna, Amitai, "Two Clearings of Goats (1 Kings 20:27): An Interpretation Supported by an Akkadian Parallel," 247–49

Berthelot, Katell, "Reclaiming the Land (1 Maccabees 15:28–36): Hasmonean Discourse between Biblical Tradition and Seleucid Rhetoric," 539–59

Blount, Justine Ariel. *See* Lewis, Nicola Denzey

Burnight, John, "Job 5:7 as Eliphaz's Response to Job's 'Malediction' (3:3–10)," 77–94

Carr, David M., "Unified until Proven Disunified? Assumptions and Standards in Assessing the Literary Complexity of Ancient Biblical Texts," 677–81

Concannon, Cavan W., "'Not for an Olive Wreath, but Our Lives': Gladiators, Athletes, and Early Christian Bodies," 193–214

Couey, J. Blake, "The Disabled Body Politic in Isaiah 3:1, 8," 95–109

Darshan, Guy, "The Origins of the Foundation Stories Genre in the Hebrew Bible and Ancient Eastern Mediterranean," 689–709

Do, Toan, "Μόνον or μονῶν? Reading 1 John 2:2c from the *Editio Critica Maior*," 603–25

Dolansky, Shawna, "Deuteronomy 34: The Death of Moses, Not of Source Criticism," 669–76

Dulk, Matthijs den, "Seleucus I Nicator in 4 Maccabees," 133–40

Ferda, Tucker S., "Matthew's *Titulus* and Psalm 2's King on Mount Zion," 561–81

Fredriksen, Paula, "Paul's Letter to the Romans, the Ten Commandments, and Pagan 'Justification by Faith,'" 801–8

Frolov, Serge, "The Death of Moses and the Fate of Source Criticism," 648–60

Gibson, Jonathan M., "Cutting Off 'Kith and Kin,' 'Er and Onan'? Interpreting an Obscure Phrase in Malachi 2:12," 519–37

Goodacre, Mark, "A Flaw in McIver and Carroll's Experiments to Determine Written Sources in the Gospels," 793–800

Hasegawa, Shuichi, "The Conquests of Hazael in 2 Kings 13:22 in the Antiochian Text," 61–76

Hendel, Ronald, "Mind the Gap: Modern and Postmodern in Biblical Studies," 422–43

Hornkohl, Aaron D., "Her Word versus His: Establishing the Underlying Text in 1 Samuel 1:23," 465–77

Irvine, Stuart A., "Idols כתבונם: A Note on Hosea 13:2a," 509–17
Jones, Brice C., "Three New Coptic Papyrus Fragments of 2 Timothy and Titus (P.Mich. inv. 3535b)," 389–97
Kirk, J. R. Daniel, and Stephen L. Young, "'I Will Set His Hand to the Sea': Psalm 88:26 LXX and Christology in Mark," 333–40
Knowles, Michael P., "Serpents, Scribes, and Pharisees," 165–78
Knust, Jennifer, and Tommy Wasserman, "The Biblical Odes and the Text of the Christian Bible: A Reconsideration of the Impact of Liturgical Singing on the Transmission of the Gospel of Luke," 341–65
Konstan, David, "The Varieties of Pity," 869–72
Larsson, Kristian, "Intertextual Density, Quantifying Imitation," 309–31
Lateiner, Donald, "Pain and Pity in Two Postbiblical Responses to Joseph's Power in Genesis," 863–68
Lewis, Nicola Denzey, and Justine Ariel Blount, "Rethinking the Origins of the Nag Hammadi Codices," 399–419
Llewelyn, Stephen R. See Wassell, Blake E.
Machiela, Daniel A., and Andrew B. Perrin, "Tobit and the *Genesis Apocryphon:* Toward a Family Portrait," 111–32
Mackie, Scott D., "The Passion of Eve and the Ecstasy of Hannah: Sense Perception, Passion, Mysticism, and Misogyny in Philo of Alexandria, *De ebrietate* 143–52," 141–63
Markl, Dominik, "No Future without Moses: The Disastrous End of 2 Kings 22–25 and the Chance of the Moab Covenant (Deuteronomy 29–30)," 711–28
Mayshar, Joram, "Who Was the *Toshav*?" 225–46
McLaughlin, John L., "Is Amos (Still) among the Wise?" 281–303
Meyers, Carol L., "Was Ancient Israel a Patriarchal Society?" 8–27
Mirguet, Françoise, "Emotional Responses to the Pain of Others in Josephus's Rewritten Scriptures and the *Testament of Zebulun:* Between Power and Vulnerability," 838–57
Miscall, Peter, George Aichele, and Richard Walsh, "Response to Ron Hendel," 451–58
Mitchell, Christine, "A Note on the Creation Formula in Zechariah 12:1–8; Isaiah 42:5–6; and Old Persian Inscriptions," 305–8
Moore, Stephen D., "Watch the Target: A Post-Postmodernist Response to Ronald Hendel, 444–50
Moster, David Z., "The Levite of Judges 17–18," 729–37
Olyan, Saul M., "Jehoiakim's Dehumanizing Interment as a Ritual Act of Reclassification," 271–79
Pajunen, Mika S., "4QPs^x: A Collective Interpretation of Psalm 89:20–38," 479–95
Pearce, Sarah Judith, "Pity and Emotion in Josephus's Reading of Joseph," 858–62
Peppard, Michael, "Brother against Brother: *Controversiae* about Inheritance Disputes and 1 Corinthians 6:1–11," 179–92

Perrin, Andrew B. *See* Machiela, Daniel A.
Rom-Shiloni, Dalit, "'How can you say, "I am not defiled ..."?' (Jeremiah 2:20–25): Allusions to Priestly Legal Traditions in the Poetry of Jeremiah," 757–75
Schwáb, Zoltán, "The Value of a Curious Translation: Revisiting Proverbs 2:5," 739–49
Stokes, Ryan E., "Satan, Yhwh's Executioner," 251–70
Vermeulen, Karolien, "Mind the Gap: Ambiguity in the Story of Cain and Abel," 29–42
Viezel, Eran, "סַנְסִנָּיו (*sansinnāyw*; Song of Songs 7:9) and the *Palpal* Noun Pattern," 751–56
Walsh, Richard. *See* Miscall, Peter
Ware, James, "Paul's Understanding of the Resurrection in 1 Corinthians 15:36–54," 809–35
Wassell, Blake E., and Stephen R. Llewelyn, "'Fishers of Humans,' the Contemporary Theory of Metaphor, and Conceptual Blending Theory," 627–46
Wasserman, Tommy. *See* Knust, Jennifer
Waugh, Robin, "The *Testament of Job* as an Example of Profeminine Patience Literature," 777–92
Wilson, Brittany E., "The Blinding of Paul and the Power of God: Masculinity, Sight, and Self-Control in Acts 9," 367–87
Wilson, Stephen M., "Samson the Man-Child: Failing to Come of Age in the Deuteronomistic History," 43–60
Winn, Adam, "Resisting Honor: The Markan Secrecy Motif and Roman Political Ideology," 583–601
Yoo, Philip Y., "The Place of Deuteronomy 34 and Source Criticism: A Response to Serge Frolov," 661–68
Young, Stephen L. *See* Kirk, J. R. Daniel